Fundraising for Social Change

FUNDRAISING
for
Social Change

Kim Klein

Second Edition, Revised and Expanded

Chardon Press

Chardon Press,
P.O. Box 101,
Inverness, CA 94937

Second Edition, Revised and Expanded © 1988, Kim Klein
All rights reserved.

Production Coordinator for the Second Edition: Nancy Adess Editing
Design: Watermark Design
Copy Editors: Nancy Adess
            Nancy A. Heneson

Library of Congress Catalog Card Number: 88-70740
ISBN 0-9620222-0-9

Printed in the United States of America

Preface to the Second Edition

At the time the first edition of this book was published, I was living in California. In 1986, I moved to Knoxville, Tennessee in order to work in Appalachia. I wanted to work in a region that would test the principles of grassroots fundraising in a rural and low-income environment, and I wanted to learn about the forms that working for social justice must take in a part of the country that is essentially a colony of the rest of the United States. Also, I wanted to get back into hand-on fundraising. Therefore, I took a job as the director of a small, public foundation, and I coordinate raising the money which the foundation gives away.

The changes in this book reflect what I have learned from that move and incorporate some reader suggestions. The facts in the book have been brought up to date, and three appendices have been added: Raising Money in Rural Areas, Dealing with Anxiety, and Using Computers in Fundraising.

Otherwise, to the best of my knowledge and experience, everything in this edition is accurate, and will work if applied with patience and thoroughness. Grassroots, community-based fundraising is not getting easier, but it *is* getting more necessary as continuing cutbacks in government and increasing economic uncertainty take their toll in the nonprofit sector.

Kim Klein
Nerinx, Kentucky
November, 1987

Preface

Like most people in fundraising, I did not start out with the intention of making fundraising my career. At the time I was introduced to the topic, I was a divinity student at the Pacific School of Religion in Berkeley, California, working on a Master of Divinity degree.

Volunteering with a shelter for battered women, I quickly learned that fundraising was a greatly needed yet uncommon skill. However, I did not decide to become a fundraiser until one evening when several female seminary students and I were talking with a remarkable woman, Peggy Cleveland, a feminist theologian and writer and former missionary. I asked her what the best thing was that women could do to promote the goals of the women's movement. Expecting her to answer with any number of options—ministry, law, politics, medicine—I was totally unprepared when she said simply, "Help women get money."

I elected to do that through fundraising. I have expanded my work to include not only the women's movement but all work for social change and social justice. I have found in fundraising a satisfying and rewarding career and I have met thousands of interesting and wonderful people working in important, life-changing areas.

Clearly, not everyone is cut out to be a fundraiser. But anyone wanting to take an active role in a nonprofit organization, as either a volunteer or a paid staff member, will eventually be called on to participate in some form of fundraising.

Fundraising is hard work, requiring planning, perseverance, and commitment. Fundraising is also empowering: successful grass roots fundraising enables organizations to take control of their own situations, to be self-sufficient, and to be accountable only to themselves, rather than to outside funding sources.

Acknowledgements

First and foremost, I want to thank my friend and colleague Nancy Adess, who read and edited this entire manuscript. Her detailed and excellent work made this book clear and readable.

I also am grateful to the thousands of organizations and individuals I have had the opportunity to train and consult with over the years—with a special thanks to the groups who allowed their materials to be used in this book. Mary Harrington and the Youth Project's Self-Sufficiency Training Project gave me the opportunity to learn to be a fundraising trainer under the expert leadership of Ms. Harrington, Joan Flanagan, Si Kahn, Kat Thomas, and many other skilled trainers and organizers.

The bulk of my theoretical knowledge about fundraising (which when put to use proved to be true) I gained from two people: Dick Schellhase, former Director of Development at Pacific School of Religion, with whom I was privileged to work in 1977-78; and Hank Rosso, Director of the Fund Raising School (San Rafael, California), one of the most knowledgeable people I have ever met and completely committed to promoting the principles of ethical fundraising.

A special acknowledgement is owed to Joan Flanagan, a pioneer in researching and teaching grass roots fundraising. Her book, *The Grass Roots Fundraising Book*, is a classic in this field.

Finally, I want to thank my partner on the *Grassroots Fundraising Journal*, co-editor and co-publisher Lisa Honig. Portions of this book are drawn from material that has appeared in the *Journal* and from what I have learned from her fundraising skills and expertise.

Contents

The purpose of this book is to provide low-budget organizations (budgets under $500,000) with the information they need to establish, maintain, and expand successful community-based fundraising programs, allowing them to move away from reliance on foundations, corporations, and government assistance.

Low-budget groups need to keep in mind that their fundraising efforts take place in a context different from those of more traditional community service organizations such as large hospitals, voluntary health agencies, or major arts groups.

First, many people will not agree with or even understand what your group is trying to do. Your organization probably has little immediate public recognition, and if you are seeking to change the status quo, people may feel threatened by your program. Even those in sympathy with what you are trying to accomplish may think that you are hopelessly naive or idealistic, and you will often be told to "face reality."

Second, you probably have little or no front money and not enough staff; therefore, you cannot afford to invest in large-scale fundraising strategies, such as large direct-mail campaigns. Without a cushion of money, you are either just holding your own or falling behind.

Third, your board, volunteers, and staff are most likely unfamiliar with fundraising strategies and may not be comfortable with even the idea of fundraising.

All traditional fundraising strategies must therefore be viewed with these three premises and their attendant implications in mind and translated into workable terms. This book does that. All of the strategies recommended here have been successful for small groups. Every strategy will not work for every group, but the discussion of each strategy will allow you to decide which strategies will work for your group and how to expand the strategies you are already using.

The appropriate staff of every organization should read the first two sections of the book to learn the context for successful fundraising. Fundraising without planning, without a strong, committed group of volunteers, without a workable organizational structure, or without understanding the basic components of all fundraising plans is practically impossible.

I will take this opportunity to deliberately state the obvious: All of the reading of fundraising literature, planning, strategizing, writing case statements, etc., cannot and will not raise money. Only implementing your plan—taking action—will raise money. So make this your motto: **"Today someone has to ask someone for money."**

OVERVIEW AND PLANNING

Chapter 1

Philanthropy in America

The Truth About Charities

The word "philanthropy" comes from two Greek words meaning "love of people." This affection is usually expressed in donations of property, money, or volunteer work to worthy causes. Similarly, the word "charity" comes from a Latin word meaning "love" in the sense of compassion, giving, and seeking to do good. The roots of these words remind us of the fundamental reasons for the work of most nonprofit organizations.

In America a long tradition of philanthropy has grown up in order to provide many services that are provided by more socialist systems of government through taxation.

The total annual income of charities in America is about $150 billion. Besides individual giving, this sum includes contracts, fees for service, sale of materials to individuals, foundation and corporate giving, and government grants and aid. If charity were a single industry, it would rank as the nation's largest income producer. Nonprofit organizations employ 5 percent of the nation's work force and use the volunteer efforts of at least 45 million more people. The total amount of money given to charity in the 1980s (about 7 percent of our national budget) exceeds the national budgets of all but 9 of the 165 nations in the world.

Two examples illustrate the size and power of some nonprofit operations: The Young Men's Christian Association (YMCA) is not only the world's largest operator of swimming pools, but its 33,000 beds are enough to rank it as the nation's ninth largest hotel chain (between Hyatt and Marriott). The Girl Scouts' cookie sales, approaching $150 million annually, now account for about 10 percent of the sales of the entire U.S. cookie industry.

The Foundation/Corporation Myth

This book will examine who gives away the money that goes to nonprofit groups and where a nonprofit organization can go for the money it needs in this rather vast market. As with many things that are critically important and use the resources of so many people, it is not surprising that a number of misconceptions have grown up about philanthropy and charities.

The most misguided of these is the idea that in private—nongovernmental—giving in America, most of the money comes from big business or foundations. The truth is that in the private sector most money given away comes from individuals. (Government is technically the largest source of nonprofit dollars; however, this book is chiefly concerned with private sector funding.)

Since 1935 the American Association of Fundraising Counsel (AAFRC) has sought to be a center of information about philanthropy. Among its other activities AAFRC studies and identifies economic and social trends in American philanthropy. Each year they compile this information in their annual report, *Giving USA* (see Bibliography). This research shows that private sector giving comes from four sources: individuals, bequests (individuals arranging their estates such that on their death the charity realizes some cash or other type of donation), foundations, and corporations. Year in and year out, varying only by a small percentage, the AAFRC report has shown that the proportion of giving from each of these sources remains constant, with gifts from living individuals exceeding the rest more than tenfold:

Giving From	Percent of Total Charitable Dollars Private Sector, Average
Individuals	84
Bequests	6
Foundations	5
Corporations	5

In 1986, the latest year for which figures are available, giving from these sources totaled $87.22 billion.

Contributions	in billions	As percent of total
Individuals	$71.72	82.2
Bequests	5.83	6.7
Foundations	5.17	5.9
Corporations	4.50	5.2

Given these facts an organization should have no trouble knowing where to go for money: individuals provide the vast bulk of support to nonprofit institutions. Foundations and corporations, which have the false reputation of keeping charity alive, are overrated as a source of funds, and the help that they can provide is often misunderstood. While foundation and corporate giving will always play a vital role in the nonprofit sector, the limitations of that role must be clearly understood. Therefore, let us examine the broad purposes of individual, foundation, and corporate giving.

Private-Sector Giving

Individuals, whether alive or through bequests, should provide the major portion of ongoing operating costs of an organization—90 percent of an organization's fundraising goal should come from individual donors. The growth of individual donations to an organization is critical to the growth and self-sufficiency of that organization; one rarely happens without the other.

Foundations usually provide seed funds for start-up costs, special capital improvements, special projects or programs, and occasionally help through a rough period in the life of an organization. Decreasing reliance on foundation giving should be implicit in the financial plans of an organization.

Corporations play different roles in different organizations. Many organizations will not be able to get any money from corporations because their work is too controversial; because there are no corporate offices in their community; because they have no corporate connections; or simply because they wish to avoid the politics of seeking corporate funds. For organizations that can qualify for corporate funding, these contributions may supplement their other funding. Corporations provide special project funds, such as capital improvements; sometimes they will provide small ongoing grants. Corporations are increasingly giving away their products or providing "in-kind" services, such as printing, from their own facilities. With rare (and well-publicized) exceptions, corporations will give small, one-time grants ($500 - $5,000). Most corporations, however, give no money away, and even

To fully understand the meaning of private sector giving it is important to look at the categories of where this money went. Again, with only a few percentage points of variation from year to year, a consistent pattern of giving has been demonstrated throughout AAFRC's record keeping. The largest chunk of philanthropic dollars goes to religious organizations, with health and hospitals a distant second, followed by education, social welfare, the arts and humanities, and civic organizations each receiving about 10 percent of the philanthropic pie.

Religious Organizations: A Model

Why do religious organizations receive so many of the private sector dollars? The answer is simple and also one of the most important to understand for successful fundraising: Religious institutions offer ideas and commitments that are of great value, but the real reason they get so much money is because *they ask for it.*

Let's look at the elements of a typical church fundraising program:*

◆ **Churches ask regularly.** In most churches a basket is passed around during the collection each Sunday. Any gift is acceptable, from small change to large checks. Everyone, whether out-of-town visitor, occasional church-

*Churches are used here because they are the dominant religious form in the United States and because of the author's familiarity with them. People from other religious traditions will see similarities in fundraising techniques.

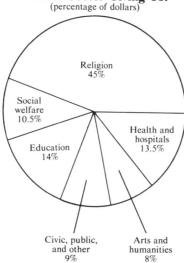

Private Sector Giving To:
(percentage of dollars)

Religion
45%

Social
welfare
10.5%

Health and
hospitals
13.5%

Education
14%

Civic, public,
and other
9%

Arts and
humanities
8%

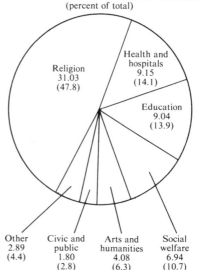

Contributions in Billions of Dollars
(percent of total)

Religion
31.03
(47.8)

Health and
hospitals
9.15
(14.1)

Education
9.04
(13.9)

Other
2.89
(4.4)

Civic and
public
1.80
(2.8)

Arts and
humanities
4.08
(6.3)

Social
welfare
6.94
(10.7)

goer, or loyal and generous congregant, has an opportunity to give, and almost everyone does. The ushers or ministers are not concerned about offending someone by asking too often. They would never say, "Don't pass the basket to Mrs. Faithful—she just bought the new carpet."

◆ **Churches make it easy to give.** In the great majority of churches, if you are a regular congregant, someone will come to your house to discuss your giving plan. He or she may ask you to tithe, or to pledge a certain amount per week or month, or to give a one-time gift to the ongoing work of the church. The option of monthly or quarterly payments allows people to give a great deal more over the course of a year than giving in a single lump sum.

◆ **Churches provide a variety of programs to which you can give as you desire.** If you are particularly interested in the youth program, you can give to that. You can buy flowers for the altar in someone's honor; you can support the music program or the overseas mission programs. Most churches have any number of scholarship funds, homeland missions, soup kitchens, and other social programs for which your donation is needed and gratefully accepted. If you are a "bricks and mortar" person—that is, you prefer to buy things with your gifts—you can buy a new window, new Bibles, a new carpet, or a whole new sanctuary.

Any size of donation is appropriate. You can belong to a church by making a gift of any amount. While some churches suggest guidelines for giving, and the Bible suggests 10 percent of income as the appropriate tithe, the church always leaves the amount of giving up to the donor.

All groups should try to copy this program of diversity in giving. In the chapters that follow I will show you how.

Chapter 2

How To Begin

Principles of Fundraising

Fundraising is an acquired taste. Probably no one says at the age of 12, "When I grow up, I want to be a fundraiser." Most people are drawn to the profession by a cause, an idea, an issue, or an organization in need of the money. They decide to help with fundraising even though it was not their first choice and even though they may have found the idea slightly distasteful or a little frightening. Many of these people find that they begin to tolerate, then like it. But because few people have actually trained to become fundraisers, most have misconceptions about it. These misconceptions usually stem from not understanding the basic principles of effective fundraising.

There are three general principles of effective fundraising:

◆ People give money to charity because it serves their self interest,
◆ Diversity of funding sources is the secret of financial stability,
◆ Anyone can learn to do fundraising.

Appealing to Self-Interest

There are more than 370,000 registered nonprofit organizations in America. In addition, some experts estimate that up to 8 million more organizations operate as nonprofit but have not sought tax-exempt status. New organizations come into existence every year, and more are created than go out of business.

Among other things this means there is a great deal of competition for the charity dollar. To employ the first principle of effective fundraising, you must carefully examine why someone would give their money to your group.

Why people give
At the level of pure exchange, people give to organizations because they like the newsletter or because they receive a free tote bag, bumper sticker, or some other tangible item. Sometimes they give to a certain group because everyone in their circle gives to that group or because it is a family tradition. Giving may be required to take advantage of something the group offers (classes, theater seats, the swimming pool).

At the altruistic level of motivation, people give because they care about the issue, they believe in what is represented by the group, they think the group's analysis of a problem and vision of a solution is correct. Often people give either because they or someone they know were once in the position of the people your group serves (alcoholic, abused, homeless, or unemployed) or because they are thankful that neither they nor anyone they know is in that position.

People give because the group expresses their own ideals and enables them to reinforce their image of themselves as, for example, feminists, environmentalists, pacifists, Democrats, etc. This association raises their self-esteem. They can say in truth, "I am a caring person," "I have deep feelings for others," "I am helping others."

Although these three sets of reasons for giving are legitimate and healthy, most nonprofit organizations appeal to two other motives for giving that, while true for the organization, will not really motivate people to give. These are: "We need the money," and "Your gift is tax-deductible." Neither of these reasons distinguishes your organization from all the others. All nonprofit organizations claim to need money, and most of them do. The fact that the gift is tax deductible is a nice touch, but gifts to thousands of nonprofit organizations are tax deductible. Neither need nor tax advantage makes your organization special.

Don't beg—offer

Use the following analogy to determine what will make your organization stand out to prospective donors: Your organization is a business—a tax-exempt corporation. As a business, the services you provide and the work that you do are like products for sale. Your prospective donors are like customers. Your organization has something they need. (Of course you need donors for ongoing financial support. But they need you for the work you do.) No grocery store whose advertising policy was, "Shop here—we need customers in order to stay in the black," would have any customers. The store's message is "Shop here: we have the lowest prices, the highest quality, we are convenient, we are friendly, we have good sales, we have variety." The message is clear: We have something you need.

Allowing yourself to imagine your donors as customers enables you to move away from **your** need to **their** need. That need, that self-interest, is what your fundraising strategies should appeal to.

Diversifying Sources

Diversity of funding sources is the secret of financial stability. In the early 1980s hundreds of cases illustrated what happened to organizations whose primary source of support was government funding. When that funding was cut or eliminated, the organizations had nothing to fall back on. Many of them severely curtailed their services; many ceased to exist.

The need for diversity is not a new lesson. Factory towns face high unemployment when their single industry has to cut back or close. People with only one skill have a more difficult time finding employment than those with a variety of skills. Yet many organizations continue to look for the ideal special event that will provide for their entire budget, or they search for the one person, foundation, or corporation to provide most of the money they need. These groups reason that if they could get one fundraising strategy going that was absolutely certain, tried and true, their money worries would be over. Unfortunately, no fundraising device is absolutely certain.

Organizations should not receive more than 30 percent of their funding from any one source. Though it would be difficult, an organization can lose 30 percent of its funding and survive, but to lose more than that would put it in serious straights. An organization could have more than 30 percent of its funding coming from membership, but not from any one member. There is no set number of sources because so much depends on the size of your budget and the sources you choose. The best rule is: The more the better.

Anyone Can Do It

The final principle, which is most critical for small organizations, is that fundraising is easy to learn. The basic principles are simple common sense; anyone can learn some aspect of grass roots fundraising. Having a diversity of sources allows all the people involved in your organization to find one or more fundraising strategies suited to their tastes and abilities. As they learn more about fundraising and experience success, they will even begin to enjoy it.

Making a Case for Your Organization

The Case Statement

The first step in preparing for effective fundraising is to develop what fundraisers call a **case statement**. The case statement, describing the need for the organization and its competence to meet the need, is an internal document for use by board, staff, and key volunteers. The case statement includes the following elements:

1. A statement of the organization's mission;
2. documentation of the existing need that your organization has set out to meet;
3. evidence that your organization is capable of meeting this need;
4. proof that your organization is well managed, financially sound (or on the way to being financially sound), and in possession of a good fundraising plan; and
5. a budget for the current year.

Once developed, the case statement can be used as the basis for preparing brochures and proposals, giving speeches, writing direct mail appeals, evaluating work, preparing annual reports, and so on. Parts of the case statement will change every year. It should be reviewed regularly to insure that everyone is still in agreement with its premises and that the words used still accurately describe what the organization is doing.

Let's take a look at each of the elements of the case statement.

Stating your mission

The Statement of Mission answers the question, "Why does your organization need to exist?" People in organization often claim, "We know why we need to exist," and then proceed to describe one of their programs. They might say, for example, "We know why we exist; to get low-income housing for senior citizens." This is not a statement of why they need to exist; this is a description of their method for meeting a need. The need they seek to meet is their reason for existing. Therefore, their statement of mission should be something like this: "There is a population of elderly poor in our community that needs affordable housing. We seek to provide that housing." They can then go on to describe how they provide that housing: Advocating to the city, buying property and turning it into low-income housing, helping seniors finance their own housing, getting federal grants to build and administer low-income housing, or any combination of these strategies.

Another example: A board member of a public interest law firm was asked for a statement of mission. She replied, "We sue banks who redline neighborhoods, which means that they will either not loan money to anyone in that neighborhood or they will charge more interest on loans made in those areas." Again, this states a method for solving a problem the group has documented. Its mission statement would be, "It is illegal for any institution to discriminate against people based on race, sex, or class. In Ourtown, there are banks practicing racial discrimination in a variety of ways, chiefly through the practice known as redlining. We seek to eliminate that practice."

Your statement of mission answers only **why**, not **how** or **what**. You can be specific, but be sure you address the need before you state what you are doing to meet it.

Documenting the need

You need documentation of the need that your organization has set out to meet. The documentation does not have to be a lengthy treatise. It can use simple statistics, surveys, and political analysis. It should be thorough enough, however, to persuade a person of reasonable intelligence and an open mind that you know what the need is and why it exists.

Here is an example:

> "Last year, there were 350 cases of children ingesting rat poison in Ourtown. A group of concerned citizens discovered that rat poison was

being used extensively in residential neighborhoods to try to bring a burgeoning rat population under control. Our group also discovered that the rat population was exploding because the antiquated sewer system was no longer adequate. Raw sewage frequently leaks out, particularly in parts of town below the water table line. We formed RATSBEGONE to educate the public about the dangers of rat poison, to pressure the city government to build a new sewer system, and to research other methods of rat control."

Proving your capability
You also need evidence that your organization is capable of addressing this need. This should include a description of your accomplishments and a list of your future plans in enough detail to provide a full understanding of how your organization works. This section should also include brief biographical sketches of each of your board members, resumes of staff, a brief history of the organization, awards it has won, letters of endorsement, etc. Many organizations also include their numbers of members, volunteers, and chapters, and any other evidence that they can do what they claim to be doing and what they want to do in the future.

Proving your management/planning ability
You need proof that you are fiscally well managed and have a good fundraising plan. (The next section discusses the development of a fundraising plan.) This part of the case statement includes an annual report, an audited financial report if you have one (or a balance sheet if you don't), and a description of how your finances are monitored.

Showing them a budget
You must produce a budget for the current year, including sources of income. This budget must be sensible in light of what you want to do. If necessary add an explanation for any items that would not make sense on their own. For example, RATSBEGONE has a budget of $25,000, covering basic operating and staff coordination expenses. However, its plans include having a full-time pest control expert working with the city government to implement an alternative pest control program, printing booklets for residents about pest control and proper use of poisons, and seeking legislation for more prominent and careful warning labels on rat poison products. RATSBEGONE also plans to continue its efforts to get a new sewer system.

At first glance, it seems that RATSBEGONE cannot possibly do all this work for $25,000. Therefore, the group prefaces the budget with the following explanations: the university has awarded a postdoctoral fellowship enabling a scientist to work full time for RATSBEGONE without cost to the group; printing and distribution costs for the booklets will be provided as a public service by the Department of Health; and RATSBEGONE has more than 50 volunteers as well as donated office space.

The board, staff, and key volunteers should all agree on the case statement, particularly on the statement of mission and the group's future plans. If the people who must carry out the plans don't like them or don't believe they are possible, they will not give their best effort. Therefore, it is worth spending a good deal of time on developing the case statement. Hurrying a statement of mission or a set of goals through the board process to save time or get on with the job will come back to haunt you in the form of commitments not kept and half-hearted fundraising efforts.

Planning for Fundraising

Developing A Budget

When asked about their budget, many small organizations will reply that they simply spend what they can raise. This budget process will do for a while, but its cost in frayed nerves, sleepless nights, and inability to expand programs makes almost any other system preferable.

The people responsible for raising money often feel too busy to make a comprehensive fundraising plan. However, a simple, straightforward planning mechanism would enable them to develop a plan quickly, so that they can spend most of their time implementing and, where necessary, modifying the plan.

The first step is to develop a working budget. A budget is simply a list of items on which you will spend money (expenses) and a similar list of sources from which you will receive money (income). A budget is balanced when the expenses and income are equal.

There is a simple, two-step process for budget preparation that most small nonprofit organizations can use effectively. The process takes into account the largest number of variables without extensive research or elaborate spread-sheets. In some organizations a single staff member prepares the entire budget and presents it for board approval, but this is a large burden for one person. Therefore, the method presented here assumes that a small committee will undertake the budget-setting program.

Step one: Expenses versus income
The budget committee should first divide into two subgroups: one to estimate expenses, and the other to project income. When these tasks are completed, the subgroups will reconvene to mesh their work (step two).

Estimating expenses. The group working on the expense side of the budget prepares three columns of numbers representing "barebones," "reasonable," and "ideal" expense figures (see figure, below). The "barebones" column spells out the amount of money the organization needs to survive. Items here generally include office space, minimum staff requirements, postage, printing, and telephone. This column does not include the cost of new work, salary increases, additional staff, new equipment, or other improvements.

Next, the group prepares the "ideal" column: how much money the group would need to operate at maximum effectiveness. This is not a **dream** budget, but a true estimate of the amount of funding required for optimum functioning.

Finally, the committee prepares the "reasonable" column: how much money the group needs to do more than survive but still not meet all its goals. These figures should not be conceived of as an average of the other two columns. For example, an organization may feel that in order to accomplish any good work, the office needs to be larger, or in order to maintain staff morale, the organization must raise salaries. Because higher rent and increased salaries aren't necessary to a group's survival, they will not be included in the group's "survival" budget; however, they are important enough to the organization's work to be included in the "reasonable" budget.

The "barebones," "reasonable," and "ideal" columns, then, give the range of finances required to run the organization at various levels of functioning.

The process of figuring expenses and income must be done with great attention to thoroughness and detail. For example, to estimate how much you will spend on printing, think through all the items you print and how many of each you will need. A simple mail appeal has at least three printed components—the letter, the return envelope, and the envelope the appeal is sent in. Planning for a newsletter, annual report, brochure, or flier must include costs of design, layout, and paste-up.

When you don't know how much something costs, do not guess. Take the time while creating the budget to find out. To assure completeness and accuracy in budgetsetting, many organizations have found it helpful to send board and staff members to training sessions on financial planning.

Projecting income. At the same time that the expense side of the budget is being prepared, the other half of the committee is preparing the income side. Crucial to this process is a knowledge of what fundraising strategies the organization can carry out and how much money these can be expected to generate. (A discussion of how to choose a fundraising strategy appears later in this chapter.) The income side is also estimated in three columns, representing "worst," "likely," and "best."

To calculate the income projection labeled "worst," take last year's income sources and assume that with the same amount of effort the group will at least be able to raise this amount again. In the case of foundation, corporation, or government grants it may be wise to write "zero" as the worst projection.

The "best" income projections are drawn up next. These figures reflect what would happen if all the organization's fundraising work was successful

Expense Columns for Sample Organization

Item	Barebones	Reasonable	Ideal
Salaries			
Director			
Fundraising coordinator			
Support staff			
Program coordinator			
Benefits and taxes			
Total Personnel			
Office rent			
Office equipment			
Maintenance			
New (specify)			
Computer			
Office supplies			
Telephone ($00.00 per month)			
Photocopy			
Printing			
Brochures			
Envelopes			
Mail appeals			
Annual report			
Newsletters			
Stationery			
Other			
Total Printing			
Typesetting			
Design and layout			
Postage			
First class			
Bulk mail			
Bulk mail permit			
Other (specify)			
Total Postage			
Bookkeeping contract			
Fundraising training for board			
Staff development			
Miscellaneous			
TOTAL			

and all grant proposals were funded. Again, this is not a dream budget. It does not assume events that will probably not occur, such as someone giving your group a gift of a million dollars. The ideal budget must be one that would be met if everything went absolutely right.

The "likely" column is a compromise. It estimates the income the organization can expect to generate with reasonable growth, hard work, most people keeping their promises, expanding old fundraising strategies and having success with some new strategies, yet with some things going wrong.

All income categories are figured on the basis of their gross: That is, the amounts you expect to earn from each strategy before expenses are substracted. The expenses must then be included in the expense side of the budget. Be sure that the committee developing the expense side of the budget includes expenses for fundraising in the total expenses of the organization (see "Sample Income Projections," below).

Sample Income Projections

Source	Explanation	Worst	Likely	Best
Major gifts				
New				
Renewing				
Membership				
New				
Renewing				
Special appeals				
Pledging				
Sale of products				
T-Shirts				
Booklets				
Bumper stickers				
Special events				
Raffle				
Dance				
Conference				
Luncheon				
Board donations				
Fees for service				
Foundations				
Other (specify)				
TOTAL				

Step two: Meet, compare, negotiate

Once income and expense projections have been completed, the two halves of the committee can share results. When the income and expense sides of the budget have been figured separately in this way, there is less chance of giving in to the temptation to manipulate the figures to make them balance. For example, in one organization in which the budget committee of the board prepared income and expenses together, the income estimates were boosted several times during the process to insure that income and expenses were the same on paper. Little thought was given to the reality of being able to raise so much more money, and the group was soon in financial trouble.

When the entire committee reconvenes, you hope to find that the "reasonable" expense column and the "likely" income column are close to the same. In that happy circumstance those figures can be adopted as the budget with no more fuss. Occasionally groups are pleasantly surprised to discover that their "likely" income projections come close to their "ideal" budget. However, compromises usually need to be made. In these cases, the expenses need to be adjusted to realistic income potential; not the other way around.

When no two sets of numbers are anywhere near alike, the committee will have to find solutions. There is no right or wrong way to negotiate at this point. If each committee has really done its job properly, there will be no need to review each item to see if it is accurate. However, with more research, committees may discover other ways to delete expenses or add income.

Two case studies that illustrate different ways of reaching a workable budget using compromise and research are discussed at the end of this chapter.

Expenses	Income
Barebones	Worst
Reasonable	Likely
Ideal	Best

Expenses	Income
Barebones	Worst
Reasonable	Likely
Ideal	Best

Expenses	Income
Barebones	Worst
Reasonable	Likely
Ideal	Best

Criteria for Fundraising Strategies

In doing income projections, groups are often stymied by not knowing what criteria should be applied in looking at fundraising strategies. While this book will later explore many fundraising strategies in depth, we will discuss here the questions that need to be asked in choosing any strategy. The following questions will give an organization a complete picture of fundraising strategies.

1. How much time will be needed to research and plan? (For example, research has to be done on which foundations to apply to even before a proposal is written.)
2. How much lead time is needed once planning is underway? (For example, to do a benefit concert up to six months can be required for publicity and arrangements, even after the performer has been booked.)
3. How many volunteer workers are needed in order to insure success?
4. How much front money is required?
5. What special knowledge is required? Who has that knowledge? (For example, groups wanting to set up deferred giving programs will need specialized information on this strategy. They may have to hire a consultant or a tax attorney.)
6. Is the plan cost-effective? (Count all staff and volunteer time and overhead expenses required. Think about what staff and volunteers could be doing if they were not participating in this fundraising strategy and if it is worth the amount of time it requires.)
7. Are there strings attached to the money earned? (For example, groups seeking free printing from a business or corporation may be required to advertise the business in their publications; an individual or corporation giving a gift may want a great deal of say in how the money is used.)
8. How much money will this strategy actually raise?
9. Is this a stable source of funding?
10. What is the worst thing that could happen?
11. What is the best that can be attained?

Some groups have found it useful to have these questions typed up for fundraising staff, volunteers, and the budget committee. Writing the questions across the top of a sheet of paper, with the strategies down the side, as shown here, provides an easy worksheet for evaluating fundraising suggestions.

Evaluation and Review

Once a budget plan is in place, the budget committee or other appropriate part of the board must review the organization's progress on a regular basis (at least quarterly). This committee should present their findings to the board in a report that is simple and easy to understand. The board needs to

Sample Chart Source	Time needed	People needed	Front money?	Special knowledge	Cost Analysis	Strings attached	Profit?	Stability?	Worst thing that could happen	Best to hope for?
Individual Donor										
Membership Dues Pledging										
Special Events										
Raffle Dance Phonathon										
Fees for Service										
Sale of Products										

know whether they are overspending or underspending, meeting fundraising goals or falling behind, and whether the income and expenses are remaining roughly equal. Much more information than this is not necessary. Putting the figures in the categories shown above usually provides all the information a board member needs to know.

If there is a large difference between income and expenses at any review period, a committee of the board, working with staff, should analyze the reasons for the discrepancies before modifying the budget. If the organization is overspending, why? If they are not on target with fundraising goals, why? Sometimes the explanation is simple, such as the organization spent a great deal of money in one quarter but will not continue to spend at that rate in the future and will thus make up the overspending. Or it could be that board members need assistance in meeting their fundraising goals. If the explanation means that expenses must be reduced, modify the budget, but make sure you have explored the other possible explanations first.

The Making of a Budget: Two Case Studies

Neighborhood Advocacy
Neighborhood Advocacy was founded ten years ago. For the past five years, they have received a federal grant of $30,000 annually. Last year, however, they were informed that federal money was no longer available. Of their total budget of $73,700, this shortfall represented over 40 percent. Their budget committee developed the following estimates:

Income
Worst $43,720
Likely $45,000
Best $50,000

Expenses
Barebones $56,500
Reasonable $73,720
Ideal $103,000

All of their income projections were below the amount they needed in order to survive. Furthermore, their reasonable budget was their actual budget from the past five years, and their barebones budget represented significant cutbacks in service. After much discussion among the board and staff the group decided that they wanted to continue operating at the current level to avoid undermining morale completely and curtailing the program. Therefore, the board asked the budget committee to develop a budget that would be between the existing "barebones" and "reasonable" options and to research further some expanded fundraising programs, including getting a loan.

The expense half of the committee then created a budget called "Barebones Two" which called for renting part of their office to another group and reducing a clerical position. The income half of the committee investigated hiring a consulting firm to help implement a large membership recruitment drive using telephone and direct mail. The strategy would pay for itself the first year and begin making money the second year. The front money required for this whole package was $10,000. The budget committee returned to the board with these figures:

Income	Expenses
Likely $45,000	Barebones One $56,500
Best $50,000	Barebones Two: $60,000
Loan $10,000	Loan $10,000

When the full board met they first adopted the "Best" income projection and the "Barebones Two" expense budget. This involved risk, and board members all realized and agreed that their level of involvement in fundraising had to increase over that of previous years. They then committed themselves to the loan: a move of considerable risk, foresight, and courage. They reasoned that the worst that could happen was that they would have to cut their budget drastically and extend the loan payments. But with some luck and a lot of hard work, Neighborhood Advocacy would never be as dependent on one source of money again.

Their final decision was to adopt their Barebones Two and Best plus Loan columns. They play to pay the loan back in the second year, when the strategy begins to make more money.

Alternative private school
Our School has been functioning for only two years. The first year the school was run entirely by volunteers, mostly parents of the students. In the second year, the board (also composed of students' parents) hired an administrator who also teaches classes. This sole staff member now needs an assistant. While the board has been successful in fundraising, and a few parents have made significant financial contributions to the school, no one is certain that these gifts will be repeated. It is also difficult for them to make fundraising projections based on past experience because they have so little to go on. A budget committee estimates these figures:

Income	**Expenses**
Worst $30,000	Barebones $28,000
Likely $40,000	Reasonable $40,000
Best $43,000	Ideal $100,000

The only difference between the "Barebones" and "Reasonable" expenses is the cost of an assistant. Even though the "Likely" income can cover the "Reasonable" budget, the board elects to adopt the "Barebones" budget for the first six months, and the "Likely" income. They reason that although their track record for fundraising is good, their fundraising program is not well enough established for them to draw conclusions about the future. Because the school has grown rapidly the board feels that taking on another staff person is ill-advised until they are sure of meeting their income goals. At a six-month income review, they will hire the assistant if they have raised at least half of their "Likely" goals. This gives the board some "breathing time" and assures the administrator that the issue of her work load is being addressed and can be solved in a short time.

Chapter 3

The Board of Directors

Roles of the Board

The broad purpose of a board of directors is to run the organization effectively. To qualify for tax-exempt status an organization must file a list of names of people who have agreed to fulfill the legal requirements of board membership. The board members are bound to insure that the organization:

◆ operates within state and federal laws;
◆ earns its money honestly and spends it responsibly;
◆ adopts programs and procedures most conducive to carrying out its mission.

The best summary of a board member's responsibility is contained in the state of New York's Not-for-Profit Corporation Law (the language of which has since been adopted by many other states). According to this law, board members must act "in good faith and with a degree of diligence, care and skill which ordinarily prudent men [sic] would exercise under similar circumstances and in like positions."

Board members, in effect, own the organization. They are the final policy makers and they employ the staff. They are chosen because of their commitment to the organization and long-term vision. As the Council of Better Business Bureaus points out, "Being part of the official governing body of a nonprofit, soliciting organization is a serious responsibility, and should never be undertaken with the thought that this is an easy way to perform a public service."

The responsibilities of board members fall into several broad categories. How any specific organization chooses to have board members carry out these responsibilities will depend on the number of board members, the number of paid staff, the sources of funding, and the history of the organization. There are no right or wrong ways to manage an organization, simply ways that work better in some groups than in others.

With that in mind, let's look at Board member responsibilities.

Responsibilities of the Board

Board members are responsible for the following:

1. Insuring organizational continuity: The board must develop leadership within both board and staff to maintain a mix of old and new personnel in both spheres.

2. **Setting organizational policy, reviewing and evaluating organization plans:** The board insures that the organization's programs are always in keeping with its statement of mission, and that the statement of mission continues to reflect a true need.

3. **Long-range planning:** The board should set aside a time, usually at an annual retreat, in which long-range plans are discussed and formed. Where does the organization want to be in 2 years, 5 years, 10 years? How big does the organization want to become? If it is a local group, does it want to become regional or national? What are the implications of world events for the group's work, and what is its response? How can the group become more pro-active, rather than reactive? These and other questions can be answered during the long-range planning retreat. Some organizations find it helpful to have a board-level long-range planning committee. This committee can raise and research appropriate questions and bring recommendations to the board for discussion and decision.

4. **Fiscal accountability:** The board approves and closely monitors the organization's expenses and income. The board makes certain that all the organization's resources (including the time of volunteers and staff as well as money) are used wisely.

5. **Personnel:** The board sets and reviews personnel policies, hires, evaluates, and when necessary, fires staff. These tasks are often delegated to the executive director. She or he then takes the place of the board in personnel matters. The board hires the executive director and evaluates his or her performance regularly. The board is also the final arbiter of internal staff disputes and grievances and should pay close attention to maintaining good staff/board relationships.

6. **Funding the organization:** The board is responsible for the continued funding and financial health of the organization.

To carry out their duties boards form themselves into smaller committees to perform specific functions. Many boards have an executive or steering committee that meets more frequently than the whole board and has authority to make quick decisions.

Board Structure and Size

There is no evidence that any particular board structure works better than another. Each structure will have its strengths and weaknesses. The structure your organization chooses will probably stem from past history and the desires of the present board members. Some groups work best with a collective structure, including open meetings, informal discussion, and decision by consensus. Other groups do better with an heirarchical structure, a parliamentarian who helps the group follow *Roberts' Rules of Order,* and a formal method of discussion and decision making. The only rule of thumb is that the simpler you can keep your structure, the better.

The size of the board also depends on the group, but there is evidence that the ideal size is between 11 and 21 members. A board of fewer than 11 members will probably have too much work, and one of more than 21 members is likely to be unwieldy, with work unevenly divided. If you already have a large board, work can be most effectively accomplished through small committees, keeping full board meetings to a minimum. A small board can also be divided into committees, which can be fleshed out with nonboard representatives recruited to participate.

Statement of Agreement

For a board to operate successfully each member must understand and respect the structure and decision-making process, as well as the mission of the organization, and must feel that she or he can fully participate in it. Achieving this understanding is difficult. One technique that many groups have found helpful is to develop a statement of agreement for board members. This statement serves as a job description and clarifies board responsibilities and authority.

Here is a generic example of such a statement:

As a Board member of _____, I understand that my duties and responsibilities include the following:

1. I am fiscally responsible, with the other board members, for this organization. It is my duty to know what our budget is and to take an active part in planning the budget and the fundraising to meet it.
2. I am legally responsible, along with the other board members, for this organization. I am responsible to know and approve all policies and programs and to oversee the implementation of policies and programs. I know that if I fail in my tasks, and if the organization becomes the subject of suit of a private person or of the federal or state government, I may be held personally liable for the debts incurred.
3. I am morally responsible for the health and well-being of this organization. As a member of the board, I have pledged myself to carry out the mission of _____. I am fully committed and dedicated to this mission.
4. I will give what is for me a substantial financial donation. I may give this as a one-time donation each year, or I may pledge to give a certain amount several times during the year.
5. I will actively engage in fundraising for this organization, in whatever ways are best suited to me. These may include individual solicitation, undertaking special events, writing mail appeals, and the like. There is no set amount of money that I must raise because I am making a good faith agreement to do my best and to bring in as much money as I can.
6. I will attend (#) _____ board meetings every year and be available for phone consultation. I understand that commitment to this board will involve a good deal of time and will probably not involve less than _____ hours per month.
7. I understand that no quotas have been set, that no rigid standards of measure-

ment and achievement have been formed. Every board member is making a statement of faith about every other board member. We are trusting each other to carry out the above agreements to the best of our ability, each in our own way, with knowledge, approval, and support of all. I know that if I fail to act in good faith I must resign, or someone from the board may ask me to resign.

In its turn, this organization is responsible to me in a number of ways:
1. I will be sent, without request, quarterly financial reports which allow me to meet the prudent person section of the law.
2. I can call on the paid staff to discuss programs and policies, goals, and objectives.
3. Board members and staff will respond in a straightforward and thorough fashion to any questions I have that I feel are necessary to carry out my fiscal, legal, and moral responsibilities to this organization.

This kind of agreement defines understandings that may never before have been verbalized; it also helps channel board members' motivation to serve the organization.

Once a board has developed this type of contract it can be read at regular intervals to remind people of their commitments. It can also be used for internal evaluation and to recruit new board members.

Such an agreement also improves relations between board and Staff. Staff know board limits and will not make demands that exceed those limits. Board members know when they can say, "No, this is not my responsibility."

Though this agreement is not legally binding, it is morally binding and provides a common ground.

Fundraising and the Board

Combating Reluctance: Diversified Fundraising

The reluctance of board members to take responsibility for fundraising can usually be traced to two sources: 1) Board members don't understand the importance of taking a leadership role in fundraising, and 2) they are afraid of fundraising. Board members cannot give themselves wholeheartedly to the process of fundraising unless these two problems are resolved.

The reason that board members must take a leadership role in fundraising is simple: they own the organization. They are responsible for the well-being of the organization and for its success. Furthermore, their supporters and potential supporters see board members as the people most committed and dedicated to the organization. If they, who care the most about the group, will not take a lead role in fundraising, why should anyone else? When the board does take the lead its members and the staff can go to individuals, corporations, and foundations and say, "We have 100 percent commitment from our board. All board members give money and raise money." This position strengthens their fundraising case a great deal. More and more, sophisticated individuals and foundations are asking organizations about the role of the board in fundraising and taking a more positive look at groups whose board plays an active part.

The fear of asking people for money is quite common. Board members are often reluctant to participate in fundraising activities because they fear they will be required to ask people for money. It's true that some fundraising strategies require board members to make face-to-face solicitations. This is a skill and thus can be learned, and all board members should have the opportunity to attend a training session on asking for money (See pp. 133-137).

In a diversified fundraising plan, however, board members can participate in different fundraising strategies. Some can solicit large gifts, others can plan special events, write mail appeals, market products for sale, etc. Everyone's interests and skills can be used. Board members inexperienced in fundraising can start with an easy assignment ("Sell these 20 raffle tickets.") and then move on to more difficult fundraising assignments ("Ask this person for $1,000."). Some fundraising strategies will use all the board members (selling tickets to the dance), whereas others will require the work of only one or two people (speaking to service clubs or writing mail appeals).

Time is not money

Board members are often saddled with two myths about their role in fundraising. First, they may feel that since they give time they should not be called on to give money. "Time is money," they will argue. Second, if an organization has paid staff board members may feel that it is the staff's job to do the fundraising. Let us quickly dispel both of these myths.

While a person's time is valuable to them, it is not the same as money. You cannot go to the telephone company and offer to run their switchboard in order to pay your phone bill. You cannot pay your staff or buy your office supplies with your time. Board members must understand that contributions of time and money are very different although equally important parts of their role.

The role of staff

Paid staff have specific roles in fundraising. These are to help plan fundraising strategies, coordinate fundraising activities, keep records, take care of routine fundraising such as renewal appeals, and assist board members by writing letters for them, discussing fundraising with them, accompanying them at solicitation meetings, and so on. Fundraising staff provide all the backup needed for effective fundraising. It is clearly impossible, however, for one person or even several people to do all the work necessary in a diversified fundraising plan. Just as it is foolish for an organization to depend on one or two sources of funding, it is equally unwise for it to depend on one or two people to do fundraising.

The final reason for all board members to participate in fundraising is to insure that the work is evenly shared. Fundraising is rarely anyone's favorite task, so it is important that each board member knows that the other members are doing their share. If some members do all the fundraising while others make policy, resentments are bound to arise. The same resentments will surface if some board members give money and others don't. Those who give may feel that their donation "buys" them out of some work or that their money entitles them to more power. Those who do not give money may feel that they do all the work or that those who give money have more power. When board members know that everyone is giving their best effort to fundraising according to their abilities, the board will function most smoothly and members will be more willing to take on fundraising tasks.

Common Board Problems and Suggested Solutions

While each board of directors will have its own problems and tensions to be resolved, many boards have a number of problems in common. They are discussed here, along with some solutions.

1. **Board members are overworked—too much is expected of them.** Nonprofit organizations use all of their volunteers to augment paid staff. The smaller the organization the more responsibility volunteers will have, becoming more and more like paid staff. To a certain point this is fine. But there comes a time when board members are taking on much more work than they had agreed to. Overload can result when board members are given new work by staff or because board work takes longer than originally planned. When board members find themselves attending three or four meetings each month and spending hours on the telephone, they begin to dread calls and meetings and to count the days until their term is up.

   This dynamic can be changed or averted altogether by adhering to the following principles:
   a) Board members should feel they can say "no" to tasks that go beyond their original commitment.
   b) Staff and board members should insure that tasks given to the board have a clear beginning and end. Thus, when additional work is essential, board members should be assured that extra meetings will last no more than a month or two and that once that task is accomplished they will not be asked to do more than the minimum for a few months.
   c) A careful eye should be kept on what the whole board does with its time. Board members (particularly the executive or steering committee) should ask, "Are all these meetings necessary? Can one person do what two have been assigned to do? Or two people what four have committed to do?"
   d) Boards should not be asked to make decisions for which they are unqualified. Sometimes consultants need to be asked for recommendations, or the board needs to be trained to handle tasks of management and fundraising.

2. **Individual board members feel overworked.** This problem can arise either because the person was given little impression of the amount of work involved beyond attending regular board meetings, or because she or he already serves on the boards of other organizations and is thus overcommitted. In the latter case he or she cannot fulfill the expectations of any of the organizations and feels overworked even while not doing very much for any one organization.

   A clear and precise statement of agreement (as discussed earlier in this chapter) will help with this problem. The statement can be used to screen out people who are overextended and to call current board members into accountability.

3. **The board avoids making decisions.** In this instance the board constantly refers items back to committees or to staff for further discussion and research. The whole board never seems to have enough information to commit themselves to a course of action. This problem is generally the result of inadequate board leadership.

   The board chair or president must set an example of decisiveness. He or she needs to point out that the board can never know all the factors surrounding a decision and yet must act despite factors changing on a daily or weekly basis.

   The person facilitating a meeting should always establish time limits for each item on the agenda. This can be done at the beginning of the meeting. Close to the end of the time allotted for an item, the chair should say, "We are almost at the end of time for discussion on this item. What are the suggestions for a decision?" If the chair or facilitator of the meeting does not take this role, individual board members should take it upon themselves to call for a time limit on discussion and a deadline for a decision.

   Very few decisions are irrevocable. Decisions can be modified, expanded, or scrapped altogether, once they are made and put into action.

4. **The board makes decisions, notes them in the minutes, and then forgets about them.** As a result of this process the board both fails to implement their decisions and usually has to decide the same issue again in a few months or years. Further, board members feel that they are not taking themselves seriously and that their work is for nothing. Three methods can be used to avoid this problem. One method is to appoint a member to keep track of decisions and remind the board of them. The secretary of the board can serve this function, or someone designated as "historian." A second, complementary, method is for decisions from board meetings (as distinct from meeting minutes) to be written up and kept in a notebook, which is available at every board meeting. The notebook can be indexed so that decisions can be easily found. The chair and executive committee should familiarize themselves with this book.

   Finally, each board member should read and keep a copy of the minutes of every meeting. Then, each member can help remind the whole of decisions made.

5. **A few board members do all or most of the work.** When this happens, those who do the work resent those who are not carrying their share. Those who don't work resent those who do because they imagine them to have all the power. Inevitably, some people will work harder than others, and some will work better. Nonetheless, the board should plan for work to be evenly shared and for everyone to take an active role, assuming that all members will work equally hard and equally effectively. Above all, board members must value everyone's contribution. The person who stuffs envelopes is as valuable as the person whose friend gives $5,000. People rise to the standards set for them. Mediocre work should not be accepted.

6. **Staff members don't really want the board to have power, or some board members don't want to share the power evenly.** Sometimes people take and keep power because they enjoy having power and building empires. More often, though, they take power because they are afraid to let go—afraid that others will not do as well as they have. This is particularly true when some board members have served for many years or when a person on staff has seen the board turn over several times. Whoever perceives that someone is hoarding power or refusing to delegate tasks (either staff or board) should address their concerns to the appropriate committee. That person should use examples, so that people can have a clear sense of what they are doing wrong and change their behavior accordingly. Generally, people will share power in the organization as others prove reliable.

All of the dynamics described above, as well as others including personality conflicts, deep political disagreements, or staff-board conflicts can be serious enough to immobilize an organization. The board and staff may not be able to resolve the problem themselves. Sometimes they can't even figure out what the problem is. Board or staff members should not hesitate to seek help in that case. A consultant in organization development or a mediator can help the group articulate and solve its problems. Although for a board to find itself in such an extreme situation is unfortunate, it is usually no one person's fault. To *not* ask for help in getting out of the situation, however, constitutes a failure of board or staff members to be fully responsible.

Some conflict can be creative, and board members and staff should not shun difficult discussions or disagreements. There is built-in tension between program and finance committees, new and old board members, and staff and board personnel. As Karl Mathiasen, a veteran board member and consultant to organizations for social change, states in **Confessions of a Board Member**, "My own feeling is that if you go to a Board meeting and never during that meeting have a time during which you are tense and your heart beats faster and you know that something is at stake—if you lack that feeling two or three meetings in a row, there is something wrong with the organization."

Recruiting and Involving New Board Members

Once an organization has a clear sense of the board's roles and responsibilities, defined the type of structure it wants (collective, hierarchy, etc.), and developed a statement of understanding or similar agreement, it can begin the formal process of recruiting additional board members. Two key tenets of board composition are: 1) Board members, while sharing a sense of commitment to the organization's mission and goals, also need to represent a diversity of opinion and skill; and 2) ideally, the combination of all the people on the board will provide all the skills required to run the organization.

Assessing the Board's Strengths and Weaknesses

To recruit board members, the current board should appoint two or three people to form a "nominating committee." (In some organizations this becomes a standing committee of the board.) This small group will assess the present board's strengths and decide what skills or qualities are needed to overcome the board's weaknesses. The following chart is an example of a way to evaluate the current board and quickly spot the gaps. Each group should fill it in with the board membership criteria it has established.

Some of the unmet criteria could probably be satisfied by one or two people. In other areas you may need several people to develop the balance you want. (For example, most community organizations will want several community activists who also embody a range of other qualifications, but will only want or need one attorney or business person.)

There is a common belief that a board should have "movers and shakers" on it. Bank presidents, successful business people, politicians, corporate executives, and the like are thought to be people with power and connections, making them ideal board members. This is definitely not necessary. There are hundreds of successful organizations whose board members are neither rich nor college-educated and who have no access to and little desire to know the movers and shakers of their community. Other qualifications and the ability to commit time to the work of making the organization successful are of far greater importance.

First and foremost, board members and new recruits must understand, appreciate, and desire to further the goals and objectives of the organization. Enthusiasm, commitment, and a willingness to work are the primary qualifications. Everything else required of a board member can be learned, and the skills needed can be brought by a wide variety of people and taught to others on the board.

In assessing what skills and qualifications your board lacks, then, don't just go for the obvious recruits. For example, suppose that no one on your board understands budgeting. An obvious solution would be to recruit an

Issue/Activity/Skill	Name of Board Member			
	Reilly	Stedman	Burger	McHenry
Budgeting				
Personnel issues				
Fundraising				
From individuals				
Special events				
Marketing				
Planned giving				
Membership				
Other				
Program planning				
Evaluation				
Publicity				
Client/former client				
Community activist				
White				
Black				
Hispanic				
Asian				
Male				
Female				
Over 30				
Over 50				
College-educated				

accountant, MBA, or corporate executive to meet this need. If you know someone in one of these areas who shares the commitments and ideals of your group, then certainly invite her or him to be a board member. But if you don't know anyone whose profession involves budgeting, use your imagination to see what other kind of person might have those skills. In one organization, a self-described housewife does all the budgeting and evaluation of financial reports. Her experience of managing a large family has taught her all the basics of financial management; she is completely self-taught. Anyone who has to keep within a budget may have excellent budgeting skills: Ministers, directors of other nonprofit organizations, small businesspersons, homemakers.

Another example: If the gap on your board is in getting publicity an obvious choice would be someone who works in the media or has a job in public relations. However, as many groups know, anyone willing to tell his or her personal story of a group or who is articulate about the issues can get media attention if a staffperson lays the groundwork. A staff member can arrange an interview, send a press release, and put together a press packet. An outgoing volunteer can then do the follow-up required to get the media coverage.

The Recruitment

Prospective board members are found among friends and acquaintances of current board members, staff members, former board and staff members, and current donors and clients. Ideally, a prospective board member is someone who already gives time and money to the organization.

The chair of the board should send a letter to each prospective board member asking the person if he or she is interested in serving on the board and giving a few details of what that would mean. The letter should state that someone will call in a few days to make an appointment to discuss the invitation in detail. Even if the prospect is a friend of a board or staff member, or a long-time volunteer, a formal invitation will convey that being on this board is an important responsibility and a serious commitment, and that it is a privilege to be invited. Whoever knows the board prospect can follow up the letter by talking to the person about being on the board. If no one knows the prospect, two people from the board should see the person. If the prospective board member does not have time to meet and discuss the board commitment, this is a clue that he or she will not have time to serve and should not be on the list of prospects.

Whoever meets with the prospective board member should go over the board's statement of understanding point by point. The current members should share their experiences in fulfilling their commitment and discuss what others have done to fulfill theirs. It is particularly important to discuss the amount of time board participation requires as well as the area of fundraising. Do not make the board commitment sound easier than it is. It is better for a person to join the board and discover that it is not as much work as was originally thought than to find that it is much more work and resent having had the commitment misrepresented.

The contact person should feel free to ask the prospective board member how he or she feels about the group and how well he or she works with people of other classes, races, or sexual orientations. Asking someone to be on the board is as serious as inviting someone to be a partner in a business, finding a new roommate, or interviewing staff. Do not expect people to change once they are on the board. What you see is what you get. Take it if it is good, leave it if it is not.

Tell the person why you are asking him or her to be on the board. Let him or her know that the nominating committee has given a great deal of thought to this choice. Give the person a few days to think it over. Ask him or her to call for more information or with further questions. Let this be an informed and considered choice. It is better for 10 people to turn you down than to get 10 half-hearted new board members.

Orienting the New Board Member

After a person has accepted nomination to the board and been elected, a current board member should be assigned to act as the new person's "buddy." The current board member should bring the new board member to the first meeting, meet with him or her (perhaps for lunch or dinner) once a month for the first two or three months, and be available for discussion. New board members have many questions that they are too embarrassed or shy to ask at the full board meeting. They will be incorporated into the life of the organization much faster if they can easily get the answers they need.

At their first meeting, the new board members should receive a packet of information including copies of the signed statement of understanding, the organization's by-laws, the case statement, and anything else that would be helpful to their understanding of the organization: an organizational chart, the current annual budget, brochures and other promotional information, and the names, addresses, phone numbers, and profiles of the other board members and of staff members.

Board members work best when they feel both needed and accountable. They will be more likely to keep their commitments when they know that keeping commitments is expected, and that others are doing so. When this tone is established at the beginning, the board will function smoothly.

A Note on Advisory Boards

In addition to a board of directors, small organizations often find it helpful to form "advisory boards" made up of people who can help with various parts of the organizations' program, including fundraising. Having an advisory board can be a helpful strategy, although it involves a good deal of work and does not take the place of a board of directors.

In some ways an advisory board is an administrative fiction. Unlike for a board of directors, an advisory board has no legal requirements, no length of time to exist, and no purposes that must be fulfilled. Such a board can consist of one person, or 200.

Advisory boards are variously named depending on their functions. They may be called community boards, auxiliaries, task forces, committees, or advisory councils. Some advisory boards meet frequently; others, never. Sometimes advisory board members serve the group by allowing the organization to use their names on the organization's letterhead. In at least one case an organization's advisory board was called together, met, and disbanded all in the same day.

You can form an advisory board for the sole purpose of fundraising. Since this board has no final responsibility for the overall management of the organization, its members can be recruited from anywhere. Furthermore, the advisory board can be completely homogeneous—something a group tries to avoid in its board of directors.

People like to be on advisory boards. It gives them a role in an organization without the full legal and fiscal responsibilities of a member of the board of directors.

Is an Advisory Board Right for Your Organization?

Organizations sometimes see an advisory board as a "quick fix" to their fundraising problems. They may reason: "Next year our group has to raise three times as much money as it did this year. Our board can't do it alone and we don't want to add new board members. So, we'll just ask 10 rich people to be on a fundraising advisory board and they'll raise the extra money we need."

There are several problems here. First, finding "10 rich people" is not that simple. If it were the group would already have a successful major gifts program. Second, a wealthy person doesn't necessarily have an easier time asking for and getting money than someone who is not wealthy. Nor will he or she necessarily be more willing to give your group money than a "not rich" person.

These are the conditions under which an advisory board is a solution to a fundraising need:

1. Although the board of directors is already doing as much fundraising as it can, it is not enough. An advisory board works best when it is augmenting the work of an active and involved board of directors.
2. An organization has a specific and time-limited project that needs its own additional funding. This can be a capital campaign, an endowment project, or a time-limited program requiring extra staff and other expenses. The advisory board commits to raise a certain amount of money overall or a certain amount every year for usually not more than three years.
3. An organization needs help to run a small business or put on a large special event every year. This type of advisory board is usually called an "auxiliary."
4. An organization wants help in raising money from a particular part of the private sector, such as corporations, businesses, service clubs, or churches. The advisory board, composed of representatives from these particular sectors, plans the campaign, the members solicit their own colleagues.

Forming the Advisory Board

If you decide that an advisory board is a good tool for your group, be sure to write out clearly what you want in this group. Use the same specificity and thoroughness here as in drawing up a statement of understanding for your board of directors. In terms of fundraising, set an amount that you want the group to raise as a goal, the number of hours you expect them to work (per month, per event, etc.), and the number of meetings they need to attend. Also, suggest ways for them to raise money. (Sometimes you won't know what to suggest, which may be why you are forming this board. In that case, be clear that there is no staff expertise to guide advisory board members.)

Be straightforward with prospects for your advisory board. Tell them your goals and choose those who can work to meet those goals.

Use the same priorities in choosing members as when forming a board of directors. Of primary importance is the members' commitment to your organization. They must of course be willing to express that commitment by fundraising.

Once you have formed an advisory board the staff of the organization must provide back-up as needed and guide the board as much as necessary. The chair or designated representative of the board of directors should receive reports from the advisory board and frequently call or write the chair to express the organization's appreciation for the advisory board's work. Advisory board members should receive minutes of every meeting, be phoned frequently, and generally treated like major donors to the organization (which they are).

Allow the advisory board to develop a direction. The first few months may be slow, but once an advisory board begins to work well, and carry out its commitments, its members can raise a substantial amount of money every year.

METHODS
AND MECHANICS
OF FUNDRAISING

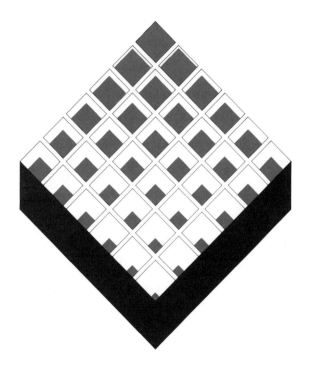

Chapter 4

Raising Money By Mail

Direct mail as a fundraising phenomenon has come into its own in the last 10 years. Always a useful strategy, direct mail has become the main method of recruiting donors for many groups. Though people's mailboxes overflow with requests from dozens of causes, and many people claim they no longer read these appeals, mail is still the best way to reach the most people for the price. Some form of ongoing mail campaign should be among the diverse strategies for almost every organization.

In this chapter, we will explain how direct mail works, as used by the large organizations that have made it so popular. Then we will explain how organizations with low budgets can use the principles of direct mail to their advantage.

How It Works

Direct mail is simple: send the same letter to 200 or more people* and hope that at least 1 percent of them respond with a donation, which is returned to your group by mail. (One percent is an average response to a direct mail appeal.) Once you have acquired donors through this method you can solicit additional gifts during the year, and so on. Donors recruited through the mail rarely know the staff or board of the organization. All communication is by mail.

Mail appeals are used to bring in gifts under $35. Occasionally larger gifts of $50 or $100 will be sent, and groups love to tell of the $1,000-or-greater gift sent in response to a mail appeal, but large gifts are not the norm.

Direct mail works like this: an organization obtains a list of people who are not donors to that group, but who are likely to become donors based on another interest that they have in common with the organization. For

---

* The letters are sent at "bulk mail" rates. This is a system whereby the Post Office will give you a discount if you send 200 or more identical pieces of mail (letters, magazines, postcards, etc). For 501(c)(3) organizations, the price per piece is about 75% less than first class postage. For commercial mailers or groups without this tax exemption, the savings are about 50%. The mail must be presorted according to rules established by the Post Office, and delivered to a Post Office in the community which is authorized to handle bulk mail. Complete instructions on how to qualify, how to sort the mail, and the varieties of permits available, can be obtained from your Post Office.

example, a wildlife group might choose donors to a humane society, or an abortion rights group might choose donors to civil liberties causes.

The organization tests its appeal on a random sample of the total list. Direct mail experts consider 2,000 names an appropriate test sample size. If the response is 1 percent or better they will appeal to the whole list. If not they will either change their mail appeal package and try again, or abandon that list.

In a successful test the original 2,000 names will yield at least 20 new donors. A full list of 20,000-200,000 names will produce 2,000-20,000 new donors. At best, the money raised will pay for the size of the mailing. However, the organization can count on more money coming in from these donors by appealing to them several times a year. Furthermore, 50-66 percent of them will renew their gift for a second year. Obviously, a 50 percent or better response is a good money maker. So whereas mail campaigns rarely make money from the first-time donors, they can be very lucrative after two or three years.

Large organizations that use mail appeals a great deal usually have a revolving fund of $5,000-$50,000 that they constantly reinvest in these appeals. Money coming in from one appeal is reinvested in the next. Major national organizations spending that kind of money generally hire direct mail consultants to design their appeals and to handle all the details of writing, printing, and mailing.

If you have read this far you are probably thinking, "Well, that counts my group out. We don't have the money, we don't have the number of people to approach, and we can't wait two years to start making money."

But now that you understand the principles of direct mail you can appreciate how they can be modified for your group. In order for low-budget groups to use mail appeals effectively they must first increase the percentage of response expected, so that they net money from first-time donors. Second, they must lower the risk so that they do not lose much money if their mail appeal fails. These goals are achieved in two ways: by writing to more carefully selected lists, and by writing to fewer people at one time. By choosing lists carefully you can increase your expected response from 1 percent to a minimum of 3 percent. In fact, groups often experience responses of 5-10 percent. By decreasing the number of people you write to at once, your outlay is lower and you will not have lost very much money if your mail appeal fails.

How small groups can use mail appeals effectively is covered in detail in the next three sections.

Developing Lists

The Categories

A list for a mail appeal is a compilation of correctly spelled names, with their correct addresses and zip codes, to which you will send your mail appeal package.

Lists are divided into three categories of expectation, which, though not rigid, describe the likelihood of people on that list making a donation. These categories are **hot**, **warm**, and **cold**.

A **hot** list contains people who have already made some kind of commitment to your organization. In order of decreasing heat, they are your current donors, your lapsed donors from the past two years (donors lapsed longer than that are barely warm), any volunteers, board, or staff members who are not donors, and finally, the close friends and associates of all the above people who are not yet donors.

A **warm** list consists of people who know about your organization and have used your services in some way, as well as donors to organizations similar to yours. The former group includes but is not limited to clients and former clients, people writing or calling for information and advice, people attending public meetings, forums, seminars or conferences you have sponsored, and people attending special events you have put on.

A **cold** list is any list that is more than a year old, or any list of people about whom you know nothing. An example of such a list is the phone book.

Organizations wanting a high response to their mail appeals write only to **hot** and **warm** lists.

List acquisition and development is a key element in the success of small direct mail appeals. To acquire lists, you must become vigilant about keeping track of names. Dozens of names come through organizations every week or month. Most of them are lost forever unless there are systems to record, categorize, and use those names. The following steps insure maximum retention of names, addresses and zip codes, and suggestions of ways to acquire hot names.

Hot lists

Because current donors are the hottest prospects available and because most people have friends and associates who share their political and ethical commitments, the first place to look for hot prospects is among the friends of your current donors. Once a year send current donors an appeal asking them to send the names of friends they think would be interested in your organization.

Some people will send only one or two names, and most people will not send any, but others will send in dozens of names. With a mailing list of 500 donors, you can be assured of getting at least 200 names from this type of appeal. Many organizations regularly remind their current donors to send in names of potential contributors by including a coupon in their newsletter and a request for names in other appeals.

Friends of board members, volunteers, and staff are also hot prospects. On a yearly basis these people should be asked to turn in a list of names, which can be compared to the current mailing list; anyone who is not already a donor can be solicited. Of course any board member, staff, or volunteer who isn't already a donor is a hot prospect as well.

Some statisticians claim that every person knows 250 people—relatives, school friends, colleagues, neighbors, and so on. Of this number perhaps only 10-20 will be suitable prospects. Nevertheless, with each volunteer or member contributing some names, you will soon have the 200 needed for a bulk mailing.

Warm lists

If your organization gives people advice, referrals, or other service over the phone or through the mail, create a system to gather those names. A notebook to log the needed information in categories can be kept by each phone. When people call, respond to their request and then ask if you can send them more information about your organization. People who don't want an appeal will decline to give their name.

Names from information requests that come through the mail can be transferred directly onto labels or also kept in a log. Every time you have acquired 200 names, send an appeal.

The people who buy any of your organization's products, such as booklets, educational materials, T-shirts, etc., are prospects for a mail appeal. Certainly, their names should be kept to advertise any new items you produce, and some of them will become members of your organization. The same is true of people who attend conferences, seminars, or public meetings that you sponsor.

Acquiring Lists

Renting and Trading

The other type of warm list is of people who belong to organizations similar to yours. To get these names requires renting or trading mailing lists. No one actually buys a mailing list. They rent it; that is, they acquire the right to use the list one time. Many organizations with large mailing lists (5,000 or more names) use the rental of their lists as a fundraising device. You may have noticed that if you give to one organization, you will receive appeals from several similar organizations within a few weeks. Your name has been rented because you are a proven "buyer" through direct mail.

You rent mailing lists either from a mailing list broker, or from another organization.

Professional mailing list brokers have a wide variety of lists available, which are used both by nonprofit organizations and by businesses. Most brokers will send you a free catalogue of the categories of names available and the number of names in each category. The variety is astounding. A quick glance through one catalogue shows these possible offerings: sports medicine doctors, corporate secretaries in corporations with budgets over $250,000, earthquake research engineers, season ticket-holders to dance performances, donors to animal shelters, women in the press, or even the fascinating category, "super-wealthy women" (236,000 nationally).

These lists come to you in zip code order. The lists generally cost $35-$60 per thousand, with a minimum rental of 2,000 names. For a small additional fee you can have lists crossed with each other, yielding the names, for example, of all the super-wealthy women who are donors to animal shelters or of earthquake engineers who are donors to historic preservation projects.

To find mailing list brokers, look in the Yellow Pages under Mailing Houses, Mailing List Brokers, or Fundraising Services and Consultants. Also, ask organizations that use direct mail services for their recommendations.

Many low-budget organizations trade mailing lists with other organizations for a one-time use. Usually, lists are traded on a name-for-name basis: 200 names for 200 names and on up. A group can also trade names for as many names as they have and rent the rest. If your organization has 500 donors, and you want another group's list of 2,000 donors, trade your 500 and pay for the remaining 1,500. Depending on your relationship with the other organization, it may rent the list to you simply for the cost of the list or the cost plus handling, or it may seek to make some profit.

Dos and Don'ts of Sharing

Organizations often feel reluctant to share their donor lists with other organizations. Some fear that their donors will prefer the other groups and stop giving or give less to their group. Studies of donors show that this is not true. In fact, donor loyalty to the first group is increased as they learn of similar organizations. Furthermore, most people who give to charity give to five or more charities. Usually all the charities are similar: they may all be in the arts or in the environment, or they may be civil rights and civil liberties causes, but there will be some similar theme in all five charities. People add charities each year. **You will not lose donors by sharing your list.**

Sometimes organizations fear that their donors will take offense at being solicited by so many groups. To insure that this does not happen simply include a line in your newsletter that says, "From time to time we make our mailing list available to organizations that we feel would be of interest to our members. If you would rather we did not include your name, please drop us a line, and we will make sure that you do not receive any of these mailings." You can publish this announcement in every issue of the newsletter to be sure that every donor sees it. Very few people will actually write in with this request. Most people like to get mail. When a survey queried people in the San Francisco Bay Area about their favorite part of the day, 71 percent said, "Opening my mail."

Do not steal mailing lists or use mailing lists that are marked "members only." Because mailing lists are fairly easy to compile and acquire, once you have the systems in place there is no need to be underhanded with others' lists. Further, your group's reputation may suffer. Almost all mailing lists, particularly those rented from commercial firms, have a certain number of "dummy" names: names that are placed to identify the use of that list. The letter addressed to a "dummy" name goes to the source of the list. Suppose you have "liberated" the list of members of a service club which has given your organization a donation. John Q. Jones is on that list. "Q" is his code for service club, and when he gets a letter using that initial, he knows it came from the service club list. He is also in a position to know or discover that no one gave your group permission to use the list. The situation can then become unpleasant and counter-productive to your fundraising efforts, especially if Jones announces at the next meeting of the club that members should not join your group.

A final rule about list acquisition and development: **Do not save mailing lists.** A list that is more than 3 months old will already be out of date. After you have used a list twice (if you have not been given a once-only arrangement), you have gotten 90 percent of the response you are going to get from that list. Throw away the names of people who have not responded. Concentrate your efforts on getting new names and refine your systems so that the names are as "hot" as possible. The list is pivotal to your direct mail success.

The Package

The mail appeal has many more elements than simply a letter in an envelope. The appeal is a package: it is "wrapped" a certain way in terms of the envelope, the writing style, and the offers made to the prospect to interest him or her in becoming a donor. The work of your organization is only one variable determining the success of your appeal.

The standard package has three parts: the letter itself, the enclosures that go with the letter, and the envelope in which the letter and enclosures are mailed (called the "outside" envelope).

Each part of the package is complementary, and all the elements work as a team to have the maximum effect on the prospect receiving the appeal. This section will examine each element separately and then discuss putting the elements together.

Principles of the Letter

As the result of careful study of every aspect of the fundraising letter a few simple principles have emerged that, if applied, will create an effective letter.

1. **People have very short attention spans.** All your sentences need to be short enough to be read in 6-15 seconds. Further, they need to be interesting enough that, after reading one sentence, the reader is willing to spend another 6-15 seconds to read the next sentence, and so on.
2. **The reader must feel involved, sought out, needed, and included.** You must speak to readers about themselves by repeatedly using the word "you" in the letter. Phrases such as "As you may have read," "as you are aware," "because you share our concern for," and "people like you" will draw people into your letter and keep them reading. References to the reader should appear about four times as often as references to your organization.

    Using the word "you" makes your letter talk *to* readers, rather than *at* them. Every time the reader sees the word "you" he or she asks if this statement actually applies. Subconsciously, readers agree with the statements. They are saying, "Yes, I am concerned, I did read, I am aware." When they have said yes in this way a number of times while reading your letter, they will be more likely to say yes to your request for a gift.
3. **People read the letter in a certain order.** People do not read a letter from beginning to end. Usually they read the salutation and opening paragraph first, the closing paragraph next, and the postscript third. Sometimes people read the postscript before the closing paragraph. Up to 60 percent of the readers decide whether or not to give based on these three paragraphs. The mission of these paragraphs, then, is to catch the reader's attention and hold it long enough to evoke an emotional, empathetic response and to assure the reader that his or her help is needed and important.
4. **People want to believe what you are telling them.** People are not reading these letters cynically. They read from their heart and they respond from their heart. This does not mean that the readers are naive or gullible, but simply that since they have taken the time to open the envelope and glance at the contents, they are people who want to respond positively if your group draws them in, your work makes sense, and your request is reasonable.
5. **The letter should be as long as it needs to be to tell the story.** Large direct mail efforts have proven that the longer the letter, the greater the response. A four-page letter generates more response than a two-pager, and six pages pull better than four. Fortunately, this rule can be suspended for small mail appeals to carefully selected lists. Since the audience is already practically sold on your group, your job in the letter is to push them to a financial commitment. You don't need to start from the

beginning to convince this audience. In fact, some potential contributors may turn away if they think you are spending an inordinate amount of money on the appeal letter. Many groups are able to put their story across effectively in one or two pages.

6. **The letter should be easy to look at.** The page should contain a lot of white space, wide margins, and a pica typeface. Break up paragraphs so that each is no more than two or three sentences long. Use contractions, write in an informal style. Do not use jargon or long, complex words.

Structure of the Letter

The opening paragraph

The first paragraph of the letter, which is also the first paragraph that is read, is used either to tell a story or to flatter the reader. The mechanism of telling a story is used a great deal in large direct mail efforts. Though often an effective strategy, it must be carefully done because Americans are increasingly skeptical of stories, of which they have heard too many.

Two rules apply to using the story opening: First, the story must be believable (though it does not have to be factual), and the characters in the story must be credible. You don't want the reader to say, "What a sad story, but that could only happen once." Second, the story must resolve itself positively owing to your group's help.

Here are two examples of the same information delivered in two different ways:

From a shelter for battered women:

◆ "While you are reading this letter, 17 women will be beaten."

◆ "While you are reading this letter, we will respond to 17 women in crisis."

From a drunk-driving education program:

◆ "Eddie Phipps was a shy and lonely high school sophomore. He had a drink with a friend one night and was amazed at the charming, funny person he became. With two drinks he felt irresistible. He began to drink every weekend. One Saturday he borrowed his parents' car and went to a party. As he drove home around midnight, his head spinning from cheap wine, he decided to see how fast he could go on the freeway. Pretty fast. Over 90, the police estimate from the impact of the collision against the cement barrier he ploughed into. Now Eddie is a statistic. One more dead drunk driver."

◆ "Eddie Phipps was a shy and lonely high school sophomore. He had a drink with a friend one night and was amazed at the charming, funny person he became. With two drinks he felt irresistible. He began to drink every weekend. He and his friends would race up and down the freeway, daring each other to go faster and faster. One day in school Eddie heard a program about the dangers of driving while drunk. Eddie decided to get help for his drinking problem from the group that had put on the program: TeenReach."

The message in the second version of each story is clear: Because the organization is there, people are getting the help they need. A positive tone is set from the very beginning.

The second use of the opening paragraph is to flatter the reader. The flattery is low key and not obsequious. You are showing the reader that you have noticed his or her commitment or interest in something that relates to your group. For example: "Because you attended our conference on the health effects of smoking on nonsmokers we want to tell you more about Clean Air, Inc." "You were one of 50 people who testified at the city council hearing on the dangers of putting a freeway through the playground of Logan Elementary School. I know you will be interested in helping us with our lawsuit to stop that project."

When readers feel that their presence, efforts, or suffering were noticed and not taken for granted or given in vain, they will want to help the organization that did the noticing.

Either opening can be effective, and the one you use will depend on your list and what your available stories or flattering comments are for that list.

The closing paragraph

The next paragraph people read, which is the last paragraph of the letter, is used to tell the reader the amount your group needs and some of the benefits of giving. For example: "For your gift of $15 we will send you our quarterly newsletter, *Community Views*, which will keep you posted on our progress. Your gift is a critical part of our efforts to insure adequate health care for uninsured people." "A gift of $20 from you today will help us reach 200 people." "Please send $25, $50, $15 or whatever you can, today. People giving $20 or more will receive a copy of an important book on this issue."

While your group may have several different membership levels, only the simplest description is used in the letter. This is a short paragraph, with the full details of benefits explained in one of the enclosures.

The postscript

This is the final sentence that people read. **The most common use of the P.S. is to suggest action:** "Join today. Your gift now is more important than ever." "Don't put this letter aside. Write your check now." The P.S. suggests an appropriate action for people to take while they are still caught up in their impulse to give. This impulse has been created by the opening paragraph, which moved or flattered them, and the closing paragraph, which indicated a reasonable size of gift and may have told them what they would get in return for their gift. In a few days, or even a few minutes, that impulse could be replaced by an impulse to have dinner, answer the phone, take the kids to piano lessons, pay the bills, or any number of other interruptions.

The P.S. can also be used to tell a story. For example:

◆ "P.S. Mrs. Jones, a long time resident of this community, was sent an eviction notice after 25 years in her apartment. The apartment building was to be razed to make way for an office building. She reported her eviction to Housing Advocacy, and we were able to stop the entire development. The money needed to buy the apartment complex and turn it into co-op housing for senior citizens was provided by thousands of people like you: people who care about the quality of life for seniors in our community."

The P.S. can be used to flatter the reader:

◆ "P.S. You may be wondering where we got your name. It was given to us by a friend of yours who told us of your interest in this issue."

◆ "P.S. We are writing to you because you cared enough to come to our community meeting last week. We hope you'll join us in our critical work."

The rest of the letter must also be good material. Use these paragraphs to tell your history, discuss your plans, tell more stories, give statistics, and list accomplishments. Use devices other than straight paragraphing to break up the text. For example, the following paragraph is the middle of a letter from the Committee for Family Planning:

Because of us:
• In 1976, a city ordinance banning birth control for teenagers was repealed as unconstitutional;
• All teenagers in this community receive sex education as a part of their biology courses;
• Teenage pregnancy, on the rise in the United States, has declined in our community;
• We remain the only independent clinic providing referrals and birth control to anyone who needs it, regardless of ability to pay.

This is much more exciting than writing the same information out in paragraph style.

Who signs the letter is not as important for a hot list as it is in a large direct mail effort. However, a real person must sign the letter. Avoid having more than one or two signatures for your letter, or it begins to look like a petition. The chair of the Board, the executive director, or a volunteer can sign the letter on behalf of the whole organization. The person who signs the letter should have a readable, straightforward signature.

The Enclosures

The return envelope

Any number of items can be enclosed with the letter, but only two are necessary: a return envelope and a return form for the donor to sign, indicating the size of the gift being made. (In direct mail jargon the return envelope is called the "response vehicle," and the return form is called the "reply device.") The purpose of these enclosures is to give the reader an easy way to express his or her impulse to give, which has been generated by the appeal letter.

There are two styles of return envelopes: With the business reply envelope the postage is paid by the organization. The donor simply puts the check in the envelope and drops it in the mail. The other type of return envelope is not prepaid—the donor must attach a stamp. The business reply envelope (BRE) costs you more than a first-class stamp, but you only pay for the envelopes that come back. You must register with the Post Office and pay a fee for a business reply permit.

There is a great deal of controversy about the effectiveness of each style of return envelope. Many direct mail consultants maintain that the additional cost of the permit and postage is more than offset by the increased number of returns. Others believe just as firmly that there is no difference in the rate of return, and that BREs are a waste of money. Despite many studies, there is no compelling evidence either way.

One factor to consider is that people are increasingly aware of the cost of a prepaid envelope to an organization. Many people used to think that BREs cost no more than a first-class stamp. Increased knowledge about nonprofit organizations has dispelled this myth. As people are more aware of the cost to a nonprofit, the effectiveness of BREs will go down.

While business reply envelopes may be an interesting experiment for a low-budget group, they are not a necessary expense. Many low-budget organizations do not use BREs and still have significant responses to their direct mail campaigns.

However, it is too much to expect that the donor will not only find a stamp, but also an envelope, and then write out your address along with their check. Studies definitively show that responses are markedly increased when a self-addressed envelope is enclosed.

The return form
The second necessary enclosure is a form on which the donor indicates how he or she will donate and gives his or her name, address and zip code. These forms are usually on card stock and are cut slightly smaller than the return envelope for an easy fit. The card's weight makes it stand out from the rest of the enclosures, and donors are accustomed to filling them out.

Another effective return form is the "wallet flap" envelope, which is an envelope and return form in one. On the inside of the back flap of the envelope, which is as big as the envelope itself, is printed all the information found on a return card.

There is no reason to think that one style of return form is more effective than the other.

The psychology of the return form is that readers are committing themselves to your organization. You have spoken to the reader all through the letter, with the use of the word "you" and allusions to the reader's interest.

Now the reader will in effect answer, "Yes, I will join," "Yes, I will give." The return form, then, also uses this language. The reader sees, "I will give," sees the choices, and chooses a gift amount that suits his or her self-image as a donor.

Here is what a return form should look like:

YES, I WILL JOIN:

_____ $15   _____ $25   _____ $50   _____ $100   _____ Other

I look forward to receiving my copy of Great Newsletter.

Name _____

Address _____ Zip _____

Or:

COUNT ME IN! I WANT TO GIVE:

_____ $ 25: Includes quarterly newsletter

_____ $ 50: Includes newsletter plus T-Shirt

_____ $100 or more: Includes newsletter, T-Shirt, and a free book

Name _____

Address _____ Zip _____

Make checks payable to: Name of Group. Send to: Group's address.

Whether you put the giving choices horizontally or vertically on the card doesn't matter. People read until they find a number they are comfortable with. Therefore, don't put the lowest gift suggestion first. Put first or second the amount you want most people to give. Unless you are appealing to a very low income group, do not suggest $5 or less as a gift. Use the category "Other" to let people write in that amount.

All other enclosures are optional. The simpler the letter is, the more responses it will pull. If your organization has received favorable press coverage, a press clipping can be an effective enclosure. People are more likely to believe what they read in the papers about your group than if you told them yourself. Newspaper clippings are inexpensive to print, as newspaper is the cheapest stock of paper available. All other enclosures, such as brochures, bumper stickers, support letters from someone else in the group, are unnecessary.

The Outside Envelope

The envelope the letter comes in is pivotal to the success of the mailing. If people don't open the envelope they will not respond to your appeal. For small direct mail appeals the mission of the envelope is to make the reader believe that it was addressed to him or her personally and was sent by first-class mail.

The most effective way to personalize the letter is to handwrite the prospect's name. With a small list and a few volunteers this is fairly simple. (Make sure the volunteers have readable, adult-looking handwriting.) If handwriting is out, typing the prospect's name right onto the envelope is also effective.

With a list of 500 or more names or a shortage of volunteers you must fall back on other strategies. Avoid using window envelopes, since those are most commonly used by large direct mail efforts. Instead, place a mailing label right onto the envelope.

Do not use a bulk mail indicia, which is the small box appearing in place of the stamp saying, "Nonprofit postage paid. Permit Number 12345." Instead, you can buy precancelled stamps of the same denomination as the cost of bulk mail per piece. You must fill out a different form from that for an ordinary bulk mailing, but there are not other differences. Most people will only notice that the letter is stamped, and will not observe that the stamp is not first class. You can also use a postage meter machine. This also looks first class, if more businesslike.

Contact the Post Office for full details about these options.

If you cannot use any of these somewhat labor-intensive methods, then you must rely on more traditional direct mail strategies. Not putting your return address on the front of the envelope but instead putting it on the back, or simply putting the address of your organization without its name on the envelope will pique some people's curiosity, and they will open the letter to see who sent it.

Using "teaser copy"—writing or drawing something on the envelope that makes people want to open it and find out more—is the direct mail method most traditionally used for the outside envelope. There are an infinite number of examples of teaser copy. If you want to see some, simply save all your direct mail appeals for a few months, and ask friends to give you theirs. Teaser copy moves the letter from the personal to the mass marketing sphere. It can be effective, however, and should not be disdained. Keep in mind, though, that low-budget groups using very hot lists have better success with the other methods discussed here.

Putting the Package Together

Be sure that your letter and enclosures are free of typographical errors. One typo can change the meaning of a sentence or more often render it meaningless; it gives a bad impression of your group's work. Although the letter itself should simply be typed, the return forms and return envelope generally should be typeset. Remember, the only impression that donors recruited by mail will have of your group will be from what they get in the mail.

Be sure that the envelope color and the paper stock for your letter do not clash. Avoid strong colors such as bright yellows or reds or any dark-colored paper. People with vision problems have a difficult time reading off of dark paper, and you don't want to lose a prospect because he or she couldn't read the letter. Use sharp contrast in your type and paper color so that the written words are easy to read.

Do a spot-check of the printed materials to be sure that they are all the same. Sometimes, a printer will have made a mistake on the middle 25 letters, which might be smeared or blank. While you can't look at every letter, you may be able to stop an error from being sent out.

Be sure that your return form fits into your return envelope. The card should not have to be folded to fit into the envelope. Put your return address on everything: the card, the letter, and the return envelope. That way, if someone loses the envelope he or she can still find you.

Fold the letter so that the writing is on the outside, rather than on the inside, as would be the case with a normal letter. A person pulling the letter out from the envelope should be able to begin reading it without having to open it or turn it around.

Make sure the response you want is obvious and easy to comply with: note on your return form to whom to make the check payable, and whether or not the contribution is tax-deductible. Specify the gift or gifts that you want. Make sure suggested amounts are offered.

Some communities have laws that require you to send a copy of your appeal to a government agency for approval before sending it out, or to list your charitable identification number on everything you send. **Be sure to investigate and comply with these laws.**

A Note on Time of Year

The time of year you send your appeal is not critically important, but some months are better than others in terms of expected response. In order of effectiveness, they are as follows:

January
February
September or October
November
March
May or June
July or December
August
April

Variations on the Mail Appeal Package

In this section we will describe six variations on the basic mail appeal package. These suggestions will not work for every organization, and not all possible variations are explored here. The point is to suggest a number of options for using the principles of direct mail fundraising. Some of these may inspire you to create other variations on the theme.

A Gift Catalogue

A gift catalogue is a mail appeal in which the organization lists items it needs and their costs. People then either donate an item or—more usually—the money to purchase an item for the group. In the latter instance the donor's gift is "earmarked" for a particular item.*

Gift catalogues work particularly well with groups such as shelters, land preservation organizations, clinics and other health services, and the like, whose shopping list can inspire donations more readily than the organization that simply needs office supplies.

The Nature Conservancy's San Francisco office, for example, successfully uses the gift catalogue in their efforts to buy and maintain ecologically significant land. A sampling of the items contained in their catalogue includes:

---

*There is an important difference between the words "earmark" and "designate" in giving. An "earmarked" gift is to be used for the purpose indicated until that need is filled; after that, it can be used at the organization's discretion. A "designated" gift can only be used for the purpose for which it is designated, even if that need has been filled. Organizations are advised to stay away from the term "designated."

- ◆ Binoculars: four pairs, $160; one pair, $40
- ◆ Classroom visits: 10 visits, $150
- ◆ Scholarships for docent trainees: cost per docent, $15
- ◆ Gates for fences: one gate, $40
- ◆ Hand lenses: 25 hand lenses, $32
- ◆ Refrigerators for houses on the preserves: two propane refrigerators, $800
- ◆ Research grants for various projects (which are described)
- ◆ Weather monitoring equipment: complete cost, $350

The budget of the organization can easily be broken down into gift categories, which are described in the catalogue. The catalogue itself may be only a few pages long. It should include an "order form" that is a variation on the reply form. People can then "order" more than one item.

Some organizations have used this concept to raise money for intangible program components, such as client care, or provision of services. A therapy collective listed these items in their gift catalogue:

- ◆ Scholarship for one family session: $40
- ◆ Complete six-week session: $240
- ◆ Parent effectiveness training
  Full scholarship: $100
  Partial scholarship: $50
- ◆ Day care for parents in therapy: $7/hr.=$ _____ (hours you wish to donate)

The actual gift catalogue can be fancy or plain. It can include pictures of the needed items or of people using the services. It can be laid out like a regular mail order catalogue or can simply list the needed items on a sheet of paper.

Generally, using your imagination in drawings and illustrations will make your catalogue more effective. Laying it out in the form of a newsletter or booklet will give it the air of a catalogue and make it stand out from regular mail appeals.

Using Your Newsletter as a Mail Appeal

If you have a newsletter or magazine with information that people want and find useful but may not be able to get elsewhere, use your publication as an advertisement for your organization. Show people what they will get for their money by sending them a copy of the publication with information on how to subscribe.

You can have a special cover made for one issue of your publication or a special issue used only for promotional purposes. This issue can contain the best of your previous issues. In this variation, the cover becomes the mail appeal. The cover includes a return form to be torn off, which is essentially a subscription form. A return envelope stapled into the newsletter is optional but will increase your returns. This appeal is not sent in an envelope.

If your newsletter is long (16 pages or more) and expensive to produce, consider making up a special short edition of it. This piece might be four to eight pages and contain one or two excellent articles plus a listing of articles and information that people would receive by subscribing. Include a subscription form, either as part of the cover or somewhere in the newsletter.

Whatever style you use, make sure it is clear that this issue is complimentary and tell people where to look for information about subscribing.

Some groups have found it effective simply to buy a rubber stamp that says, "Complimentary copy—please subscribe." They can send these complimentary newsletters to names they have acquired along with their regular mailing of the newsletter, or as a separate mailing. If the newsletter is good enough that simple message can be enough to generate donations.

Phantom Event

In a phantom event people are invited to a special event which is not going to happen. This event is described in detail, and the prospects are invited to stay home and miss it. The appeal is sent in the style of an invitation, with an RSVP used as the return form:

T he Board of Directors of Californians for Action invites you to their first annual gala nonevent. The City Council, Robert Redford, Tom Hayden, and other notables will not be there. In fact no one will be there. You will not have to mingle with people you barely recognize. You will not have to eat soggy hors d'oeuvres, buy a fancy outfit to appear in, or travel after dark.

Please join us in staying home.

Time: 6-10:30 p.m.

Date: June 14

Cost: $58.95. Send us the $50 and keep the $8.95 to buy a bottle of wine to share with a loved one.

We look forward to not seeing you.

RSVP by June 1 using the enclosed card.

Phantom events work because they catch people off guard, they amuse people, and because, in fact, they appeal to the many people who don't enjoy large social events.

The Brief Message

Organizations working on issues that are familiar to most people, or whose mission is totally self-evident, can use the brief message format. Your appeal and return form are all on the same piece of paper, and a return envelope is enclosed. The Arthritis Foundation, Northern California Chapter, used this method effectively. (See illustration.)

```
NORTHERN CALIFORNIA CHPT.              ARTHRITIS
203 WILLOW ST., STE 201           IS AMERICA'S BIGGEST
SAN FRANCISCO, CA 94109                  PAIN.
```

MR. MCDONALD, PLEASE JOIN THE NORTHERN CALIFORNIA CHPT. IN
THE FIGHT AGAINST ARTHRITIS... $10 OR MORE MAKES YOU A
MEMBER... FOR 3,814,000 ARTHRITIS VICTIMS IN OUR STATE,
THANK YOU... JEFFREY SMITH, TREASURER

I'LL HELP. I ENCLOSE THIS SLIP WITH MY GIFT OF:
$_____ □$50 □$25 □$15 □$10 □$5 $10 OR MORE MAKES YOU A MEMBER

```
                                    NORTHERN CALIFORNIA CHPT.
MR. JERRY D. MCDONALD               P. O. BOX 44580
901 N. INTERNATIONAL                SAN FRANCISCO, CA 94144
RICHARDSON, CA   75081

                                    N851.232C2
```

Courtesy of Arthritis Foundation (National Office).

The brief message conveys the following: "I am not going to use a whole sheet of paper and precious minutes of your time. You know who we are. You read the paper and hear the news. Join us. We need you." Brief messages are effective when the group or the group's work is well known and requires little explanation, and because the message uses the word "you" effectively. The reader is pulled in quickly and asked to decide almost before there is time to think about it.

Pictures

Organizations that serve animals or people in distress can express their message more poignantly through photographs or drawings than with words. A picture can take the place of many pages of text. The ubiquity of television has caused what we see to have more impact than what we read, and photographs appeal to that reality. The pictures can be part of the letter or a separate enclosure. For pictures to be effective they must be real and they must not be deliberately sappy or maudlin. Photographs must not demean the people in them.

Sometimes photographs are used to jar people's sensibilities. This can be effective when carefully done. Showing an animal caught in a leg-hold trap, for example, is far more moving than a wordy description of the trap and its effect. A picture of the bodies of victims of Central American death squads provides vivid evidence of a situation that many people find hard to credit.

Drawings such as an artist's rendering of a new building are usually used to augment the text of a letter. Again, the drawing must depict something real and be well done. It does not generally replace as many words as a photograph.

Promotional Items

Many long-established organizations use promotional items to draw in donors. The method works because people open the envelope to get what's inside—stamps, bumper stickers, pencils, address labels, etc. It also works by generating a feeling of obligation to reciprocate with a donation. Because these items are expensive it is generally better to use them as a part of a thank-you package, if at all. With the exception of groups that have always used these items, they do not seem to increase the rate of response relative to their cost.

Use of Benefits and Premiums

An organization that intends to have a large base of donors who repeatedly give small gifts must establish a workable benefits program. The purpose of a benefits program is to give donors something tangible for their donation. Benefits are important for the simple reason that Americans are consumers. We are accustomed to getting things for our money, and even nonprofit organizations compete for the consumer dollar on this level.

Although supporting the work of the group gives the donor a feeling of good will, this feeling lasts only a little while, and the donor needs a reminder of the gift and of the work of the group. A thank-you note is the first reminder. It should go out within 48 hours of receipt of the gift. (See pp. 76-78 for a full discussion of thank-you notes.) The second reminder is the item or items that the group will send the donor regularly.

Donors: What They Are, What They Get

In setting up a benefits program the organization must define what relationship their donors will have to the organization. If you decide that you want your donors to have a feeling of ownership and involvement in your organization, you should consider establishing a membership. Each donor is then called a member. If your by-laws already specify the rights of members, and if you do not wish to give donors voting or other rights specified by your by-laws, simply amend your by-laws to include a class of nonvoting members, number unlimited. If you do not wish to have members, you might establish giving categories such as "friend," "supporter," "benefactor," etc.

After you decide what to call your donors, you must decide what you are going to give them, and whether donors who give more money will get more attention. Most organizations find it useful to have three donor categories to reflect greater contribution amounts. Each category has incentives to join at that rate. The categories might be:

◆ Basic: $15-$25—includes basic benefits package;
◆ Larger: $50-$500—includes basic package plus a book, T-shirt, or other incentive;
◆ Major Donor: $500 and up—includes the above, plus regular reports on the progress of the organization and individual attention.

Generally, you will be recruiting the lower categories of donors through the mail, with occasional donors of $50 or more. A major donor requires face-to-face soliciting, with a correspondingly more comprehensive benefits package.

The Basic Benefits Package

The most common benefit is a newsletter. Appropriately, this benefit regularly reminds donors of your group, raises their level of awareness about your group's work, and provides information not available elsewhere or a point of view not generally expressed in the mass media. Other possible basic benefits include a T-shirt, bumper sticker, membership card (which doesn't have to entitle the member to anything), discounts to special events, or other educational materials. There are two guidelines for choosing benefits for donors: 1) the fulfillment costs (that is, how much money it costs your organization to produce and send the item you promise) should never be more than one-third of the lowest membership category, and 2) while you can always add benefits, you cannot take them away.

In deciding on a benefits package, then, start with small benefits that you know your organization can continue to afford, and that you have the staff or volunteers to handle. The difference between a bimonthly newsletter and a quarterly one will not be nearly as important to the donor as it will be to your budget and time.

If you decide to have incentives for larger donations, try to find something that promotes your organization. A book about the work you do or that is related to a topic you address is excellent. Books can usually be purchased directly from the publisher in quantities of 100 or more for 40 percent off the cover price. Paperback volumes are fine. Paperweights, tote bags, bookmarks, bumper stickers, T-shirts, and the like are all acceptable as well. Specialty merchandising firms can send you catalogues of available items and can print your logo or message on them at low cost.

The psychology of a benefit is this: the donor sends a gift, and your organization, in gratitude for the gift, sends a **free** benefit. The donor is not buying the benefit, which costs much less than his or her donation.

Premiums

Premiums are additional thank-you gifts for donating within a specified time period. Announcement of a premium is often included in the mail appeal letter at the postscript, whose main purpose is to move the donor to act: "P.S. Send your gift by December 15, and we will send you a special edition of a calendar created by a local artist for our group." Or, "P.S. We have a limited number of signed lithographs that we will send to the first fifty donors. Join today."

Premiums are particularly useful in getting renewal gifts. The majority of these donors are probably going to give anyway; the premium simply encourages them to give sooner rather than later. You don't want the renewing donor to put your appeal in the pile of bills to be paid later or to lose the appeal, so you offer them a premium for acting promptly.

The best premiums from your organization's point of view are ones that you already have. For example, suppose you are doing a concert, and ticket sales are slow. Offer renewing donors a free ticket for renewing by a certain date. Or suppose you have had too many calendars printed and cannot possibly sell them all before the beginning of the new year—offer them as a premium.

In using premiums for acquiring new donors, remember to add the cost of the premium to the cost of the mail appeal. This will lower your net income, but if you gain even one or two percentage points in response, the cost will be offset.

Appealing to Current Donors

Too often, appeals to current donors are overlooked. Years of testing have proven that some donors will respond every time they are asked, another group will give less automatically but more than once a year, and that donor renewal rates are higher for all donors (even those who do not respond to extra appeals) when they receive several appeals a year. Once your organization has acquired donors, it should appeal to them several times a year.

Many groups have discovered that with repeated appeals they can raise enough money from their current donors to be able to scale down their recruitment of new donors. Many large organizations appeal to their donors 8 to 12 times a year. For small, low-budget groups, 4 to 5 appeals a year seem to have the maximum effect.

The Multiple Appeal

Multiple appeals are successful for a number of reasons. First, a person's cash flow can vary greatly from month to month. In one month, a person receiving an appeal from a group he or she supports would like to give more, but just paid car insurance and so throws the appeal away. If the organization were to ask again in two months the person might have more money available and make a donation.

Second, different people respond to different types of appeals. Sending only one or two appeals a year does not allow for the variety of choices donors want. Organizations often discover that donors who regularly give $15 a year will give $50, $100, or more when appealed to for a special project. People who respond to specific project appeals are often called "bricks and mortar" people. They "buy" things for an organization: media spots, food for someone for a week, a job training program, a new building.

We rarely know why people don't respond to appeals. Despite this lack of knowledge many people are willing to make the assumption that the donor doesn't want to give, when any of the following might be true:

◆ The donor has been on vacation and mail has piled up, so anything that is not a bill or a personal letter, including your appeal, gets tossed.
◆ The donor is having personal problems and cannot think of anything else right now, even though he or she might be quite committed to your group.
◆ The appeal is lost in the mail, or the donor meant to give but the appeal got lost or accidentally thrown away before it could be acted on.

Donors do not feel "dunned to death" by multiple appeals. On the contrary, they get a sense that a lot is happening in the organization. Their loyalty is developed when they know that their continuing donations are also needed. Most important, they have an opportunity to express their own interests when a particular appeal matches their concerns.

Once an organization has accepted the idea of sending multiple appeals, they often wonder what they are going to say in each one. The following section contains 12 ideas to help you choose some approaches. Some of these appeals are taken from or modeled on specific groups' letters. Some will suit one organization better than another, but almost any organization should be able to find one or two ideas that they could modify and use for their group.

Seasonal appeals
1. **End-of-year:** "As you close your books for this year, please remember _____ (organization). This is your last chance to make a tax-deductible donation to our group and count it for this year's taxes."
2. **Beginning-of-year** (written as a testimonial): "One of my New Year's resolutions was to give more money this year to _____ (organization). I realized that, like many of my resolutions, this one could fade if I didn't act now. So I sent an extra $25 on January 5. I imagine that many of our members made a similar resolution. Perhaps you did. If you are like me,

time may pass without action. So join me, and send that extra donation now."

Holiday appeals

1. **Lincoln's Birthday:** "President Lincoln was only one of the more famous people to be killed with a handgun. I know you want to end this senseless outrage. An extra donation from you, sent today, will give us the extra funds we need to work on _____ (special program) against handguns/ crime in the street to strengthen our community organization activities/to escort people who are alone across campus."

2. **Valentine's Day:** "Do you often think of important people on Valentine's Day? Do you remember them with flowers, candy, or cards? I know I do. This year, I thought of other important people in my life—the people at _____ (organization). They really depend on us, their members, for the financial support they need. Will you join me in sending an extra donation? You can send flowers or candy as well. Simply use the enclosed card."

3. **Labor Day:** "A time to take the day off. But what about all the people who want to work—the 10% percent of the population that is unemployed? For them Labor Day is another reminder of their joblessness. Our organization is providing training to thousands of people so that they can get good jobs in areas needing workers. Remember the unemployed this Labor Day with a gift to _____."

4. **Columbus Day:** "Columbus discovered America. This is one part of American history almost everyone knows. The problem is that this is only a half-truth: Columbus discovered America for white people. There were already people here—our people. We are Americans. Yet our history since Columbus has been one of genocide, displacements, and oppression. At Native American _____, we are determined to reclaim Columbus Day. You have helped us in the past. Will you help us, on this holiday, to continue our vital work?"

5. **Thanksgiving Day:** "We would like to make Thanksgiving Day a little brighter for hundreds of people in our city who cannot afford to buy food. With your donation of $14.50 we will provide a family with a turkey and all the trimmings. Please give whatever you can."

6. **Christmas/Hannukah/end of year:** "We are just $400 short of our goal to buy a new furnace for our runaway house/send our staffperson to the state capitol to work for the bill we have been working so hard on/ distribute thousands of leaflets telling seniors how to get their homes insulated for free. Can you help us meet our goal with a special end-of-year donation?"

Old stand-bys

1. **Anniversary:** Our organization is now entering its third/fifth/fiftieth anniversary of service to the community. Celebrate with us by sending 1 dollar/10 dollars/100 dollars for each year of our existence. For your

gift we will be pleased to send you a special anniversary parchment, suitable for framing. In addition, for those donating $1,000 or more, there will be a special reception honoring _____ (famous person), who has been so helpful to our cause."

2. **Famous Person:** "I'm _____. You may have seen me on television. In my personal life, I am very concerned about birth control/tenants' rights/ public education. I believe the _____ (organization) defends our rights in this area. Please join me in supporting them." (Famous person can be truly famous, such as a movie star, or someone well known only in your community and widely respected there.)

3. **Another member:** "My name is _____. I have been a member of _____ for five years. In that time, I have witnessed the continuing erosion of our rights and the seemingly malicious efforts of our leaders to take what little we have left. All that stands between them and us is _____ (organization). In the past five years, our organization has succeeded in _____ and _____. That's why I am giving a little extra this year. Fifteen dollars is not a lot, but it really helps, and if everyone gave just $5, $10, or $15 it would really add up. Will you join me?"

4. **Urgent need:** "We have an urgent need to raise $2,000 to alert the public to the hazards of chemical dumping currently being proposed for the east side of town. This little-known bill, which has the support of our supervisors, will bring unwarranted health hazards to over 1,000 people. The town council is trying to slide this bill through without our knowledge, and thus our protest. Help us stop this outrage now, with an extra donation of $15, $25, or whatever you can send."

Setting Up and Maintaining A Pledge Program

Pledging is the secular equivalent of the church tithe. Tithing is a religious custom of both Judaism and Christianity in which people donate a certain amount of their income (usually 10 percent) to their church or synagogue. Since few can afford to give the entire 10 percent at once, most donors give the amount promised over the period of a year. A pledge is the same thing: a donor wishes to give a certain amount of money that is greater than he or she can give all at once. Therefore, the donor "pledges" the amount, and fulfills the pledge with regular payments.

The main advantage to an organization of a pledge program is that people can give more by spreading their payments over time. Further, a sizable pledge program means a reliable monthly income.

There are also clear advantages for the donor. People who are committed to an organization can give more than their annual dues by pledging. Many people who could not afford a $60 gift all at once can certainly pledge $5 each month. Even people who can afford a larger gift of $50, $100, or more can be encouraged to give still more by repeating that gift twice a year, quarterly, or monthly.

The Pledge Appeal

There are a variety of ways to introduce the idea of pledging to your donors. The best way is to send a special mailing to your current donors asking them to pledge. The appeal letter explains that the reader is a valuable supporter, and your organization wants to give him or her an opportunity to give more without undue hardship. Groups often find it helpful to provide incentives for pledging. This can be done by creating a special category for people who pledge, such as "gifts-of-the-month club," "donor club," or "sustainer club." People who pledge can also be given something not available to other members, such as a T-shirt, a special newsletter, or a book.

In addition to being the subject of a special mailing, pledging should be an option in all your mailings. The idea of pledging sometimes takes a while to catch on, but when donors see this option in many different places and grow accustomed to the idea, eventually some of them will pledge.

The pledge appeal includes a pledge card or form and a return envelope. The purpose of the pledge card is to get the donor to specify an amount he or she will give per month or per quarter. The pledge forms should also remind donors that you will mail them stamped, self-addressed envelopes when the pledge is due.

Keeping Track of Pledges

When someone pledges, record the information on that person on a 3″ × 5″ card and keep all the pledge cards in a separate file. The pledge card should contain the donor's name and address, the amount pledged, and the date the pledge was made, along with an indication of how often payments will be made. It should also have a column noting when the pledge payments are due. Note pledge payments made beside the date they were due. A quick glance will tell you whether the donor is behind in payment.

People pledging monthly and those pledging quarterly can be kept in separate sections of the file box. Once a month someone goes through the box, fills out the appropriate pledge note (see below), and places it with a stamped return envelope in an envelope addressed to the donor. Putting this package together and sending it out is the extent of work required for collecting the pledge.

The pledge package should go out 7-12 days before the date the pledge is due. People may drop out if their pledge reminders arrive at different times every month.

This pledge note should be preprinted, and the blanks filled in for each person pledging. Make sure the amount noted as the pledge is correct, the donor's name is spelled correctly, and only one envelope goes out each time.

Most groups find that they collect between 80 and 100 percent on their pledges. If a person has been reminded three times without paying, assume

Dear _____ ,

Your monthly/quarterly pledge of _____ is now due. Thank you for your ongoing support.

Sincerely,

Name of Director or President

Amount pledged _____   Amount given to date _____

that he or she is not going to pay. Drop these people from the program rather than hound them for payment.

At the end of the year send a personal letter with the final pledge note asking the donor to renew his or her pledge. Include a renewal form. The letter is simple and straightforward, such as:

Dear _____ ,

This is the last payment on your pledge of $250. Your ongoing support has been tremendously important to us this past year. I am writing to thank you for your commitment.

I also hope that you will renew your pledge. We will continue to send you reminders, and you will receive _____. I enclose a form for you to fill out if you wish to renew.

Thank you for all your support.

Sincerely,

Name of Director or President

Two Don'ts of the Pledge Appeal

Organizations are sometimes tempted to try cost-cutting measures on their pledge programs. They may, for example, send a donor who has pledged $10 a month 12 envelopes at one time expecting the person to return one envelope containing a payment each month. People cannot be expected to remember to pay their pledges or to keep track of the envelopes you have sent them. Even though churches give congregants a box of envelopes for the entire year, they have the advantage of reminding people weekly to turn in their pledges. Further, for people who don't come to church regularly, the church will send a letter reminding the congregant to pay.

Other organizations leave the stamp off the return envelope, reasoning that if the donor can afford and is committed enough to pledge, he or she can afford a stamp. This is technically true, but a stamp makes it easier for the donor to send in the pledge payment and is a small way to show the donor your appreciation. Do not set up a pledge program only to undermine it with these types of penny-pinching measures.

Pledge programs are easy to set up and maintain. Though they require attention to detail and more ongoing attention than regular mail appeals, the payoff can be great. A pledge program is a logical extension of any existing donor program.

The Mechanics of Collecting Direct Mail Donations

Two systems for collecting money from donors require little or no paperwork on the part of the donor and insure immediate collection of the pledged amount of money. These two systems are electronic fund transfer and credit card transactions. In this section, we will discuss both of these methods.

Electronic Transfer of Funds

Simply stated, electronic fund transfer (EFT) allows the transfer of funds from one account to another via a computer network. Prior to 1978, when President Carter signed the EFT Act, a piece of paper such as a bank check or a money order was necessary to transfer money from one party to another. Since the EFT Act, transferring money electronically has become quite popular and is being used in a variety of different ways.

The most common fund transfer method to develop recently is the Automated Teller Machine. Available at most banks in urban areas, these machines allow the customer to conduct routine banking business 24 hours a day, including cash withdrawals.

Direct deposit programs, another form of EFT, account for nearly 60 percent of social security payments. Government funds are transferred directly to the recipient's account, and they can use their money on the actual date of payment with no fear of loss, theft, or mail delay.

Many people are now paying their telephone and credit card bills, insurance payments, and the like by authorizing their bank to transfer the amount owed directly to the creditor or company. Even retail stores are using "debit cards," which look like credit cards but allow payment to be made instantly from the purchaser's checking account.

Many people feared that consumers would not like any form of EFT because of computer phobia and the impersonal nature of these transactions. On the contrary, consumers use EFT a great deal, and it is an increasingly accepted way to pay bills and conduct business with banks. Including the use of automated teller machines, consumers in 1983 made more than 28 million electronic fund transfers per month!

In the future various forms of electronic fund transfer will become more common than using paper money or checks. The advantages are obvious: no checks, no mail delays, no billing, and instant transfer of the money. The costs of stamps, envelopes, and checks, and the time involved with that form of payment are eliminated. In fact, the only paperwork is the authorization form for the bank and checkbook balancing for the consumer.

The system of electronic fund transfer is run by a nationwide network of automated clearinghouses regulated by the National Automated Clearing House Association (NACHA). The clearinghouses receive debit and credit requests on magnetic tape and send them to the receiving financial institution by computer.

Advantages of EFT

Charities are beginning to use EFT for pledge programs. EFT is simple for both the donor and the charity. The donor signs an authorization form which is sent to the charity, authorizing the donor's bank to transfer a certain amount of money on a monthly or quarterly basis to the charity's bank account. Each deduction is listed on the donor's bank statement, and an annual statement summarizes all EFT transactions. For the charity there is no more opening mail, processing the check, and sending pledge reminder forms. The charity simply sends the authorization form to their service clearinghouse.

Another advantage to organizations is that the rate of pledge fulfillment is nearly 97 percent, compared to 75 percent from regular pledge programs. Depending on the number of donors pledging, this increase can pay for the cost of maintaining the EFT system.

Two public broadcasting stations that offered EFT as a giving option in the 1979-1980 pledge drives analyzed the effectiveness of this program. Their study showed that the average pledge made through EFT was $74. Previously, most of their donors had given a single gift, average $28. The stations also noted a renewal rate of 89 percent from EFT donors compared to 70 percent from their non-EFT donors.

While there are no striking disadvantages to an EFT program, only organizations with a strong, well-developed donor base should begin using them. EFT payments are another element in your bookkeeping. The authorization forms must be dealt with promptly and effectively. Records must be kept on EFT donors, and these donors must be sent the same benefits and premiums as others in their category. Your record-keeping system must be very efficient, and preferably computerized, before you are ready to institute an EFT program. Also, as discussed below, the number of donors using EFT must be high before it is cost-effective for either the bank or the organization.

Setting up an EFT program

You can contract with a professional firm to set up an EFT program, or you can do it yourself. To do it yourself ask your bank for assistance in setting up the program. If you are in an urban area or deal with a branch of a large bank, getting this assistance should not be a problem. In rural areas, however, or with small banks, personnel may not be familiar with EFT or may not want to take the time to help you with it. In fact, many groups report reluctance on the part of all banks to help them unless they have at least 500 donors who will be using EFT as their method of payment. If you have someone in your group who works in a bank, it may be easier to get the assistance you need.

There are several professional services nationally that can take care of all these details. They have the volume of business needed through all their clients, plus they have the computer setup, the forms, and the knowledge of how to do it. Generally, these firms charge a setup fee and a fee per individual or percentage per transaction that decreases with volume. Using such a firm is usually not cost-effective until you have 1,000 or more people using EFT—a number out of the range of most small nonprofits groups.

It is important for low-budget groups to be aware of EFT and to see it in their future. As use of EFT becomes more common costs will go down. More and more banks will be willing to help you set it up, and possibly firms will start specializing in EFT programs for low-budget organizations.

Charging Donations With a Credit Card

Paying for goods with cash is becoming less and less common. Checks were the first item to replace cash, although they stand for actual cash. After checks came credit, which allows people to defer payments and to go into debt easily.

More and more people have credit cards; many have more than one credit card. The use of fraudulent credit cards is on the rise, but so is buying on credit, and the frequency of both phenomena will continue to grow.

Many nonprofit organizations have long offered donors the option of giving with their credit card. The return form includes a space for the donor's credit card number and the amount of the gift. Groups that use credit cards report strong donor acceptance. Often donors will give more by credit card than through check payments.

In deciding whether or not to use credit cards, you first must discuss the political ramifications of credit. Some groups do not want to use credit cards because they do not want to perpetuate the American practice of encouraging people to spend money they don't have. Other groups argue that donors are adults and can make their own decisions.

What you should expect

If you decide to use credit, set it up through your bank. The bank will run a credit check on your organization to see how many of your organization's checks have bounced, whether you pay your rent and other bills on time, and what your assets are. They will also visit your organization. This visit is largely to see if the organization actually exists and is what it claims to be. Two or three (depending on bank policy) of your board members must act as trustees for the organization, agreeing that they will supervise the maintenance of this program, and that to the best of their knowledge, the organization is sound enough to undertake such a program. The bank will also run a credit check on those individuals.

The bank takes between 3 and 5 percent of every transaction made by credit cards, although sometimes groups with a friend in the bank have succeeded in having that percentage lowered or waived. The bank will familiarize you with the procedures it wishes you to follow.

Advantages for the organization

There are two main advantages to credit cards for an organization: Cash flow is speeded up, and collection of pledged amounts of money is almost 100 percent. If your bank has a policy of holding personal checks for a period of time, credit card payments can be a big help in avoiding that cash flow delay. The other advantage is that you will gain some donors who otherwise would not have joined the organization at all or who will give more than they would have given by check.

Like electronic fund transfer, credit card giving is worth knowing about and looking into. A smaller number of donors is needed for credit cards to succeed than for EFT. The setup charges are low, and some banks have no setup fee. There are bookkeeping ramifications, however, and your organization must be financially efficient to benefit the most from this system.

What To Do With the Responses

The process of raising money by mail does not end when you get the gift. The next section will discuss recording the gift, and keeping up with donors. This section focuses on two aspects of dealing with the responses to a mail appeal: The thank-you note and evaluation of the mailing.

Thank-You Notes

Thank-you notes acknowledging receipt of the gift and its importance to the organization are the backbone of a successful donor campaign, particularly for small organizations without the money or staff to offer lavish benefits. Without thank-you notes, you will greatly reduce the number of donors repeating their gifts and you will have few donors upgrading their gifts. Since getting donors to repeat and upgrade gifts is a primary reason for acquiring donors in the first place, you can see why thank-you notes are so important.

All gifts, no matter how small, should be acknowledged. Many donors send a small gift (for example, $10) even if they could send $50 or more. While they have liked what they read in the appeal, they may want to see what the group will do with their donation, what the newsletter is like, and so on. If the group responds positively to these donors—a prompt thank-you, a good newsletter, other appeals during the year—they will be more likely to upgrade their gift to their true capability. Other donors giving small gifts may be giving a large percentage of their income. You will have no way of knowing this, but a note from your organization affirming the importance of all gifts will be greatly appreciated by these donors. Appreciation and loyalty in itself are reasons to send the note, but it also happens that when the donor's financial situation improves, he or she will remember your group with a larger gift.

Ideally, thank-you notes are personal; nicely done form notes, however, are better than nothing. Postcards are acceptable for thank-you notes, but a postcard should not state the amount of the gift. Major donors should therefore always receive a personal letter.

Thank-you notes are brief and easy to write. Volunteers can write (or type) and sign them. Here are some generic examples of thank-you notes:

◆ **Personal postcard:**

Dear Ms./Mr.,

Thank you so much for your membership gift to _____ organization. It is not only a help financially, but also a great morale boost! We look forward to staying in touch. Your newsletter begins with the _____ issue, which you will begin receiving shortly.

Again thanks,

Name of Volunteer

◆ Personalized letter:

Name
Address

Dear Mr./Ms.:
    Your generous gift of $_____ arrived today. Thank you! As you know, our organization relies on gifts from our supporters to continue our work. Your gift will go a long way in helping us _____ (state the mission of your group).
    You will begin receiving your newsletter with the next issue, coming out in _____. Please feel free to write or call any time with any comments or questions you may have.
    Again, on behalf of the board and staff of _____ , thank you for your help.

                                Sincerely,

                                Name of Volunteer

◆ Form letter:

Dear Friend,

    Thank you for joining _____. As you know, we rely on members for the bulk of our financial support. Your gift is important to us.
    Within a few weeks, you will begin receiving _____.
Please feel free to keep in touch.
    On behalf of the board and staff, thanks again.

                                Sincerely,

                                Name of Volunteer

For donors who are renewing or giving an extra gift a personal thank-you is a must. The thank-you note only has to be two or three sentences, but the donor will feel noticed and appreciated, which insures a loyal and long-lived relationship. Certainly, if you knew you could earn $25 in two minutes, using skills you already have, without doing anything illegal, and in the process make somebody feel good, you would do it. That is what writing a thank-you note is all about.

Sometimes groups feel that thank-you notes are trivial, waste time and money, and that donors don't really care one way or the other. Studies show, however, that donors repeat their gifts when they feel wanted and needed, and that in candid surveys donors admit to preferring groups that send them thank-you notes.

Evaluating Your Appeal

In order to know if your appeal has been effective, and why, and which of your appeals are the most effective, you must "track" and evaluate them. The process of tracking is simple: You want to find out how many people responded to your appeal, how much money it brought in, and what the average gift was.

The simplest method for keeping count of the number of responses is for the person who opens the mail to code each response on a tally sheet.

Simply mark each response under the week or month that it came in. The heaviest response will come during the first four weeks, and 95 percent of the responses you will be getting will be in by the end of two months. The rest will dribble in over the next six months.

At the end of two months add up the number of responses and the amount of money you earned. Evaluate the appeal in these categories:

◆ Total response, including number of pieces and amount of gross receipts
◆ Number of donors in each category, i.e. members, major gifts, etc.
◆ Percent of response (divide the number of responses by the number of
◆ pieces mailed)
◆ Average gift (exclude major donors or your average will be skewed)
◆ Gift you got most often (also called the MODE gift)
◆ Cost of mailing
◆ Ratio of income to expense (divide the money you grossed by the money you spent)
◆ Any narrative comments

For each mail appeal use a separate folder to file a copy of the appeal, copies of the enclosures, and the evaluation form. If you decide to repeat the mailing, you will have all the information you need in one place. After several mailings, you can pull out all the evaluation forms and see what they have in common. Do some types of lists seem to respond better than others? Did the mailing with a premium offered do better than those without? Does one set of facts or one particular story seem to stir more people to give?

Remember to test only one variable at a time. You cannot find out if more people respond to a BRE over an unstamped envelope in a mailing that is also testing the story approach over the low-key flattery approach. Also, you must use portions of only *one* list to test responses. You cannot test one variable on a list to a service club and another variable on a list to a group of health activists.

If you have mailed fewer than 2,000 pieces, you will not have a statistically significant evaluation. However, using your instinct and what information you are able to garner you should be able to make some educated guesses about what is working and why.

Without evaluation all fundraising is simply shooting in the dark. To get the maximum benefits from a mail appeal program, evaluation is essential.

Fundraising by Telephone

Basic Technique of the Phone-A-Thon

A basic fundraising axiom is that the closer you can get to the prospect the more likely you are to get the gift. Phoning, as we all know, is "the next best thing to being there." A phone-a-thon can be a very successful fundraising strategy.

In its simplest terms, a phone-a-thon involves a group of volunteers calling people to ask them to support your organization with a donation. A phone-a-thon is an excellent way to involve volunteers in fundraising because it teaches them how to ask for money but is less intimidating to them than soliciting donations in face-to-face situations.

Phone-a-thons can be good money-makers. They are usually inexpensive to produce and have a high rate of return. Anywhere from 10 to 25 percent of the people reached will contribute. (These percentages can be higher if you are calling lapsed donors.) Compared to a direct mail campaign's response rate, which is often 2 to 5 percent, a phone-a-thon has much greater potential for raising money. The costs involved include printing and postage, any toll call charges, and food and drinks for volunteers doing the calling. (If you choose to pay your callers your costs will rise a great deal. I recommend and focus here on using volunteers.)

A phone-a-thon can be organized by one or two people. It takes several hours of preparation followed by a 5-hour time block for the event. Several people are needed to make all the calls. The following formula will help you figure out how many people will be required.

Preparation

To prepare for a phone-a-thon, the organizers take these steps:

1. **Prepare the list of people** who will be called. These potential donors are people who have expressed an interest in your organization, have benefited by something you have done for them, or are past supporters of your organization. People attending community meetings you have organized,

alumnae or former clients, and members of and donors to other organizations are all prospects. Get their names and look up their phone numbers. (Organizations in small towns or rural communities or organizations that serve a specific neighborhood or geographic constituency may be able to use the phone book as their source of names, but generally this is too "cold" a list.)

List the names and phone numbers, with any code that is necessary (e.g. L = lapsed, CL = client, etc.) on sheets of paper. Include columns noting what information you will want the telephone volunteer to record. A list of names might have the following headings at the top:

Name, Address, and Code

Yes	No	More info	Not home	Address verified	Other

Explain how to use the code when giving instructions to the volunteers at the time of the phoning.

2. **Set a date** for the phone-a-thon. Pay attention to other events in your community—don't call, for example, on an evening when everyone will be at a birthday party or benefit auction for another group. Most people find that calling on a Tuesday, Wednesday, or Thursday night between 6:00 and 9:00 p.m. at the beginning of the month (near payday) works best. Some groups call on weekends with success, but calling on a sunny weekend afternoon may bring people racing in from their yard or interrupt them while entertaining and may irritate more people than necessary. No one is sunbathing on a Wednesday evening at 8:30. Pay attention to what's on television: Don't call during the Superbowl, on an election night or during the Academy Awards.

3. **Write a script** for volunteers to read as they phone. Generally volunteers can "ad lib" after the second or third call, but initially a script gives them a feeling of security. The script should be brief and to the point:

"Hello, my name is _____, and I am a volunteer with Good Organization. May I speak with you for a minute?" (PAUSE for answer.) "Thank you. I am calling tonight as a part of a phone-a-thon. Are you familiar with our work?" Or "Did you read about us in the *Daily Blab*?" Or "Did you receive our recent appeal?" (PAUSE for answer.) *If the answer indicates little familiarity with the organization's work, say* "We are a group of concerned people working on . . . " *and give a two-sentence or 15-second summary of your work.* (PAUSE.) *If there is no reaction or a positive reaction from the person being called, continue.* "Our goal tonight is $_____. We are asking people to help us with a gift of $15 or more. We will send you our quarterly newsletter (or other benefit). So far, _____ people have pledged $_____. Would you care to make a donation?" (PAUSE for answer.) *If the answer is positive, continue:* "We are trying to keep track of how much we have raised. What amount may I put you down for?" (PAUSE for answer.) "Thank you very much. I'll send you a reminder in tonight's mail. Let me just verify your address." (*Read the address.*) "Thank you again. Good night."

In addition to the script, write up a list of questions that volunteers may be asked, with suggested answers. Include questions and statements such as "Why haven't I heard of you before?" or "I sent you guys money and never got anything."

4. Prepare three letters (samples of each are given below) and appropriate enclosures:

◆ **A letter for people who say "Yes."**

Dear _____ ,

   Thank you so much for joining Good Organization with your gift of $_____ this evening.
   As you probably know, Good Organization is primarily supported by donations from people like you. Your gift will help us continue our work of _____. (Describe in two or three sentences.)
   Please fill out and return the enclosed card with your check in the envelope provided.

Sincerely,

Name of volunteer

◆ **Return card format:**

Name _____

Address _____ Zip _____

   Enclosed is my pledge of $_____. I look forward to receiving the newsletter and other benefits of membership.
   Make checks payable to: Good Organization.
   Mail to: Our Address

(The return envelope should have a first-class stamp affixed.)

◆ **"Sorry we missed you" letter*** to people who weren't home or who had their answering machine on:

Dear _____,

   Sorry we missed you this evening. We tried to call you because we wanted to ask you to join/renew/tell you more about Good Organization.
   Good Organization is . . . (brief summary of not more than three to five short sentences). We have been working on these issues since 19____. Our main program goal for this year is_____.
   I hope you will want to join us in our important work. For a gift of $_____, we will be pleased to send you our quarterly newsletter, *The Right-On Times*. For a gift of $50 or more we will include a beautiful/important book/calendar/picture.
   Please take a moment to read the enclosed brochure, then fill out the membership form and send it with your check today. Your gift sent now is more important than ever.

                              Sincerely,

                              Name of volunteer

◆ **Letter to people with questions about the organization:**

Dear _____,

   Thanks for talking with me this evening.
   I am enclosing the information we discussed, which I hope will answer your questions. Please feel free to contact our office to discuss our organization further if you wish.
   I hope you will decide to make a donation after reading this information. I am sure you know, as I do, how important our work is. Please do whatever you can.
   An envelope and membership form are enclosed for your convenience. I look forward to hearing from you.

                              Sincerely,

                              Name of volunteer

---

* If these letters go by bulk mail, each one must be exactly the same. In that case use the salutation Dear Friend.

Enclosed with both the second and third examples is a card or form that the donor will fill out, a brochure about your organization, and a return envelope. It is not necessary to stamp any of these envelopes.

To decide the quantity of each letter to have printed, count the number of people you will be calling and assume that two-thirds of them will be home. Of this number, anywhere from 10 to 25 percent will say "Yes" and need the "yes" letter; 25 to 30 percent will say "Send me more information," and need the letter described in (c); and the rest will say "No." The other one-third will need the letter described in (b). Much depends on how good your list is, but this formula should give you enough letters without having lots of them left over. If you do not date the letters and avoid using any reference to a month or day, you can use the same letters at other phone-a-thons throughout the year.

5. **Determine how many phones and how many volunteers you will need.** To do this, estimate that one person can make 20 phone calls in an hour and that people will work no more than three hours. Therefore, one person can make 60 calls in an evening (including calls to people who aren't home) and fill out the appropriate follow-up letters.

To get by with fewer phones, people can work in teams of two to a phone. In this arrangement, as soon as one person has made a call and is filling in the appropriate letter, the other person begins a call. This way the phone is always in use. Sometimes a phone team agrees that one person will do all the talking and the other will do all the writing. Phone teams can make about 30 calls per hour per phone, or 15 per volunteer per hour. Since most people will not call for three hours straight, you will need one or two extra volunteers to make maximum use of the phones available.

Suppose you have 600 names to call. If one person made all the calls it would take 30 hours (600/20). If each person has his or her own phone it will take 10 volunteers with 10 phones to get through the calls in one evening, plus one or two extra volunteers to spell people (30/3 hours of calling). If people need to share phones it will take 40 volunteer-hours (600/15 calls per hour), or 14 volunteers on seven phones (40/3 hours of calling), plus one or two extra volunteers.

You may wish to conduct the phone-a-thon over two nights. This has two advantages: You can call more people or use fewer volunteers, and you can call people on the second night who weren't home on the first night.

Sometimes small organizations decide to conduct a phone-a-thon from the volunteers' homes. While there is nothing wrong with this method and just as many calls can be made, it is more fun and generates more momentum to have everyone in the same office. That way, successful calls or rude responses can elicit immediate praise or sympathy, as appropriate. A group effort is also helpful in keeping track during the evening of how much is being pledged. (If you have to use individual homes, have at least two people at each home.)

For national or regional organizations, phoning can be done from different areas to save long distance costs. An excellent example of a national phone campaign is included in the last section of this chapter.

6. **Find a place.** You will need one room or a suite of connected rooms with one or more telephones in each one. Depending on the number of telephones in your organization's office and the number of volunteers you have, you may have enough lines there. Real estate offices, travel agencies, law firms, large social service organizations, mail order businesses, and so forth are good candidates to let you borrow their telephones for the evening. You will be trusted not to disrupt or take anything, to clean up before you leave, and in most cases to pay for any long distance or toll calls.

7. **Recruit volunteers.** Use the phone-a-thon as an opportunity to bring in some new volunteers. Often people who have limited time or who cannot volunteer during the day can be recruited to work one evening on a phone-a-thon. It is a straightforward commitment which begins and ends and does not require preparation or follow-up. Ask volunteers to meet for a training session 30 minutes before phoning begins.

The Night of the Phone-A-Thon

The committee planning the phone-a-thon should arrive at the place where the phoning will take place 30 minutes early. Be sure that desktops or table-tops where volunteers are to sit are cleared off so that your papers do not get mixed up with the papers of the person who uses that desk during the day. Put a stack of the three different letters, their enclosures, the return envelopes, the mailing envelopes, and a couple of pens on each desk. Put a list of names and a script by each phone.

Bring in juice, coffee, and snacks. Pizza, sandwiches, or other simple dinner food should be provided if volunteers are arriving at dinner time. The food should be kept in one part of the office, and volunteers should be discouraged from having food by their phones. Pay attention to details like bringing in napkins, plates, and eating utensils. In a borrowed space take out your own trash.

After all volunteers have arrived, have been introduced to each other, and have had a chance to eat, go through the phoning process step by step. Go over the script and make sure people understand and feel comfortable with it. Review difficult questions they might receive and simulate a few phone calls (one from each of the categories: yes, maybe, no). Be sure people understand the different letters, know what to write on each, what enclosures go with them, and what information needs to be noted on the list of names. (A call that reaches an answering machine is treated as a "Sorry we missed you.")

Each volunteer or phone team goes to a desk. The committee that has planned the phone-a-thon begins calling immediately. When a few people are on the phone, shy volunteers will feel better about beginning to call. Try to avoid a situation where everyone in the room is listening to one person's phone call unless that person feels comfortable with that role.

A staff person or a phone-a-thon committee member acts as a "floater." He or she answers questions and fields difficult phone calls. The floater also continually tallies how much money has been pledged and announces the changing total to the group. The scripts are then changed to reflect new totals. The floater can also be preparing "Sorry we missed you" letters for bulk mailing if that will be used.

Each individual should be encouraged to take breaks as they need to, but the group as a whole will not take any breaks.

At 9:00 p.m. stop the phoning. The first step in wrapping up is to finish addressing all envelopes and to gather up the list of people who were phoned. If a bulk mailing is being done with the "Sorry we missed you" letters, try to do that quickly or do it the next day at the latest. Gather up any leftover forms, envelopes, letters, and cards. Tally the final amount pledged and let the volunteers know how successful the evening has been. If the amount pledged is below your goal, explain that you set your goal too high. Do not let the volunteers leave feeling discouraged.

The callers should be able to leave by 9:30 p.m., leaving the planning committee to do any final cleanup.

After the Phone-A-Thon

Within two or three days, send all the volunteers a thank you note for their participation. If you borrowed a space to conduct the phone-a-thon, write the owner/manager a thank-you note. Thank everyone for whatever they did to make the event a success.

During the next two weeks you should collect about 90 percent of the pledges made. As each one comes in, a thank-you note should go out. At the end of two weeks go through your list and see who said a definite "Yes, I will give" but did not send their money. Send them a gentle reminder.

This is accompanied by a return envelope and a reply form. Most organizations do not find it worth the time and cost to remind people of their pledge more than once.

Tally up the final amounts received and write an evaluation of the event. The evaluation should note how many people were called, how many pledged, how many pledges were received, how many volunteers participated, where the phone-a-thon was held, how that space was arranged (if donated), and it should also include copies of all the letters and return forms used. File all this away so that the next time you do a phone-a-thon you won't have to start from scratch.

◆ "Reminder letter:

Dear _____,

   This is just a note to remind you of your pledge to Good Organization made on the night of _____. In case you misplaced our letter and return envelope we enclose another. Thanks again for your pledge of $_____.

Sincerely,

Name of volunteer

Getting Publicity for Your Phone-A-Thon

A phone-a-thon may be a good time to generate some publicity for your group. Publicity can make the community more aware of your group's work and can alert listeners or readers to the fact that many of them will be receiving phone calls from your organization on a specific day or evening. The organization's address and phone number can be included in all publicity so that people can call or send in their donations.

   How much publicity a group is able to generate for a phone-a-thon will depend a great deal on the group's success in getting publicity for any of its works. Chances are that if an organization has never had any stories in the local newspaper or on radio or TV, they will not get coverage for their phone-a-thon. However, if the group does have a relationship with columnists, talk show producers, station managers, and so on, it may be able to use those contacts to get publicity for a phone-a-thon.

   Unless you are on very good terms with press people, the phone-a-thon alone will not be a newsworthy event. While a short press release or a public service announcement (PSA) describing the phone-a-thon may be used, an article or an interview will not come out of the phone-a-thon alone. It would be best, therefore, to use the occasion of the phone-a-thon to emphasize a new program, tell a human interest story, or have some other newsworthy reason to get press attention in which you mention the phone-a-thon.

   In all of your publicity emphasize the need for community support. Stress that your organization relies on the community for the bulk of its support or wants to rely on the community (if you don't now). Talk about what a gift of $15 to $25 will do for the group so that people have a sense that a small gift can make a difference.

Use a Public Figure

One way groups have interested the press is by having one or two famous people participating in their phone-a-thon. "Famous people" include not only national celebrities but also people only well known in your community, such as the mayor, city council members, well-respected community activists, the president of the community college, or a major corporate executive. The novelty that someone "famous" would help your organization lends credibility to your group. Also, almost everyone is flattered to be called by someone famous. If you decide to ask public figures to participate, be sure that they are well liked by your constituency.

Public fixtures can simply come for the first half hour of your phone-a-thon and make a few calls without making an enormous time commitment to the event. It is an easy way for both you and them to gain goodwill while they show their support of nonprofit organizations and of the work of your organization in particular.

Court the Media

If you can't get any publicity through your press contacts, simply send a letter to the editor of the local paper. Be sure to send it in time for publication (particularly if you are a rural group dealing with a weekly paper). Many groups have found that letters to the editor are an effective way to get publicity for many issues. Again, give the address and phone number of your organization and the date of the phone-a-thon.

If you do get any publicity (even a simple press mention or public service announcement aired), write or call the press person with the results of the phone-a-thon and emphasize what a difference their publicity made. Include with your letter a press release or PSA announcing the success of the phone-a-thon and a statement of thanks to the community for being supportive. A letter to the editor can also follow up publicity. It is important to sound successful even if your phone-a-thon was not as successful as you had hoped.

Consider the Disadvantages

There are drawbacks to extensive publicity that should be taken into account before seeking it. Publicity for a direct service organization may generate more clients than donors. One organization, whose purpose was to advocate for people with work-related injuries and to help them get the benefits they deserve, got a full-page interview about their work and their upcoming phone-a-thon in the local paper. The night of the phone-a-thon more than half of the calls were from people needing the organization's help. Volunteers were swamped; almost no outgoing calls were made, as all lines were full. The phone-a-thon was a financial failure; but the experience certainly demonstrated the need for this group's work.

A second disadvantage of publicity is that phone calls may keep coming in long after the phone-a-thon is over. If you have borrowed a space and the phone number you announced belongs to the business that owns the space, they will have to forward your calls. If you gave your office number, your staff or daytime volunteers will need to respond to those calls in addition to doing their regular work. While handling the calls is not too time-consuming, making sure the right information goes out and keeping track of pledges and so forth can mean a lot of time.

If you have taken all these contingencies into account, publicity may turn a good phone-a-thon into a giant fundraising success.

Other Uses of the Phone-A-Thon

There are three common uses of the phone-a-thon technique in addition to that described in the first section of this chapter. They are as follows: using the phone only to get prospects, following a mail appeal with a phone-a-thon, and using the phone-a-thon to renew lapsed donors.

Phoning for Prospects

This takeoff on a sales technique means phoning a large number of people, giving basic information about your organization, and asking if the person would like to know more. If the person says yes, he or she turns into a prospect. There is no attempt to solicit a gift at the time of the phone call. The purpose of the call is to create a "hot" list for fundraising mail appeals.

During the telephone conversation the caller can determine the degree of interest by asking the prospect some open-ended questions about their knowledge of the organization and their philosophical support of its work. When interest is present the prospect will be sent more information about the organization and a list of ways that he/she can help, including giving money. Some groups use this opportunity to seek new volunteers, get support for or against a piece of legislation, ask for items that the program needs (for example, a shelter might ask for food or clothing), and so forth. A return envelope is included.

This strategy does not raise money per se. Instead it acquires donors. The costs of phoning and of any mail and follow-up may well be only slightly less than the total amount received as gifts. Nevertheless, the organization now has a group of new donors, many of whom will renew the following year, who may give in response to appeals during the current year. (See also discussion on donor acquisition in Chapter 4.)

This strategy is best for new groups that do not have an established constituency or for groups that have little name recognition even if they have existed for some time. It also works well for political organizations seeking to familiarize people with their candidate or their election issue.

This method differs from an ordinary phone-a-thon in the script and the training of volunteers for calling. The purpose of the call is only to determine interest and to get permission to send more information. Therefore, the script would be something like this:

> "Hello, I am Jane Smith, a volunteer with Shelter for the Homeless. I would like to talk to you for a minute, and I will not be asking you for money. Is this a good time?" (PAUSE.) "Thank you. I'll try to be brief. Have you ever heard of our program?" (PAUSE.) *If the answer is "No" or "I don't know very much," continue:* "Shelter for the Homeless is a 30-bed facility for homeless single people and families. It also provides job counseling and referral, meals, and child care so that parents can look for work. Did you know that there are more than 2,000 homeless people in our community and more arriving every day?" (PAUSE.) "Many people find our program excellent, but we know that others disagree with our approach or feel that some of the people using our services are freeloading. What do you think?"

Generally, the answers fall into three categories:

◆ People who are basically in favor of your work
◆ People who like your program generally but have a specific objection to something about it
◆ People who feel that everyone should help themselves and that your program is undermining the moral fabric of the country.

For answers in the first category the caller in this example might say:

> "I'm glad you feel that way. The shelter relies on community support for over three-fourths of its budget, and it is good to know that members of the community like what we are doing. I wonder if I could send you a brochure and some other information about our services and about different ways that citizens can help us. There is no obligation, and no one will call you afterwards, but you may find the information interesting." (PAUSE for answer.)

If the answer is yes, then verify the name and address, thank the person for his or her time, and say good night.

If the answer falls in the second category, the specific objection in this case might be:

> "I support the ideals of your program, but the problem is that more people move to our community because you are here. We can't continue to absorb people this fast."

The caller needs to agree with the prospect in some way in order to acknowledge that the prospect's objection is valid. In this case, the caller could say:

> "It does seem that the more services that are provided the more people there are who need them, and that it is an endless cycle." (PAUSE.) "But in our case it is interesting to know that no more people are moving here now than before we opened the shelter." OR "Communities with no services for the homeless are experiencing as fast a growth rate of that category of people as in our community. In fact, sometimes people call us from other states, and we are able to discourage them from moving here because our economy is so tight right now. Then they don't have to come and learn that the hard way."

When a person's objection is acknowledged as valid and then corrected or new information supplied, he or she generally becomes more receptive. If the person says something like "I didn't know that" or "I am glad to hear that," ask if you can send him/her more information just as for prospects in category one.

In case of answers in the last category, simply say "I appreciate your candidness. It helps us to know why people don't like our program. Thanks for your time. Good night."

The training of volunteers for this type of phone work is much more detailed. Volunteers must be able to listen, to deal with difficult questions, and to know when to give up. Each will take longer than calls in a fundraising phone-a-thon. Callers must be clear that they are only calling to determine interest, not to convert people.

Callers should practice with difficult questions and their answers in depth and familiarize themselves with many facts about the organization and the issues.

No list is needed for this phone-a-thon. The phone book can be used or you can do a random calling of any list of people.

Phoning After a Mail Appeal

This method is quite straightforward. A mail appeal is sent to a list of prospects. After two weeks all the prospects who have not sent money are called. The purpose of this method is to increase the return from the mail appeal.

The script is the only part that is slightly different from a regular fundraising phone-a-thon, in that a sentence is added, such as, "I am Joe Reilly from the Greenbelt Project. We recently sent you a letter about our work. Did you have a chance to read it?" Depending on the answer, the rest of the script is the same as that described in the first section of this chapter. If the person has read the letter and seems in favor of your goals, skip right to the question, "Will you be able to help us with a gift of $_____?"

Do not indicate in the original letter that the prospects will be called. You want as many people as possible to send in their gift without being called.

Phoning for Renewals

In average organizations about one-third of the members do not renew their memberships from one year to the next. As a result, organizations spend most of their renewal budget trying to woo these recalcitrant members back into the fold. Usually an organization will send the member two or three renewal letters one month apart, each notice firmer than the one before. The third notice usually explains that the membership has or is about to lapse unless the member pays now. If there is still no response the organization removes the member's name from its mailing list.

The phone-a-thon can be used in place of either second or third renewal notices. It is particularly useful for organizations with a large number of local members. Although it does not save the cost of printing and postage, it does provide a way to have much more personal contact with members than is generally possible.

Many organizations have renewal phone-a-thons twice a year. They find that while the response to a second or third renewal letter is 2 to 5 percent and sometimes less, the response to phoning is at least 10 percent and can be as high as 30 percent. This means that these organizations are cutting their member losses by 10 percent or more. Instead of having a 66 percent renewal rate they will be retaining members at a rate of 75 or 80 percent.

Groups that have had trouble with their recordkeeping systems and that may not have accurate records as to when members are due to renew can also use the phone-a-thon to clear up their records.

A renewal phone-a-thon is almost exactly like a regular fundraising phone-a-thon.

First, identify from your mailing list all the people whose subscriptions have expired within the last six months, not including those who have had less than a month to renew. (Unless your organization is in a terrible financial bind and you really need the money, a person will feel harassed if you call too soon after your first renewal notice is sent.)

Next, prepare the letters to thank people for renewing and to contact people who weren't home when you called, as discussed in the first section of this chapter. Both of these letters are brief. The point is to remind the member of his or her commitment to give; there is no need to convince the person of the worthiness of your organization. Each letter is accompanied by a return envelope and a return form (pledge card).

When volunteers call the lapsed donors they will generally hear the following reasons for not renewing: People are out of work, forgot about it, thought they had renewed, or didn't receive the renewal letter. In some instances they were just about to renew and are glad you called.

It is important to believe whatever the member might say. For example, people who claim to have renewed but whom you have no record could be asked to produce a canceled check; however, it is easier and more productive in the long run simply to take their word for it and to reinstate them on the mailing list.

When someone says that they no longer agree with the "course you are taking" or that they have a disagreement about a particular issue, ask them to explain. It may shed light on how the public perceives something you have done, or you may be able to clear up a misunderstanding.

At the end of the phone-a-thon make sure you have carefully sorted all the names into those who have renewed, those who requested to be taken off the mailing list, and those who were not home. Deal with complaints that same evening:

> "Dear Mrs. Upset,
> We are sorry you have not received your newsletter for the past two years. Here are all the back copies you have missed. We will enter your name on our mailing list for the next year as a complimentary member. Your past support means a lot to us, and again, we apologize."

Case Study of a Phone-A-Thon

The phone-a-thon in this example was conducted by DES Action National, a nonprofit organization dedicated to finding people exposed to the drug DES and to giving them health information and referrals to health care. DES Action has 25 groups in the United States and national offices in New York and San Francisco. Despite the size of the national organization, its budget is relatively small (around $115,000), as most of the work of the organization is carried out by volunteers.

DES Action publishes a quarterly newsletter called the *DES Action VOICE,* read by more than 2,000 people. Subscriptions to the *VOICE* provide the bulk of income for local chapters, which receive two-thirds of the $15 annual subscription fee.

As is common with subscriptions, about one-third of the subscribers do not renew. The phone-a-thon described here was an attempt to improve the renewal rate. The phone-a-thon was conducted by the national office with 10 of the larger chapters participating by calling lapsed members in their areas. Presented here is information developed for the local chapters participating in the phone-a-thon, followed by the results of the phone-a-thon.

This phone-a-thon makes an excellent case study for two reasons: First, it was a clever way to call subscribers all over the country without incurring the long distance phone bills, as the chapters tried to make all calls from one of the national offices; and second, the phone-a-thon was successful because the information provided to volunteers participating in the event was thorough. They needed only to follow the instructions for the phone-a-thon to work.

Materials Sent to Participating Chapters

HELLO and welcome to DES Action's FIRST ANNUAL TELEPHONE RELAY.

The purpose of this letter is to confirm the details and arrangements for the relay. Also, attached are copies of the letters we will be using, and your list of lapsed donors.

DATE: OCTOBER 24, MONDAY, 6-9:30 p.m. your local time

CONCEPT

DES Action has a large subscriber list which provides a high percentage of national and local income. As is common with national non-profits, every year about ⅓ of the subscribers do not renew. In the past two years, we have instituted sending two extra renewal appeals for people not responding to the first one. This has helped a great deal. We now have a total of 810 subscribers who have lapsed in the past year.

On an experimental basis, we have called a local sample of these subscribers, asking them to renew. We have received 15-50% positive response.

For the National office to call all over the country would be too expensive, but local groups calling in their area would make this renewal method possible. Thus, we decided to do this PHONE RELAY.

HOW IT WORKS

The relay starts on the East Coast. Groups there will begin calling their lapsed subscribers at 6 p.m. Eastern Standard Time. At 7 p.m. EST, they will call a group in the midwest, where it will then be 6 p.m., and they will report how much money they have raised so far. Midwest groups will then begin calling. At 9 p.m. EST, east coast groups will end their phone-a-thon, tally up their results, and call the Midwest. In turn the Midwest will call California at 8 p.m. with their results so far, and at 9 p.m. with the final results. California groups will begin calling at 6 p.m. Pacific Standard Time, and end at 9 p.m. The phone-a-thon will have gone on for 6 hours total, three hours in each of three time zones. With each successive tally of how much has been raised, callers can tell the people they talk to how much has been brought in, thus increasing excitement.

WHAT DO WE NEED TO DO?

A phone-a-thon is not complicated, however there are tasks that must be done ahead of time, and some things to do that evening. The following is a list of tasks in chronological order.

1. Read this material and make sure you understand everything.

2. Take the list of lapsed donors in your area and find as many phone numbers as you can. Between the phone book and "information," you should be able to find most of them. (For those whose number you can't find, see Instruction #7)

a) Some groups do not have many lapsed donors in their area. In that case I have included names of donors from the rest of the state and some surrounding states. You may call those people, or put together a list of your own. If you do elect to call in other states, YOUR group will be asked to incur the cost of the call, but will be CREDITED FOR ANY RENEWALS YOU GET.

3. EITHER: Find a place that has two or three phones. Ask the local YWCA, or someone with an office if you can use their phones for the evening. Obviously, you will reimburse them for the cost of the calls made in that evening.

   OR: If you can't find a place with more than one phone line, you will do the phone-a-thon from someone's home. Have two or three people at each house so that it will be more fun, and people can trade off calling.

4. Get as many volunteers as you need. A rule of thumb is that one person can make 20 phone calls in an hour. Some people won't be home, and most people talk only briefly, which is why you can make so many calls. Count the number of people you will be calling, and divide by 20. This will tell you the number of hours it will take. Then divide by 2 or three (depending on how many hours you want each volunteer to work) and you will have the number of volunteers you need. The more volunteers you have, the more fun it will be, and if you have several phones, you'll get done earlier.

5. Photocopy the pledge letter and the "Sorry we missed you" letter onto your own stationery. They are typed so that they can be copied onto half or full sheets of stationery as is. If you wish to retype them, and change the content, mentioning local group accomplishments or something, that's fine.

   In order to figure out how many to print, assume that 2/3rds of the people will be home, and 2/3rds of those will say yes. The rest will need, "Sorry we missed you letters." You will have extra copies, but don't type a date onto the letter, and that way you can use them at other times.

   I have sent each of you DES Action return envelopes with your group marked on the lower left corner. We are doing this to save you the trouble of sending the checks and orders to us, and will also expedite processing the renewals. (Groups that are incorporated will use their own return envelopes.)

6. Get together around 5:30 or 6 the night of the phone relay. Go over the materials, and make sure everyone feels comfortable with the script and the process.

   I recommend that two people work each phone. When one person finishes her call, another can dial. The phone is always in use. While one person is talking, the other is filling out the appropriate letter, and addressing the envelope.

Each phone team, or each person working the phone should have:
a) a list of the people she is to call
b) copies of the letters to send
c) return envelopes and outside envelopes
d) the script (which follows.)

7. If you can't find someone's number, or they are not home when you call, send them the "sorry we missed you" letter.

YOU ARE NOW READY TO BEGIN PHONING.

How many people will say, "yes, I'd like to renew?"

This is difficult to predict and will vary from place to place. The important thing to remember, so that you will not be disappointed, is that MOST PEOPLE will either not be home or will say NO. Many people do not renew their subscription to the VOICE for reasons outside our control—they have lost their job, they have high medical expenses, they find the issue too depressing, etc.

We are hoping that each group will get ONE in FIVE people to say YES. A 20% response from the phone-a-thon would be terrific.

What if the person we call says,

"I did renew already." Say, "I'm sorry to have bothered you. Your renewal must not have caught up to our computer yet. Let me verify your address." Then, make sure National has the correct address, and note on the sheet of names and addresses that the person claims to have renewed. (From time to time we do make this mistake. If the person is not telling the truth, they must want the VOICE badly, so that's fine.)

"I've never gotten my VOICE, and that's why I didn't renew." Say, "I'm sorry to hear that. I will let the National office know. Let me verify your address, and we will send you the most recent issue, and extend your subscription." Then note that on the sheet of names.

"I'm always getting fundraising appeals from you. You seem to spend all your money on fundraising." Say, "Sometimes it seems that way. You will be interested to know, however, that our fundraising costs are only 2% of our total budget. Most of our fundraising is done by volunteers, and much of the paper and printing is donated. We have found that our subscribers respond positively to extra requests for donations, and we always need money to continue our work. Will you be able to renew this year?"

What if they say,

"I have to think about it." Say, "OK, but may I send you a subscription form anyway, and then if you decide to renew, you'll have it right there?"

What if they say,

"Yes." Say, "That's great. Thank you. I'll send you a subscription form and a return envelope tonight, and will look forward to hearing from you."

Then, fill out the "Thank you so much for renewing" letter, sign your name and send it with a return envelope by first class mail.

Note on the sheet of names and addresses that they promised to renew. If the National does not hear from them in a week or two, we will send them a reminder. The National office will thank them on your behalf when the check does arrive. You will be notified of the collection rate from the phone-a-thon, and also the final total pledged.

THE SCRIPT (Call and ask for the person who is the subscriber. When he/she answers, say,

Hello, my name is _____, and I am a volunteer with Des Action (local chapter). May I have a minute of your time? (Or, is this a good time to talk for a minute?) Tonight Des Action local affiliates all over the country are calling subscribers who seem to have let their subscriptions to the Des Action Voice lapse. So far we have raised $_____. I am hoping you will renew your subscription with a gift of $15.
(Pause—answer any questions or respond to comments they have.) If the answer is positive, say, OK, thank you very much. See above. If the answer is no, say, "Thanks for taking the time to talk with me this evening. If you ever change your mind, feel free to contact our office.

◆ **Pledge Letter**

Dear _____ :
   Thank you so much for renewing your subscription to the DES Action VOICE this evening.
   As you probably know, DES Action National and its 31 local affiliates are primarily supported by donations and subscriptions from people like you.
   Your gift will help us continue our work of finding DES exposed people and keeping them informed of the latest medical and legal findings.
   Please fill out the enclosed card and send it, with your check of $15 or more, in the enclosed envelope.
   Thanks again.

                    Sincerely,

                    DES Action volunteer

◆ "Sorry We Missed You" Letter

Dear _____ :

Sorry we missed you this evening. We tried to call you because our records show that your subscription to the DES Action VOICE has expired.

We called to ask you to renew with a gift of $15 or more. Volunteers from all over the country were calling people in their area, asking them to renew. Groups on the East Coast started the phone-a-thon, and it ended in California.

As of _____ p.m. _____ time, we had raised $_____.

I hope you will want to renew. The DES Action VOICE is the only ongoing source of information about DES exposure. New medical and legal findings make it important for DES daughters, sons, mothers, and others concerned about the drug to have this important publication.

Your gift will also help us to continue our work of finding DES exposed people. We estimate that up to half of them (3-6 million people) still do not know of their exposure and the health risks they face.

If you wish to renew your subscription, please fill out the enclosed card, and send it with your check, in the enclosed envelope.

Sincerely,

DES Action volunteer

Results

Analysis of the geographic distribution of *VOICE* subscribers showed that they were clustered in metropolitan areas and that many local DES Action groups did not have any lapsed subscribers in their area. Therefore, the phone-a-thon was only conducted by those groups with lapsed subscribers in their location.

Three groups that might have participated elected to have a phone-a-thon on another night because they couldn't get enough volunteers on the night the national relay was scheduled. All told, seven local chapters using an average of three volunteers each called 600 people, 300 of whom were home. Renewal rates varied between 25 and 35 percent per chapter, 100 people agreed to renew, and 80 actually did so.

In addition, those who were not home and those who were not called were sent the "Sorry we missed you" letter, which generated another 35 renewals. The gross income for this event was $1,600, which was divided among the groups according to their results. Twenty-one volunteers worked three hours each, for a total of 63 volunteer hours. The net income, then, was approximately $25 per hour. The group was pleased with the results of the phone relay and plans to make it an annual event.

Chapter 6

Other Methods of Fundraising

Canvassing

Canvassing is a fundraising technique that involves a team of people from your organization going door to door requesting contributions for your group's work. The canvassing technique is used extensively by local groups and by local chapters of state or national organizations.

While part-time or temporary canvasses can be run with volunteers, most canvassing is a full-time operation involving salaried or commissioned employees who work 40 hours a week and solicit in neighborhoods on a regular, revolving basis. Well-run canvasses can bring in from $50,000 to $500,000 or more in gross income. Because they are labor-intensive, however, the high overhead of most canvasses absorbs at least 60 percent of their gross earnings.

Advantages and Disadvantages

There are three main advantages to canvassing as a fundraising strategy: First, an established, well-run canvass can provide a reliable source of income to your organization, and this income can be quite substantial. Second, the face-to-face contact with dozens of people each evening can bring in more new members than almost any other strategy; this volume of personal interaction is not duplicated in any other fundraising strategy. Third, canvassers bring back to the organization the public's opinions and perceptions of what your organization is doing.

There are also disadvantages to a canvass. If it is done on a full-time basis it requires separate staff and office space as well as extensive bookkeeping and supervision. As with a small business, canvass income can be unreliable if the top canvass staff is not good or if too many canvasses are operating in an area. The canvassers themselves can give the organization a bad reputation if they are unkempt, rude, or unpleasant to the people being canvassed. A final disadvantage is that many donors do not like the concept of canvassing because of the high overhead involved. While the amount of gross income can be impressive, much of that is lost to overhead costs.

Elements Needed to Run a Canvass

Four elements must be present for an organization to operate an effective canvass. First and most important, **the organization must work on local issues**. People give at the door when they perceive that an issue affects them and their neighborhood. The work of your organization can have national impact and your organization might be a branch of a national group, but in door-to-door canvassing you must explain how this issue affects the resident directly.

Second, **people must feel that even a small donation will make a difference**. Most people make a cash donation to a canvass, and even a check will rarely be for more than $25. People must feel that their small donation is needed and will be well used.

Third, **people must feel confident about your organization**. Their confidence will be inspired by your organization's accomplishments, which must be clear and easy to discuss. Newspaper articles about your work are a major boon to canvassing. A specific plan of action that can be explained simply and quickly and that sounds effective is essential. The work of some organizations lends itself to canvassing. Work on issues of general importance and interest to the majority of people, such as health care, the Equal Rights Amendment, or antinuclear organizing is good. Litigation can work if the suit is easy to understand, if there is a clear "good guy" (your group) and "bad guy." Complex regulatory reform, issues requiring historical background, legal knowledge, or patience in listening to a long explanation do not lend themselves to canvassing.

Finally, you must be able to **distinguish your organization** from any other organization doing similar work without implying any disrespect for the other organization. In some communities where there are not only two or more groups working on similar issues but also several groups canvassing, potential donors get confused and then angry that they are being solicited so often for issues that seem interrelated. People will explain to your canvassers that they just gave to your group last week, that someone from your organization was just there. No amount of protest from you will change their minds. The only thing that will help is to clearly distinguish your group from any other.

All these requirements for a successful canvass, except the focus on local work, are also necessary for many other fundraising strategies, particularly mail appeals and phone-a-thons, where the object is to get the donor's attention quickly and hold it long enough to get the gift.

Setting Up

Know the laws and regulations

First, check state and local laws and ordinances concerning canvassing. If canvassing is heavily regulated in your community, it may not be worth the time involved to comply with the regulations. Some communities have tried to stop canvassing operations altogether by means of ordinances governing what you can say when soliciting door to door and establishing strict qualifications for canvassers, including expensive licensing. If your canvass violates even a minor subregulation it could be forced by the city or state to cease operation and may bring bad press for your organization. Some of these ordinances have been challenged in court and most of them are unconstitutional, but most organizations have too much work to do to also take on costly and lengthy legal battles in this area.

State laws governing canvassing can be learned by contacting the attorney general's office, which generally monitors all rules related to charitable solicitation. Many states publish handbooks on canvassing regulations.

Local ordinances are sometimes more difficult to discover, since several city departments may have jurisdiction over different parts of the canvassing operation. Contact the police department and ask for notification and application procedures for a canvass. Be sure to write down whatever the person tells you, and get his or her name so that if you get a different story from another police official you can refer to this phone call.

Contact the city attorney's office for information regarding solicitation of money for charity. Sometimes the mayor's office has some jurisdiction over these matters. In general, informing as many people as possible about your canvassing operation will ensure the least amount of interference later.

Study the demographics
After making sure that you can comply with the law you must determine if your community's geography and population density and the income range of the people being canvassed are favorable to a canvass. Gather demographic data on your area: For various neighborhoods, find out the population density, the property values, how many of the people are homeowners, what type of work most people do, what the income levels are, and so forth. This information is available from various sources, including driving around and getting a sense of the neighborhoods, asking local people, reading the newspaper, talking with volunteer and board members who have lived in the area, and consulting with the Chamber of Commerce.

REMEMBER one important caveat in assessing demographic data: A canvass rarely does well in an affluent neighborhood, and canvassers sometimes conclude that "rich people" are "tightwads" and "do not care at all." Affluent people do not make contributions at the door. Their charitable giving is usually done through major gift solicitation or swank special events. Canvassing operations do best in middle- and lower-income neighborhoods, where giving at the door is acceptable.

The other demographic item you need to evaluate is whether the population is dense enough per square mile to make it worthwhile to canvass. Canvassers need to be able to reach 80 to 100 homes per night. This means that there must be enough people in the area and that the terrain must be flat enough to allow canvassers to walk quickly from house to house. It is much harder to run a successful canvass in a rural area simply because of the distance between houses and because of the lack of people.

Staff

Once you have determined that your area can support a canvass, you are ready to hire canvass staff and prepare materials.

The staff for a canvass varies from place to place but generally includes several individuals with the following roles:

◆ **Canvass director:** Supervises the entire canvass operation, including hiring and firing canvassers, researching areas to be canvassed, and mapping out the revolving canvass for the area to be canvassed in a year, keeping the organization in compliance with the law, keeping up to date on new laws, and planning and updating materials.

◆ **Field manager(s):** Transports and supervises a team of five to seven canvassers. Assigns the team to various parts of the neighborhood, collects the money at the end of the evening, and trains new canvassers on the team. This person also participates as a canvasser at the site.

◆ **Secretary/receptionist/bookkeeper/office manager:** Manages the office, including keeping records of money earned by each canvasser, replacing canvass materials as needed, scheduling interviews with prospective canvassers for the canvass director, answering the phone, and generally acting as back-up person for the canvass operations. This person does not canvass.

◆ **Canvassers:** The people actually carrying out the canvass. We will look at their role in some depth.

Role of the canvasser

Canvassers work from 2-10 p.m. five days a week. They usually have a quota—an amount of money they must raise every day or every week. Their pay is either a percentage of what they raise (commission), a straight salary, or a base salary plus commission.

Canvassers must represent the organization accurately and be respectable ambassadors for the organization. The individual canvasser is often the only person from the organization whom donors will see and may well be the only face they will ever associate with your group.

Because the pay is low and the hours long and arduous there is a high turnover in canvass staff. In the summer, college students help expand the canvassing staff. In the winter months recruiting canvassers is more difficult.

Canvassers must be equipped with various materials. These include any identification badges or licenses required by the city or state, clipboards to carry the materials to be given away, brochures about the organization, return envelopes, newspaper clippings about the work of the group, and a receipt book.

Many canvasses use a petition to get the attention of the person being canvassed. The canvasser will ask, "Would you sign a petition for . . ." and briefly explain the cause. While the person is signing, the canvasser will ask for a donation as well.

Canvassers should try to get the gift right at the door. However, for people who insist on "thinking about it" or discussing it with a roommate or spouse, they can leave a brochure and a return envelope. A brochure should also be given to people making a donation, because on reading it some of them will send an additional donation.

All of the information is carried on a clipboard, which makes it easy to display and lends a degree of authority to the canvasser. People are more likely to open their doors to someone who looks like he or she has a good reason to be there.

When canvassers begin their work day they are appraised of the neighborhood they will be canvassing and told of any new information or special emphasis on issues that they should present to this neighborhood. They then have a late lunch/early dinner and are driven by their field manager to the canvass site. They begin canvassing around 4 p.m. and end at 9 p.m., when they are picked up by their field manager and taken back to the office. They turn in their money, make their reports, and finish around 10 p.m.

Because canvassing is hard work, essentially involving face-to-face solicitation with a "cold" list, it is critical that the rest of the organization's staff and the board members see the canvass staff as colleagues and as integral to the total operation of the organization. To help build this support, many organizations require noncanvass staff to canvass for an evening every couple of months.

Second only to quality of canvass staff in ensuring the success of a canvass is an efficient record-keeping system. After each neighborhood is canvassed an evaluation of the neighborhood should be filed along with the demographic data on that neighborhood that led to its being chosen as a canvass site. These data can then be reevaluated in the light of the canvassers' experience. Any special considerations, such as "no street lights," can also be noted in the evaluation.

Many people worry that theft by the canvassers will be a problem. Theft occurs no more often by canvass workers than by any others. Careless bookkeeping, however, can cost money and can give the impression that money has disappeared. At the end of the evening, both the canvasser and the field manager should count the money brought in. The amounts are entered under each canvasser's name on a "Daily Summary Sheet." The money and the summary sheet are then placed in a locked safe, and the secretary/bookkeeper will count the total again in the morning and make a daily deposit to the bank. At the end of the week the bookkeeper tallies the total receipt of each canvasser and prepares the payroll sheet.

Canvassers who fail to bring in their quota for more than a week must be retrained or fired. Strict discipline is important in a successful canvass, and keeping performance records will help to maintain a good canvass team.

Canvassing is an excellent strategy for some groups, and if done properly it can be extremely lucrative. However, there are many pitfalls, and it is neither a simple nor a low-cost strategy. Canvassing changes the nature of the organization. It doubles or triples staff size and requires office space and additional equipment. Only groups that have thoroughly researched the pros and cons of canvassing should consider beginning a canvass.

Fees for Service and Products for Sale

Fees for service and products for sale are related fundraising strategies, because they both involve principles of selling—selling either services or tangible products.

Fees for Service

Collecting fees for service is a common way for groups to help offset the cost of their programs. Tuition, ticket prices, registration fees, and admission charges are all examples of fees for service. The fee almost never covers the entire cost of the service provided.

A fees-for-service system is fairly easy to set up. Examine the work of your organization and see what services you provide (such as counseling, referral, health examinations, meals, shelter, clothing, employment opportunities) and what these services would cost at commercial rates. Start your fees at no more than half the commercial rate. Publish these rates in your newsletter and on posters and brochures around the community. Community health clinics and counseling centers often find that many people come to them because they like the quality of care they receive rather than because they need free service. These people will gladly pay.

Nonprofit organizations sometimes fail to charge for services out of a concern that people who need the service and can't pay will be excluded. A sliding-scale fee-for-service plan can deal with this problem. Those whose incomes are at the bottom of the scale are charged a nominal fee or no fee at all. Your plan can have several levels, with suggested fees based on both income levels and the type of service provided.

The best system for instituting fees for service is to show the client the fee scale, including suggested amounts for each service and each income level, and let him or her make the decision about what to pay. Don't question their decision and you will never embarrass your clients.

Products for Sale

Most organizations have T-shirts, bumper stickers, or buttons for sale, which both raise money and, more importantly, promote the group or a specific issue it is working on. While the income from most of these products merely covers their cost, with their main value being promotion, some products can be money-makers. Educational materials, calendars, jewelry, toys, holiday cards, and so forth can be sold at a good profit and bring in a reasonable income.

Most organizations lose money on their products because they do not take into account all the costs involved in having products for sale. They may charge more than the cost of the product itself but fail to account for staff time in distributing the product, postage and envelope costs if the product is mailed, development and advertising costs, and storage of the inventory. Therefore, to realize any profit a product must be marked up 100 percent above cost.

Products will not sell themselves. They require a marketing plan. Before getting deeply into product sales (beyond simple T-shirts, buttons, and bumper stickers), consult with other nonprofit organizations with products for sale. Find out what they have learned so that you don't have to repeat their mistakes.

Though they will rarely make as much money as the other strategies discussed, products for sale and fees for service are useful adjuncts to a diversified funding plan.

Setting up a Small Business

With recent, massive reductions in government funding for nonprofit organizations, many groups have been advised to start small businesses. The idea seems sound: Sell something people want to buy and use the profits to finance your organization. For many years nonprofit organizations have run small businesses—thrift stores, gift shops, ticket sales for performances, concessions, and so on. Some nonprofit organizations have well-known multi-million-dollar businesses, such as the Girl Scouts' cookies, the Salvation Army's second-hand stores, and UNICEF's gift shops.

Despite these glowing examples of success, the unfortunate fact is that most nonprofits that have started small businesses have failed in this endeavor. Their failures were caused by the same factors that cause 9 out of 10 small businesses to fail: Undercapitalization, poor management, inability to respond to market conditions, and underpricing of goods.

First, The Problems

In addition to the problems that come with starting any small business, nonprofit organizations have several other problems. First, the staff and board members are not generally business people themselves. In fact, they may have a distaste for business and capitalist ventures and feel uncertain about the politics of starting a small business. Further, staff and board members are usually already putting in a great deal of time and may be feeling pressed to work harder. Almost any staff person knows the feeling of being constantly behind in his/her work, always barely catching up, always conscious of tasks that never get done. Board members, squeezing in time for the organization between jobs, families, and other commitments, know this feeling also. To establish and supervise a business on top of these time commitments is often impossible.

To start a small business an organization must be financially sound. A successful small business takes three to five years to show a profit and should not be seen as a "quick fix" to financial difficulties. Even after three to five years of development a small business can provide, at the most, 10 percent of an organization's budget.

Charles Cagnon, in his study of small business ventures, *Business Ventures of Citizen Groups*, explains:

> Many non-profits have an annual budget of over $100,000. It would require a remarkable business to make an impact on a budget of that size. For example, a typical business would have to receive gross revenues of nearly $1 million in order to earn $50,000 in net profits which could safely be removed from the business and applied to the non-profit. (Even though some industries are more profitable than others, a 5% net profit is a conservative rule of thumb.) A business which would produce $1 million in gross revenues could easily require 20 employees, particularly in the retail and service industries which citizen groups are likely to consider. . . . To put it another way, for a business to contribute a modest $5,000 to the non-profit's budget, the business would probably have to generate $100,000 in gross revenues.

In figuring out the profit margin from a business, groups must keep in mind that not all the profit can be given to the organization's work: Some money must be reserved for business slumps and to reinvest in the business to ensure its long-term growth.

Types of Small Businesses for Nonprofits

There are two broad categories of business that a nonprofit may engage in under existing tax law. One is called a **"related" business**. In a related business the profits from the business are exempt from income tax. To qualify as a related business the business activities must "contribute importantly" to the accomplishment of the organization's mission. While there is no limit on how much can be earned from a related business, salaries cannot exceed general market levels for comparable work.

To constitute a business the work must be carried on regularly. Therefore, an organization can sponsor a completely unrelated special event on an infrequent basis and it will not be considered taxable business.

The other broad category is an **"unrelated" business**: that is, the product or services sold do not advance the mission of the group. In that case the organization must pay tax on the business's income at a regular corporate rate. A serious problem with an unrelated business is that if the business activity is "substantial" compared to the nonprofit activity, the nonprofit may lose its tax-exempt status. This happens in cases where the business becomes so consuming that the purpose of the organization seems to be to run the business rather than to run the organization.

There are a few circumstances under which income tax is not collected from businesses, including:

◆ The bulk of the work is done by unpaid volunteers.
◆ The products sold have been donated to the nonprofit.
◆ The revenue comes from the rental of property for which little or no property management services are provided.
◆ Revenue comes from interest, dividends, investments, or royalty income.

The key element the Internal Revenue Service uses to evaluate the continuation of the organization's tax-exempt status is the determination of whether the nonprofit organization has an unfair advantage over a profit-making business and is thus engaging in "unfair competition." Because a nonprofit organization's related business does not pay income tax, it can reinvest that money to expand the business faster than a for-profit concern.

To avoid the accusation of unfair competition and to avoid losing your tax-exempt status, your group can opt to incorporate the business as an entirely separate entity and pay income tax. The business then donates its profit to your organization.

REMEMBER: The laws governing businesses are complicated and somewhat vague. Groups should always consult an attorney and business advisor about their own situation before proceeding with a business.

Are You Ready for a Small Business?

Several elements must be present in an organization before it is ready to start a small business. First, the organization should have a strong donor base, regular special events, and an ongoing program of recruiting new donors. The organization should not *need* the money from the small business. A small business is a diversification strategy for a group that has already diversified to the more traditional fundraising strategies and is looking ahead five years or more to other strategies.

An organization must also have people who are very committed to the idea of a small business, many of whom probably own or have owned successful small businesses of their own. These people can constitute a planning group to do the research necessary to decide if and what kind of a small business is appropriate. An organization with all of the above in place can then consider starting a business.

The organization must have or borrow the start-up capital to open the business. This almost always takes more money than is planned and longer to recoup than is anticipated. Undercapitalization—lack of enough start-up capital and enough money to put into the business after it starts and before it begins to show a profit—is a major reason for small businesses' failing. Nonprofit organizations, which often live from month to month, are obviously not going to have the financial reserves to risk on starting a business. Even for groups that are financially sound and have some financial reserves, deciding to risk them on the gamble of a business is a difficult decision. Borrowing the money does not solve your problem because the money must be paid back. The board of directors, some of whom will sign for the loan and may even put up collateral for it, are personally liable for the loan. So a small business may mean not only risking all the assets of the organization but some of the personal assets of volunteers as well.

The Risks

An organization must reflect on several major risks in undertaking a business venture. The most obvious risk is that the business will fail. If the business goes bankrupt the nonprofit corporation and its board of directors may be liable for any debts the business has incurred. If the product is faulty, the staff unfriendly, the price too high, the place dirty, and so forth, there is the danger that the business will give the organization a bad reputation. A bad business reputation attached to your organization will not only affect the success of your business, but it will also hamper your fundraising and organizing endeavors.

A second risk is that the business will not fail but will be so marginal that it becomes a financial and emotional drain to the organization. All of its profits will have to be reinvested into the business or, if it operates at a loss, the organization will have to decide whether to invest more borrowed money in it. This is a drain in many ways, not the least of which is the stress involved in deciding whether to persevere, hoping that time will make the difference and the business will become successful, or to cut your losses and bail out. If you decide to persevere, how long do you keep the business going? What will progress look like? All the fancy business plans in the world cannot ease the anxiety involved in running a business.

A further risk, as discussed above, is that the organization will lose its tax-exempt status.

The Gains

The advantages of a successful business are tremendous. First, of course, the organization can count on a reasonable amount of income from the business on a regular basis. Second, the skills acquired in learning how to run the small business are useful in all aspects of fundraising and financial management for the entire organization. Many organizations that have small business ventures have discovered that the management of the overall organization is greatly strengthened. When an organization is strong and well managed it is more attractive to donors and more money can be raised.

Third, just as an excellent and repeating fundraising event increases visibility for a group on an annual basis, a business does so on a daily basis. A good business draws people in who may never have heard of your organization. Some of these people may become more involved with your group as donors and volunteers, and others will simply patronize your business because they like what you sell even if they don't care about the goals of your group.

For direct service organizations a business can sometimes provide valuable training and job experience for clients.

A small business is something that almost every organization should think about, read about, and consider. Many established groups have small business ventures as part of their 3- to 5-year plans, to be started once several other fundraising strategies are established and reliable.

Payroll Deduction Programs

Using payroll deduction programs has proven to be one of the most efficient and effective methods of raising money for some organizations. More than $1 billion is pledged through payroll deductions every year. The pioneer agency for this type of fundraising is, of course, the United Way, with affiliates in almost every town of more than 25,000 people in the United States. Ninety percent of the billion or more dollars raised through payroll deduction goes to the United Way, with the rest going to Combined Health Agency Drives (CHAD), United Arts Funds, Black United Funds, and other service and alternative funds.

A payroll deduction plan is a cross between a pledge program and an electronic funds transfer program. Employees specify how much money they want to give per pay period, and the amount is deducted from their wages. On a quarterly basis the employer sends the collected money to the federation, which keeps a percentage to cover its own costs and distributes the rest to its members.

There are several ways to benefit from payroll deduction programs, including becoming a beneficiary of the United Way or of one of the other federated funds in your area. Even if a group isn't a federation agency, it can receive money through a Donor Option Plan from any of the funds.

Because the United Way is the oldest, largest, and most powerful federated fund, direct service groups should start by applying to it for funding before pursuing any alternative workplace solicitation program. If you are turned down you have a strong case with the other federated funds or a case for starting your own fund. If you are accepted you need go no further.

United Way

What it is, what it does
The United Way of America is actually a federation of United Ways around the country. While United Ways have many things in common, each has a great deal of autonomy. Each nonprofit organization will have to approach the United Way in its community. United Way supports direct service organizations and groups providing health education. It does not support arts or environmental groups unless the work of the group has to do with health education.

Application forms and details of the application process can be obtained from your local United Way. The process is usually long and tedious, involving an extensive written application, site visits, and reviews by various United Ways committees. The bulk of United Way funding has customarily gone to a variety of "mainstream" direct service organizations, such as Boy Scouts, Red Cross, Salvation Army, YMCA, and YWCA. Traditionally the United Way has not funded women's or minority organizations, groups with advocacy programs, or groups working for social change.

In some communities the United Way has been severely criticized for its lack of responsiveness to social change and social justice concerns, and it has responded by making significant changes in funding policies. In some communities the United Way leadership is progressive. In those circumstances United Way has funded shelters for battered women, groups working with the disabled, gay health clinics, and some advocacy programs.

To find out what the United Way is like in your community, talk to groups that receive United Way funding and to those that have been turned down by United Way. If possible, meet some United Way officials and discuss your organization's needs with them. If it seems from this research that your group falls within United Way guidelines, then proceed to apply.

Pros and cons
There are obvious advantages to getting United Way funding. First, it is usually a sizable amount of money, which can be counted on from year to year. Even though groups must reapply each year and allocations do change, once an agency is accepted by United Way it will usually continue to receive grants for many years.

For organizations truly interested in self-sufficiency and in diversifying their funding sources, there are many disadvantages to United Way funding. First, organizations receiving United Way funding are not allowed to do their own fundraising from September to November. This so-called "blackout" period is when the United Way conducts its payroll solicitation. To lose three of the best months of the fundraising year is a serious drawback.

Unless the allocation from the United Way is two or three times larger than what your organization could raise in that time, it is not worth submitting to this structure.

Second, many donors will not give to organizations receiving money from the United Way. People think that agencies supported by United Way need no other funds. Third, many Americans simply do not like the United Way. They do not like being pressured to give at their workplace, and they see the United Way as wasteful and bureaucratic. While this perception is false for some United Ways it is true for others, and the poor reputation of the United Way can tarnish your organization's own reputation.

The Donor Option Plan. There is another way to receive United Way funding: Through United Way's Donor Option Plan. This plan is not available in every community, but when it is available it allows employees to designate the agency they wish to receive their contribution. Even if your organization does not qualify to be a United Way-funded agency, you may still get some money through the Donor Option Plan. The United Way does not promote the Donor Option Plan and sometimes tries to discourage employees from using it. The United Way sometimes maintains that the Donor Option program is expensive for them and complicated to manage. They will ask local groups not to advertise it and not to solicit gifts through Donor Option. Nevertheless, there is nothing the United Way can do if you do advertise Donor Option plans to your donors. Ask your donors to notify you if they have given to you through Donor Option, so that you can check up on the pledge if the United Way does not notify you.

Alternative Funds

If your organization cannot or does not wish to receive United Way funding but still wishes to pursue a payroll deduction plan, you will want to explore alternative funds. First, find out if there are any in your community and what their grant-making capabilities are. Some alternative funds are not yet able to make large grants but have excellent technical assistance programs. Others are giving away money but may not yet have gained access to many employers and must raise money in other ways besides payroll deduction.

Starting an alternative fund
If there is no alternative fund in your community you can start one. This is a major undertaking and, like a small business, takes several years before it will pay off. However, it can be lucrative if you have the time and the skills required. Setting up an alternative payroll deduction plan is simple in theory. Your organization calls together similar organizations to form a federation. The federation acts as an umbrella for the member groups and other groups that may apply. The federation gets employers' permission to solicit donations from employees and distributes the money after taking out of the

collected funds what they need to operate the federation. The overall fundraising costs are much lower than if each group were to try to do this type of fundraising on its own.

There are many decisions to be made in forming a federation. Who is a member? How does the federation choose new members? What will the application process be? How will the money be distributed? Will it be divided evenly among all the members, or given out according to each agency's need, or given out in accordance with the wishes of the donor, or a combination of these three approaches?

Once the federation has made these decisions (which can take many meetings and many months of negotiation and discussion), it has to gain access to the workplace to solicit the funds. Since the United Way has had a virtual monopoly on employee contributions for some time, it is understandably reluctant to share the stage with alternative funds. Employers may find it easier to limit access to the United Way only. Interestingly enough, however, studies show that when employees have several choices of funds to give to, and when they have Donor Option programs, total giving goes up. Some United Ways have discovered to their surprise that they did better when other funds were also allowed to solicit.

Finally, because a great deal of money can be involved and because the politics of the organizations forming an alternative federation are often in clear conflict with the United Way or with the employer involved, groups may find themselves embroiled in legal battles to protect their right to free speech in soliciting employees.

> Because most organizations will be asked by individual donors, foundations, or corporations whether they have applied for funds from the United Way and if not why not, all groups need to explore the possibility of becoming a member of a federated fund even if the exploration leads them to the conclusion that such a move would be unwise. The group can clearly present its reasons for not being involved. Knowing why you have rejected a fundraising strategy with such a large possible payoff is important for convincing donors that you are knowledgeable and responsible.

Adbooks

An adbook provides a way for your organization to raise money from businesses and corporations by selling them advertising space in a booklet, program, menu, or other printed item. The adbook is then distributed to a group of people who will be likely to patronize the businesses that advertised there. Businesses whose owners may not care about the issues you represent may still buy an ad because they know your constituents use their business or want them to do so.

Adbooks are a superb fundraising strategy if they are well done on a regular basis. Some organizations use this concept as a way to underwrite conventions, luncheons, concerts, or any special event where a program or printed agenda would be appropriate.

Adbooks are lucrative because the business buying the ad is paying 200-1,000 percent more for the space than its actual printing cost. An adbook can be as simple as a folded sheet of paper with ads on all sides, or as complex as a full-scale paperback booklet printed in color. An adbook can also include coupons.

One advantage of adbooks is that they train volunteers to ask for money face to face while giving the donor a concrete value for his or her money. Some volunteers who are reluctant to ask for outright monetary donations are willing to approach business people to buy ads. They know that business people want and need to advertise and that they are always looking for creative ways to reach more people. The advantage to the advertiser is that the cost of space in your adbook is almost always less than the cost of an ad of comparable size in a newspaper. Even though a newspaper reaches more people, the people you reach are "hotter" prospects.

What Will it Look Like?

An adbook, like all fundraising strategies, requires careful advance planning. The first step is to plan what shape and size your adbook will be. While the exact number of pages will be determined by the number of ads you sell, you must know what the distribution of the adbook will be, what the book will look like, and what the cost of the ads will be. If it is an adbook for a special event, the distribution will be simple: all those attending will receive one. However, if it is an adbook to be distributed widely you will need to decide if you will send one to all your donors, put the adbook in stores, hand it out in your neighborhood to people on the street, or use some other distribution strategy.

What Should it Cost?

There are no set formulas for determining how much ads should cost. Check with other groups in your area that have done successful adbooks and see what they have charged. The price of the ads will depend in large part on how fancy your adbook will be. If it is printed in color on glossy paper the ads must be more expensive than if it is simply printed in black and white. There should be some variation in price between ads on the cover of the adbook and those on inside pages. Cover-page ads (including the back cover and the two inside covers) are usually at least twice the price of ads within the book because the exposure is so much better. Some groups charge more for ads in the centerfold as well, since they too will have more exposure.

The ads are sold either by dimension in inches ("display ad") or by the number of words ("classified ad"). A display ad is prepared by the advertiser and sent to you "camera ready," that is, ready to go to the printer. For a classified ad, the advertiser sends the ad copy and you have the message typeset for inclusion in the book. Display ads are sold as full page, half page, one-third page, quarter page, and sometimes one-eighth page (depending on how big one-eighth of a page would be). Some groups choose only to have display ads so that they will not have to design classified sections.

It is a good idea to give businesses and individuals the option of buying a single line in your book and calling those advertisers "friends" or "sponsors." These listings are less expensive—$15 to $25. They do not advertise the person or business buying them but simply show that the person or business is supportive of your organization.

Once you have designed your adbook and set prices for the ads, prepare sample pages to be given to volunteers in selling the ads. A sample layout for an 8½ × 11″ format is shown.

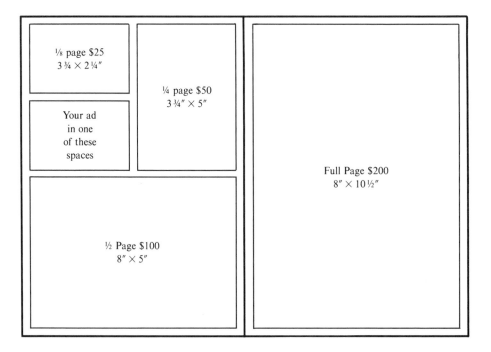

The next step is to set a time line for ad sales. If the adbook is for an event, the event will be the distribution point, and the deadline for final sales must be at least two weeks ahead to allow for typesetting, paste-up, and printing of the book.

The time line can be prepared in the same way as for a special event, with a master task list and a budget. (See Chapter 9.) A large adbook will require about a 6-week sales period. The week before sales begin will be needed for planning and preparation of materials and training of the sales force. Two weeks at the end of the sales period will be needed for layout, proofreading, and printing. Thus, the total length of the time line is nine weeks.

Getting Ready to Sell

Make a list of businesses and individuals who might want ads. Ask all volunteers, board members, and staff to list all the businesses they patronize, companies they work for, companies their spouses and friends work for, and businesses that would serve a large cross section of your donors. (For example, a women's organization would be sure to include women's clothing stores, beauty salons, and women's bars.) To help people recall all the possible businesses they patronize, give them a list of suggestions, including banks, restaurants, vegetable stores, supermarkets, butchers, clothing stores, bakeries, liquor stores, and such people as your doctor, mechanic, therapist, hairdresser, accountant, and plumber.

Place each name you receive on a 3″ by 5″ card with the address of the business and a contact person there, the name of the person who uses the business, and any other information that will be helpful to the sales person. (For example, Joe's Auto Supply, Joe Jones, owner, 512 Main St., board president's brother-in-law; also, Sally buys everything for her motorcycle there.)

Divide these cards among the volunteer sales people. If possible, volunteers should be assigned businesses and individuals they know, as they will have a better chance for success.

If you are a neighborhood or community group, it may be easier to have each volunteer simply approach every store on a square block of the neighborhood.

In addition to their prospect cards, the volunteers each need a supply of brochures describing the work of your organization, sample ad sheets with order forms to give to each business, return envelopes in case the business owner wishes to mail in their ad or payment, and receipt books for payments received at the time of sale.

Prepare the volunteers for difficult questions they may encounter, and provide possible answers including convincing arguments. Each volunteer should stress how many good prospects the adbook will reach, how inexpensive the ad is, and how much members of your organization enjoy the business, store, or service where the volunteer is selling.

Selling the Ads

Depending on the type of business you are soliciting and the general style of your community, volunteers may first want to call the business owner or manager and make an appointment. In soliciting ads from corporations or large firms, sending a letter with a follow-up phone call and visit will be imperative.

Two or three volunteers should act as "team leaders" for the rest of the sales force. The team leaders play the same role as the planning committee for a special event. While they should sell ads, their main function is to encourage people on their team and to make sure that volunteers are making their calls. Volunteers must understand that they will be turned down more often than not. It will take from five to eight solicitations for every sale. As is the case when soliciting major gifts, you rarely know exactly why you were turned down. Don't spend a great deal of time thinking about it: Simply go on to the next prospect.

As sales are made a progress chart should be posted at the office, and progress reports should be given to salespeople to encourage them. Once a week every sales person should be given a list of the businesses that have already bought ads. They can take this list with them on solicitations; business owners may be persuaded to buy an ad when they see the names of colleagues who have done so.

Thank businesses immediately after they send in their ads and their money. When the adbook is produced send them a copy. Encourage your members to tell the business that they read about the business in your adbook and to thank the business for supporting the organization. Some businesses will not send payment until the adbook is published. Careful records will show which bills remain outstanding, and those businesses can be billed again after they receive a copy of the adbook. Because they have filled out and signed an agreement specifying the size and wording of the ad, it is extremely rare for business people not to pay.

Producing the Adbook

After all the ads are in and the sales period is over, the book must be produced. Groups usually find it helpful to have a second set of volunteers handle the production and distribution details. The sales force has done their task. A graphics designer or person with layout skills should be asked (or paid) to help ensure that the ads are laid out straight, that all the ads fit properly on each page, and that all the ads fit in the book. Attention should be paid to putting ads that look nice together on the same page and to having some "white space" on each page so that the ads don't look crowded and unreadable. Great care should be taken to proofread all copy and to keep the display ads and all the copy clean. There must also be space, either throughout the adbook or in a specific section of it, for the conference agenda or information about your group and a membership form.

The final laid-out book is then ready for printing. Someone who knows about paper stock and the printing process should help select the paper and ink and specify the printing process. (Generally letterpress is preferable to offset.)

The first year you produce an adbook is the most difficult. Businesses are taking a chance that you will do what you say in terms of quality and distribution of the book. If your adbook is successful and people patronize the businesses they have read about there, repeat sales will be easy to get. Be sure to save some copies of the adbook to use in next year's sales effort so businesses can see exactly what they will get for their money. If they like what they see, they will be more inclined to buy.

Adbooks can be lucrative, both because the ads bring in much more money than the cost of printing them and because they are a repeatable commodity. They are good for training volunteers in fundraising techniques and for building community relations with businesses. If they are not well done, however, the reputation of your group and the willingness of any business to support your group again will be greatly impaired.

Raising Money from Religious Institutions, Service Clubs and Small Businesses

Religious institutions, service clubs and small businesses are worth pursuing to augment your fundraising plan. They can be asked to support specific projects or to give specific items such as office supplies, raffle prizes, or the use of space. (These groups should also be approached as audiences for speaking engagements to broaden your visibility.) Religious groups, service clubs and small businesses are useful for funding community groups, neighborhood projects, and projects with low costs. With rare exceptions, national organizations will not get money from these groups, which concentrate their giving on local projects.

Once you have received money or services from any of these sources, you have a good chance of having the gift repeated. Few groups, however, will find any of these to be major sources of funding; many groups will be unable to get money from them at all. The more your organization's work challenges the status quo, particularly on issues of distribution of wealth, the less likely you will be to get money from businesses and service clubs.

Religious Institutions

In Chapter One, we noted that religious institutions receive most of the money given away by the private sector in America. From that evidence they would seem to be a source of funds for community groups and, indeed, they give away several billion dollars a year to secular organizations. However, most houses of worship use the money they raise to pay for their own programs: maintaining buildings, paying staff, providing dues to their national offices, allocating scholarships for seminary students and supporting various mission programs in America and abroad.

If you are going to be successful raising money from religious institutions, keep these points in mind:

1. **There are few clearinghouses for information on religious funding sources,** so it is difficult to find out which religious groups give and under what circumstances. (See bibliography for some guides.)

2. **Religious institutions vary widely in structure.** Some are local branches of national organizations; some are fairly autonomous, with linkages to a national structure; others are completely autonomous, with little or no accountability to a regional or national structure.

   All local churches and synagogues can give contributions if they choose. In some cases, there are also regional or national programs for making contributions, or ecumenical efforts focussed on one population or set of issues. The best known of these are the Catholic Campaign for Human Development, the United Church of Christ's Board of Homeland Ministries, the United Methodist Voluntary Service, the Jewish Fund for Justice, the American Friends Service Committee (Quaker), the Unitarian Universalist Service Committee, and the ecumenical Commission on Religion in Appalachia (CORA). Many orders of nuns and priests provide funding to local groups as well.

3. **Certain denominations take stands on specific issues.** One obvious example is the Catholic Church's stand against freedom of choice in abortion and birth control. Most churches have reaffirmed their position that homosexuality is incompatible with Christian life. All churches place a strong emphasis on the integrity of the family, the importance of marriage, and other traditional values. With laudable exceptions, churches do not participate in social change; in fact, many stand in the way of progressive thought or action.

Generally, in order to seek a gift from a religious institution, a non-profit organization must have a relationship with the minister, rabbi, or the leading laypeople in the local organization. Then, there are several avenues for obtaining local funding:

◆ A minister or rabbi can give a group money (generally up to $500) from a discretionary fund that he or she is allowed to distribute.

◆ In churches which take up a collection, the minister or leading lay-people can call for a "second collection": After the collection for the church has been taken at a Sunday service, the minister or representative from your group will describe your work to the congregation, and the collection plate will be passed again. The proceeds from this second collection will go to your group.

◆ Within most churches and synagogues there are various guilds and clubs, each of which does its own fundraising, many of which give the money away as they wish. Generally, any house of worship will have at least one women's guild, several mission programs (the money from which can be used for "domestic" missions), and youth projects.

◆ Churches and synagogues may make their facilities available free of charge. These can include meeting rooms, office space, use of the photocopy machine, limited use of the telephone, and so forth. For groups just getting started, these services can be invaluable, as the church or synagogue can also act as your mailing address and may agree to receive phone messages for you until you are established.

Service Clubs

Every city, town, and village in America has service clubs whose members are active in civic and community affairs and that often raise funds for various community causes. The most common service clubs are Rotary, Kiwanis, Lions, Toastmasters, Oddfellows, Shriners, Moose, and Elk (men's clubs), and Junior League, Soroptomist, Job's Daughters, Zonta, and the Garden Club (women's clubs).

Sometimes service clubs simply adopt an organization or a program for which they then sponsor an annual fundraising event. Organizations adopted for such support are usually Boys' and Girls' Clubs, camps, scholarship funds, school programs, or vocationally specific programs (such as a trip to Washington, D.C., for young people wanting to go into politics, specially equipped vans for disabled people needing to get to college classes, and so forth). Service clubs will also give funds to buy equipment and will occasionally give to capital campaigns.

A group can approach a service club either by knowing someone in the club who knows the club's fundraising program and who will advocate for your group or by offering a speaker from your group for one of their monthly meetings. If you don't know anyone in a service club, write or call the club for the name of the volunteer in charge of the program for monthly meetings, and then write or call him or her and volunteer a speaker from your group. Most groups will gratefully accept your offer.

Clubs' politics, commitment, and size and level of activity vary greatly from community to community. Therefore, research the clubs in your town to find out what, if anything, they can do for you.

Small Businesses

Groups seeking money from corporations and large businesses are often surprised by the generosity of small-store owners and sole-proprietor businesses compared with the usual lack of response from bigger operations with more money.

Small businesses are best approached for in-kind rather than cash donations. Businesses can give raffle prizes, buy ads in an adbook, give your group items at wholesale cost (or at greater discounts for volume purchasing), underwrite special events, and buy tables at your luncheons or dinners. The key element in getting a business donation is to show the business person that his or her business will materially benefit from supporting your group. For example, in soliciting a raffle prize, stress how many people will see the raffle ticket with the business's name on it and how many will read the listing of supporting businesses in your newsletter. One raffle prize is a small investment for all that advertising.

Businesses that sell supplies that your group uses, such as office supplies or paper products, sometimes find that they need to discontinue a product line that isn't selling or to reduce inventory. Be sure you let them know that you will be glad to receive donations of such products.

Businesses can also extend credit to your group enabling you to buy needed items and to pay when your cash flow is better. As long as you are trustworthy and keep in touch with them, businesses may be willing to carry a debt for quite some time.

Most business people belong to one or more business associations that meet regularly and need speakers. By being invited to one of these meetings you can meet many business people at once. Use the same procedures as for getting a speaking engagement with a service club.

The economic conditions of your community and the health of small businesses generally will affect your ability to raise funds or services from them. If you show, however, that it is in their self-interest to help you, you will be able to expand your fundraising to these areas.

CAMPAIGNS AND SPECIAL EVENTS

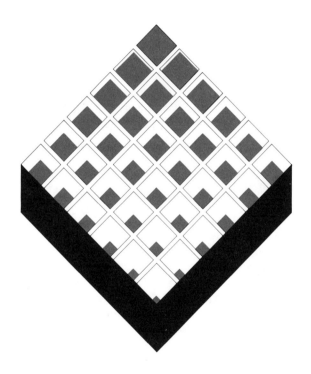

Chapter 7

Major Gifts

Asking for Money

Asking people for money is both the hardest and the most important part of fundraising. Every organization committed to financial self-sufficiency requests money from people in a variety of ways—direct mail appeals, special events, adbooks, and so on. But the most difficult fundraising method of all is for board, staff, and volunteers to ask people directly for large donations. A major gifts program is a strategy to obtain donations of $50 or more from a large number of people. Experience has shown, however, that it is impossible to have a large major gifts program without face-to-face solicitation.

To do effective major-gift soliciting people need to know why they fear asking for money and how to overcome these fears.

Why We're Afraid to Ask for Money

If the idea of asking for money fills you with anxiety, disgust, dread, or some combination of these feelings, you are among the majority of people. If asking for money does not cause you any distress you have either let go of your fear about it or you grew up in an unusually liberated household.

To identify the source of our fears we must look at both the role of money in American society and at the attitudes about asking for anything that have been generated by the strong puritan ethic that is our American heritage.

Politeness and the puritan ethic

Most of us were taught that the following four topics are taboo for discussion with anyone other than perhaps one's most intimate friends: money, sex, religion, and politics. The taboo is far stronger for money and sex than for religion or politics. Many of us were taught to believe that inquiring about a person's salary or asking how much he or she paid for a house or a car is rude. In many families the man takes care of all financial decisions. Even today it is not unusual for wives not to know how much their husbands earn, for children not to know how much their parents earn, or for close friends not to know each other's income. Many people know nothing about the stock market—for example, the difference between a bear and a bull market, or what the rising or falling of the Dow Jones average means for the economy.

Not only do most people lack basic knowledge of how to handle money, but they have no desire to learn more about money. We have been carefully taught that "nice" people don't care about money. The hidden message is that "good" people only deal with money insofar as they must to live. Many people, misquoting the New Testament, say, "Money is the root of all evil." In fact, Paul's letter to the Phillippians states, "Love of money is the root of all evil." Money in itself has no good or evil qualities. It is a substance, not a moral being.

Money is shrouded in mystery and tinged with fascination. Most people are curious about the salary levels of their friends, how much money people have inherited, how the super-rich live. Consequently people speculate a great deal about the place of money in others' lives. Money is like sex and sexuality in this regard: kept in secrecy and therefore fascinating. Just as much of what we learned as children and teenagers about sexuality turned out to be untrue, so it is with money. Our assumptions about it are for the most part based on speculation.

One major effect of money being treated as taboo is that only those willing to learn about it can control it. In America an elite class controls most of the nation's wealth, either by earning it, by having inherited it, or both. It serves the interest of this ruling class for the rest of us not to know about money. As long as we cannot understand this substance, without which we cannot live in America, we will never control the means of production, we will never be able to finance our nonprofits adequately, and we will never ourselves have the power that knowledge about money provides.

Because we are political activists and participants in social change, it is imperative that we learn about money—how to raise it effectively and ethically, how to manage it carefully, and how to spend it wisely.

The idea of asking for money raises another set of hindering attitudes, which are largely the inheritance of a predominately Protestant culture. The puritan ethic, which lives today, conveys a number of messages that guide our feelings and actions: If you are a good person and you work hard you will get what you deserve. If you have to ask for something you have not worked hard enough and you probably don't deserve it. If you have to ask for something you are a weak person because strong people are self-sufficient.

Specific fears

With these two very strong taboos operating against asking for money, it is a wonder that anyone ever raises a dime! Understanding the source of our discomfort is the first step toward overcoming it. The next step is to examine our fears of what will happen to us when we do ask. When people look at their fears rationally they often find that most of them disappear or at least become manageable.

Fears about asking for money fall into three categories:

◆ those that will almost never happen (*"The person will hit me"*; *"I'll die of a heart attack during the solicitation."*);

◆ those that could be avoided by training and preparation ("*I won't know what to say*"; "*I won't know my facts, the person will think I am an idiot.*"); and

◆ those that definitely will happen sometimes ("*The person will say no.*").

In the case of being refused occasionally, one can make the fear of it manageable by asking, "If the person says no, is that the end of the world? Will I have to leave town, change my identity, permanently hang my head?" Clearly, the answer is no.

While each individual will have his or her own fears and anxieties about asking for money, most people have three fears.

1. **The person will say no.** Rejection is the number one fear. It is also something that will happen to any solicitor, at least as often as the prospect says "yes". Therefore, it is important to get to the point where you don't feel upset when someone says "no." You do this by realizing that when you ask someone for a gift you are seeing them at a single moment in their lives. A thousand things have happened to the person prior to your request, none of which has anything to do with you, but many of which will affect the person's receptiveness to your request. For example, the person may have recently found out that one of his or her children needs braces, that the car needs new tires, or that a client is not able to pay a bill on time. This news will certainly affect the prospect's perception of what size donation he or she can make. Events unrelated to money can also cause the prospect to say no: A divorce proceeding, a death in the family, a headache. As the solicitor, none of these things is your fault. In fact, you probably couldn't have known them ahead of time. If you feel personally rejected you have probably misinterpreted what happened.

   Everyone has the right to say no to a request. Most of the time you will not know exactly why your request was turned down. Your job is not to worry about why this prospect said no, but to go on to the next prospect.

2. **Asking a friend for money will have a negative effect on our friendship.** Many people feel that friendship is outside the realm of money. To bring money into a friendship, they feel, is to complicate it and perhaps to ruin it. Friends are usually the best prospects, however, because they share our commitments and values. They are interested in our lives and wish us success and happiness. To many people's surprise, friends are more likely to be offended when they are *not* asked. They can't understand why you don't want to include them in your work. Further, if it is truly acceptable to you for a person to say "no" to your request, your friend will never feel put on the spot. Your friend will not feel pressured by your request, as if your whole friendship hung on the answer. When asking friends, then, make clear that **yes** is your favorite answer, but **no** is also acceptable.

3. **The person will say yes to my request, then turn around and ask me for their cause. I will be obligated to give whether I want to or not.** This quid pro quo ("this for that") could happen. However, if someone you ask for

money gives some to your organization, you are not obligated to that person. You have not materially benefited. You presented your cause, the person was sympathetic and agreed to help support it. The cause was furthered. Beyond a thank-you note and a gracious attitude, you owe this donor nothing. If the donor then asks you to support his or her cause, you consider the request without reference to your request. You may wish to support the person or the cause, but you are not obligated to do so. If you think that someone is going to attach strings to a gift, don't ask that prospect. There are hundreds of prospects who will give freely.

> Far from being a horrible thing to do, asking someone for money actually does them a favor. People who agree with your goals and respect the work of your group will want to be a part of it. Giving money is a simple and effective way to be involved, to be part of a cause larger than oneself.

Many volunteers find that it takes practice to overcome their fears about asking for money. To begin soliciting donations does not require being free of fear: it only requires having your fear under control. An old fundraising saying is that if you are afraid to ask someone for a gift, "kick yourself out of the way and let your cause do the talking." The point is this: If you are committed to an organization you will do what is required to keep that organization going, including asking for money.

Planning a Gifts Campaign

Before beginning to solicit major gifts, your organization must define how much money it wishes to raise from large gifts, the minimum amount that constitutes a major gift, and how many gifts are needed.

In the ideal gift campaign you would determine that you need, for example, 200 people to give $100 each. You would send 200 letters, make 200 phone calls, and get your money. Unfortunately, 200 people will never behave in the same way. Most will give nothing, some will give less than $100, and a few will give more.

Apportionment of Gifts

Over the years fundraising experts have observed a pattern of how gifts come into organizations. Based on that pattern, it is possible to project for any fundraising goal how many of each size gift you should seek and how many prospects you will need to ask to get each gift.

This is the established pattern:

◆ Sixty percent of an organization's income comes from 10 percent of the donors.

♦ Fifteen percent to 25 percent of its income comes from 20 percent of the donors.

♦ The remaining 15-25 percent comes from 70 percent of the donors.

In other words, the vast majority of the gifts you get will be small, but the majority of your income will come from a few large donations.

For example, if your organization must raise $50,000 from grass roots fundraising, you should plan to raise $30,000 (or 60 percent) from major donors, $7,500-$12,500 or (15-25 percent) from middle-range donations, and the remaining 15-25 percent from every other fundraising strategy.

Many low-budget groups define a major gift as any gift over $50. While not a large gift, $50 is larger than the average gift groups receive, which is generally $10-$25. Fifty dollars is also an amount that most employed people can afford by pledging $15 a quarter or $5 a month. It brings being a "major donor" into the realm of possibility for most volunteers.

Size of Gifts

A second observation concerns gift size and the number of prospects needed to achieve the goal. The two top gifts must provide 10 percent of the total goal. In the example of a $50,000 campaign, the two top gifts would each be $2,500. The rest of the major gifts are then figured on a gift range chart. Given that 60 percent of the money will come from 10 percent of the donors, the major gift range chart for a $50,000 campaign would be as follows:

Major Gift Range Chart

Gift Amount	No. of Gifts	Prospect/Donor Ratio	No. of Prospects
$ 2,500	2	5:1	10
1,000	5	4:1	20
500	10	4:1	40
100	50	2:1	200
50	200	2:1	400
$30,000	267		670

The gift range chart, which can be seen as a triangle, is not a blueprint for the campaign. Its purpose is to show what an average major gifts campaign would look like. The numbers can be changed—the ranges moved up and down depending on the group. If you have a top prospect who can give $5,000, your gift-range chart triangle would be longer and narrower. If the biggest gift you can get is $500, you might need more gifts of that size and more gifts of $100, etc., or you may need to lower your goal. Your triangle would be short and wide.

Gifts of $1,500 or $250 are also appropriate sizes but are not included on this average chart because most people don't think in those amounts.

Materials, Volunteers, and Prospects

Besides a goal for your major gifts program, and a gift range chart, three more elements need to be in place before the campaign can begin. These are materials, volunteers, and prospects.

Materials include brochures, stationery, and return envelopes. Volunteers will also need a roster of the board members and their affiliations, a copy of the case statement, and a list of difficult questions they may face, with suitable answers.

Volunteers must be trained to ask for money (discussed on pages 133-137). They do not have to have previous experience nor do they need to know very many prospects themselves. They do not have to be board members, but some board members should be part of the major gifts effort. Most groups find it helpful for all the volunteers who will be soliciting major gifts to meet before the campaign. At this meeting the fundraising coordinator describes the process of the campaign, reviews the materials, and helps the volunteers practice asking for money. At this meeting volunteers can discuss their fears about asking for money and ask any questions about the organization. The meeting also serves as a pep rally for the campaign. Group meetings should be held every two months or so for these volunteers so that they can discuss their experiences and renew their enthusiasm for the campaign. Fundraising staff should announce how far the organization has moved toward its goal—always a morale boost—and encourage people who are hesitant to complete their assignments.

Some of the prospects to be solicited need to be identified before the campaign. Some will be identified by the volunteers themselves and others will be identified by other donors as the campaign progresses. The next section discusses the process of prospect identification.

In planning a major gifts campaign, keep in mind that the first year of recruiting major donors will be the hardest. Do not set your goals too high; you don't want volunteers to be demoralized by failing to reach an unrealistic goal. Major gifts recruitment does not have to have a campaign format—that is, a formal beginning and end. Major gifts recruitment can be an ongoing program, with different volunteers helping for different periods of time. The most important step to take in a major gifts program is to start it. Even if you only have one prospect, ask that prospect. If the largest gift you can imagine someone you know giving is $50, start with $50. A major gifts program builds on itself; simply establishing the groundwork for the program will begin the process of getting major gifts.

Prospect Identification

Traits of the Qualified Prospect

How do you know if someone would be likely to give $50 or more to your organization if asked? Look for positive evidence of three qualities—that the person is acquainted with someone in your group, that he or she is committed to your cause or to a similar cause, and that he or she is able to make a major gift. When you have this information you have a "qualified prospect": Someone who should be asked for a gift. Let's examine each of these elements.

Acquaintance: You cannot approach total strangers with your request. The prospect must be acquainted either with someone in your organization or with someone who will allow you to use his or her name to approach the prospect. The person who actually asks for the gift may not know the prospect at all, but there must be someone whom the prospect and the solicitor both know.

Commitment: There must be reason to believe that the prospect would be interested in your organization. Be creative and broad-minded in assessing this quality. For example, a board member of an organization working with victims of child abuse was encouraged by another donor to approach a wealthy woman known to support the local symphony and museum. For various reasons the donor did not wish to approach this woman herself but told the board member to use her name. In seeking to understand why someone involved in the arts would be interested in child abuse, the board member found out from the donor who suggested the woman's name that the woman had been a victim of child abuse herself. She eventually donated quite a large amount to this project. A blanket assumption about her interests would have resulted in no request.

Another example: A board member of a wilderness preservation program knew that his neighbor, a retired real estate developer, gave substantial donations to the local hospital and to his alma mater. Though the board member assumed that his neighbor's former profession would preclude an interest in wilderness preservation, he invited his neighbor to an educational event sponsored by the program. There the neighbor heard about the need for preservation and about some of the group's current projects. He was delighted. Having been a Boy Scout and then an Eagle Scout, he had enjoyed camping and outdoor experiences. Now that he was retired he wanted to become reinvolved in outdoor activities. Not only did he become a donor to the organization, he eventually became a member of the board.

The final piece of evidence you need to establish commitment is evidence that the person gives away money at all. Someone who is not in the habit of giving to charity will be unlikely to break that habit by giving to your organization. The acquaintance of the prospect should know what groups the prospect belongs to. Searching through membership lists printed in other organization's newsletters, lists of donors printed in convention or performance programs, and the like will also let you know whether a prospect is a donor to any group.

Ability: Because of the secrecy surrounding money, ability is sometimes difficult to judge. Nonetheless, it is critical to determine a specific amount or a specific range of giving for each prospect. You cannot approach someone and simply ask for a gift or a donation without stating specifically how much your organization needs and how much you hope this prospect will give. The prospect should not have to guess what to give. When you name an amount or a range of gift the prospect can make an informed decision.

There are two levels of evidence of ability: primary and supporting. Primary evidence is information about how much this prospect has given to other causes and how this prospect spends his or her disposable income. Primary evidence includes a person's hobbies (photography, scuba diving, coin collecting are expensive); whether the person would spend $500, $1,000, $1,500 or more on a single antique or piece of art; whether the person holds season tickets to the opera or football team; whether he or she goes away for the weekend frequently, and where; and whether he or she eats out often, and where.

Supporting evidence is information about such things as the kind of car the prospects drive, where they live, and what their occupation is. Supporting evidence, if used alone, can be misleading. Some people living in expensive homes, driving expensive cars, and holding down high-income jobs are, in fact, in debt over their ears. Conversely, people living modestly can be quite wealthy.

Finding Prospects

Information gathering
Evidence of acquaintance, commitment and ability is best gained from the person who knows the prospect. However, there are several sources that can provide valuable back-up information or confirm what you have been told. The wealthier a prospect is the more research you should do. Sources such as the telephone book can provide correct spelling of names and, where listed, addresses. The *Yellow Pages* can provide information about profession, company affiliations, even an indication of the affluence of the company based on the size of the advertisement they buy. Other sources, which will be of varying value depending on whom you are researching, are the *Who's Who* series (which include *Who's Who in America* and more than 25 other special subjects), Standard and Poor's *Register of Corporate Executives and Directors*, property rolls at the county or city assessor's office, records of contributions to political candidates or issues (available at the courthouse), the business, social, and obituary section of the local newspaper, and membership lists of local clubs and organizations. Visiting your local business library and exploring the reference section is time well spent.

The prospect record

The prospect record shown below presents a way of gathering this information systematically. You will want to design a form that addresses the specific needs of your organization or community; this one includes most questions you would need to know. You will not need much information other than whether or not the person is employed to determine their ability to give $50. Gifts of $250 will require knowing whether the person either gives away or regularly spends such an amount. Gifts of $500 and up require more research.

Prospect Record

Date of Research:_____

Name _____

Address: Business _____

Home _____

Phone: Business _____ Home _____

Occupation _____

Length of time in current occupation _____

Employer _____

Education _____

Church/service club/professional associations: _____

_____

_____

Political party _____ Active? _____

Marital status _____ Children _____

Approximate annual income _____

Other sources of income _____

Other evidence of wealth (i.e., second home, expensive car, vacations, style of dress, hobbies, etc.): _____

_____

_____

_____

Interest in nonprofits, including donations to nonprofits: _____

_____

_____

Other interests (recreation, social interests, hobbies): _____

_____

_____

Evidence of interest in our program _____

Who knows this person? _____

Who should approach him/her? _____

Gift potential _____

Ability is the least significant of the three factors. Knowing the prospect and knowing his or her commitments and values is much more important than knowing his or her level of ability. Many people with ability will never give you any money, and others with seemingly little ability will dig deep and give substantially because of their commitment.

To find prospects, start with yourself. Will you give $50 or more? Whom else do you know who could give that amount? Next, move out to the board of directors and other volunteers or staff in the organization. Statisticians tell us that every person knows 250 people—no doubt some of these people can and will give large donations. Another place to look for prospects is in your current donor list. Most people have friends roughly on par with their own economic standing. Your $50-, $200-, and $500-donors will know other people who could give in that range. While many of your donors will decline to give you names, they will not be insulted, and some of your current major donors will help you expand your major donor rolls.

Soliciting the Gift

Most people discover that doing face-to-face soliciting rekindles their commitment to the organization. They remember why they became involved in the first place and their excitement about the organization's work. Occasionally people discover that their commitment is no longer strong and that they would be happier in another organization.

Approaching the Prospect

The first step in soliciting gifts from others is for the solicitor to give. The size of the gift is not important: What matters is that the gift is substantial for that person. When solicitors go out to ask, they must feel that they are not asking the prospect to do any more than they themselves have done.

After the solicitor has made his or her financial commitment, the prospects have been thoroughly researched, and the best prospects have been identified, the solicitor can begin the process of "getting the gift."

There are three steps to approaching the prospect:

1. a letter describing the program and requesting a meeting to discuss it further, followed by
2. a phone call to set up a meeting, and then
3. the meeting itself in which the gift is actually solicited.

Obviously, if you are approaching your spouse or your best friend you can skip the letter and perhaps even the phone call. In some cases the letter will be enough, and there will be no need for a phone call; in others the letter and a phone call will be enough, and there will be no need for a meeting. Deciding whether a meeting or follow-up phone call is necessary will depend on your knowledge of the prospect. However, it is always better to err on the side of doing too much.

The letter

The letter should raise the prospect's interest, giving some information, but not enough for a truly informed decision. The letter should be brief, not more than one page. Its purpose is to get the prospect to be open to your phone call, in which you will request a meeting. In other words, the letter introduces the fact that you will be asking for a large gift for your organization and that you want the prospect to be willing to give you a short amount of time to explain why you want this gift and why you think this prospect will be interested. No commitment to give or to be involved in any way is asked for in the letter—only a request for the prospect to discuss the proposition of a gift with the solicitor. The elements of the letter are shown on the following page.

The letter is straightforward. Wally knows what the request will be, including the amount. He knows what the money is for. If giving to this organization at all is out of the question, he can decide that now. If giving a lead gift is out of the question, he has been given the option of giving a smaller gift in the sentence about "a slew of $250-$500" gifts. He has been flattered, and his importance to the campaign has been stated. Yet there is nothing he needs to do at this point except wait for the phone call. No action has been requested—in fact, he has specifically only been asked not to decide.

The phone call

If you say you are going to call you have to call. Rehearse the phone call beforehand to anticipate questions or objections the prospect may have. Be sure you know exactly what you are going to say from the very first hello. Many people find it useful to write down what they will say, in the same way that one writes a script for a phone-a-thon.

The phone call is the most difficult part of the solicitation. First, it is pivotal to getting the meeting. Without the meeting you will probably not get as large a gift as you might have and you might not get a gift at all. Second, you have no visual clues about the prospect. You can't tell if he or she is frowning, smiling, in a hurry, or busy. Third, you can't rely on how people sound on the phone. People who are easygoing may sound brusque or harried on the phone. Many people simply do not like to talk on the phone, and their dislike of being on the phone may come across to you as a dislike of talking to you or a reluctance to discuss their gift.

To insure that you have not caught the prospect at a bad time, ask if this is a good time to talk or if the prospect has two minutes right now. Be sure not to read meaning into statements that can be taken at face value. For example, do not hear, "I don't want to give" in a statement such as "I'm very busy this month," or "I have to talk to my spouse before making any

Mr. Wealthy Committed Acquaintance
Important Office Building
Thriving Downtown, Healthy State

Dear Wally,

Establish relationship to prospect and to organization.

For several years you have heard me talk about _____ (local community organization). As you know, I have recently been elected to serve on their board of directors. At a recent meeting, we made a decision to launch a major gifts campaign, the main purpose of which is to help LCO become financially self-sufficient. In the future, we want to depend on a broad base of donors rather than on foundations and government grants.

Establish briefly what you want and why.

The goal of the campaign is $15,000 the first year. We need two lead gifts of $750, plus a slew of gifts in the $250-$500 range. The lead gift should be from someone of standing in the community, whose word carries weight. I am hoping you will consider being one of the leaders in this campaign.

(One more paragraph on the work of the organization.)

Don't decide; just listen to me.

I know this is a big request. Before you make any decision about it, I would like to meet with you and discuss LCO's programs and the need it fills in our community. I can't convey my excitement about this organization in this letter, nor can I do it justice.

I'll call you next week to set up a time. Hope you are well. Enjoyed seeing you and your family at the baseball game last week.

Sincerely,
Al
Almost As Wealthy

decision." Instead, in the first instance say, "I can understand that. How about if I call you next month, when things might have slowed down for you?" In the second instance say, "Would it be possible for me to see you both in that case?"

The purpose of the phone call is to get the meeting. Again, the prospect does not need to decide about his or her gift until the meeting. Rehearse with a friend the possible objections and difficult questions you can imagine coming up in your phone call and what you would say in each one.

If the prospect tries to put you off, do not assume that he or she is saying no. In fact, the wealthier the prospect is, the more likely he or she is to be trying to determine how serious you are about your organization. If you take the first putoff as a final no, it will appear to the prospect that you are not serious either about the group or about the prospect's gift.

The Meeting

Once you have an appointment you are ready to prepare for the face-to-face solicitation. This is not as frightening as it seems. First of all, the prospect knows from your letter or your phone call that you will be talking about making a contribution. Since he or she has agreed to see you the answer to your request is not an outright "no." The prospect is considering saying yes. Your job is to move the prospect from consideration to commitment.

The purpose of the meeting is to get the gift. As the solicitor, you must appear poised, enthusiastic, and confident. If you are well prepared for the interview, this will not be too difficult. Board members and volunteers can go with each other or bring a staff person to such a meeting to provide any information the solicitor doesn't have. If you do go in pairs, be sure you know who is going to actually ask for the gift.

Meeting etiquette

The more the prospect is encouraged to talk the more likely he or she is to give. Be sure that you have a true discussion with prospects, and that you do not lecture them or do all the talking. Ask the prospect open-ended questions, and try to draw out any objections he or she might have.

Toward the end of the half-hour interview, or when the prospect seems fully satisfied with what you have said, you are ready to close—that is, to ask for the gift. Repeat the goal of the campaign, and the importance of the work of the group in one or two sentences. Then, looking directly at the prospect, ask for a specific gift: "Will you help with $2,000?" Then be quiet. At this moment, you give up control of the interaction—a control that you have had from the moment you sent your letter. At last, you are asking the prospect to make a decision. Wait for the prospect to speak, even if you have to wait several minutes. Keep looking at the prospect. You can breathe easy now, because you have said everything you need to say and you have put your best foot forward. Look relaxed and confident.

The prospect's response

At this point the prospect will say one of five things.

1. **"No, I can't help you."** Although this is an unlikely response at this point, it should be treated with respect. Thank the prospect for his or her time and leave. Send the prospect a thank you note thanking him/her for agreeing to see you and for his/her candidness.
2. **"I'd like to help, but the figure you name is too high."** This is a yes answer, but for a smaller gift. You can say, "Would you like to pledge that amount and contribute it in quarterly installments over a year's period?" Or you can say, "What would you feel comfortable giving?"

"What would you like to give?"

3. **"That's a lot of money."** This statement is not a decision. This statement says, "Remind me again of my role in this campaign." Your answer: "It is a lot of money. There are not many people we could ask for that amount. Your gift will be a trendsetter. Your gift will be very important in helping us reach our goal." Then be quiet and let the prospect decide.

4. **"I need to think about it."** Some people truly cannot make up their mind on the spot, and if pushed for an answer will say no. Ask the prospect, "What else can I tell you that will help you in your thinking?" and answer any remaining questions. Then say, "May I call you in a few days to see what your decision is?" Set a time when the prospect will be finished thinking and will give you an answer.

5. **"Yes, I'll help."** Arrange for how the gift will be made (by check, by pledge, by stock transfer; now, later), say "Thank you," and leave.

Coming to closure

After the prospect has made a commitment, verify how he or she will be paying: Through a pledge, through a check given to you then and there, by sending a check later, with a gift of stock, etc. Once these arrangements are made, thank the prospect again and leave.

Immediately after the interview send the donor a thank-you note. Another thank-you note should come from the organization when the gift is received. Although it is frightening to ask someone for a large gift, it is also thrilling when the prospect says yes. It is also a good feeling to know that you were able to set aside your own discomfort about asking for money for the greater purpose of meeting the needs of your organization. Knowing that you can talk comfortably about the financial goals of your organization is indeed an empowering experience.

Renewing and Upgrading Major Donors

As this book has repeatedly stressed, the main purpose of acquiring donors is to develop a loyal group of supporters who give money to your organization every year and who increase the amount of their donations regularly.

This process of donors renewing and upgrading their gifts does not happen automatically. Rarely do donors think of renewing their gifts without being reminded, and they almost never think of raising the amount of their donation on their own. In order for these things to happen, major donors must receive special attention from the organization in a systematic way. It is ineffective to write to major donors only when you want them to renew their gifts. They need to feel that they are an integral part of the organization throughout the year.

Keeping in Touch

An organization needs to be in contact with its major donors three times a year besides the time when the donor is asked to renew his or her gift. Generally, this contact is the job of the person in charge of fundraising.

There are several easy ways of keeping in touch with major donors that make them feel personally appreciated and do not cost the organization much in time and money.

First, send donors a holiday card during December. The card wishes them happy holidays or happy New Year. Unless you are a religiously identified organization make sure the card has no religious overtones, including cultural Christian overtones such as Santa Claus, elves, and Christmas trees. The fundraising coordinator, chair of the board, or board member with a personal relationship to the donor should sign the card on behalf of the organization and, if possible, write a brief note on it.

Second, send donors a copy of your annual report, accompanied by a personal note. The note can be handwritten or typed and need not be lengthy. It can simply say, "I am sending you a copy of our annual report because your ongoing and generous support has helped to make the programs described in it possible." Or: "Sending this along because I know how interested you will be in seeing our progress. Your generous gift is a big help to us, and we look forward to staying in touch with you." It doesn't matter if you don't know the donor at all—a personal note will make him or her feel appreciated.

The third contact comes from taking an opportunity that arises during the year. If you have positive press coverage; if you win a victory in your organizing, legislative, or litigative efforts; if you are commended by a citizen's group, service club, or politician; take the opportunity to send a special letter to donors telling them of this event. This letter can be brief and does not have to be personal. A newspaper clipping can be reproduced for all of the donors, the victory can be summarized, or additional information can be given to them beyond what is in your newsletter.

If no such obvious opportunity occurs during the year, you will have to create another contact. Sometimes groups send major donors an invitation to their annual meeting or other special event, including a personal note to the donor. Sometimes groups prepare a mid-year report simply called "Special Report to Major Donors" describing the organization's progress in meeting its financial and program goals and thanking the donors for their support. This report, which need not be more than two or three pages long, should again be accompanied by a personal note. Each of these notes can be similar in content, but they should be personalized. If you use a word processor, use a letter quality printer, not a dot matrix printer.

By keeping in frequent touch with your major donors, you will lay the groundwork necessary to approach them for a renewal of their gift the second year they give and a request to increase the size of their gift the third year of their giving. You have established a rapport with the donor, even if you have never met the person.

The Renewal

Near the anniversary of the donor's gift send him or her a letter asking for a renewal. The letter should be personal (that is, typed separately for each donor) and should be signed by the fundraising coordinator. For gifts of $500 or more a follow-up phone call with an offer to meet with the donor is important, although most donors will not need a meeting in order to renew. If the donor is a friend of someone on the board or in the organization, the fundraising coordinator should still send a letter requesting a renewal of the gift, but the friend of the donor should make the follow-up phone call.

The renewal letter should be no more than one page and should summarize the highlights of the previous year or the goals of the coming year. The letter should stress the importance of the donor's gift both in the past and in the future. The letter should be sent with a stamped return envelope marked to the attention of the person who signed the letter.

Just as in soliciting the gift for the first time, if you say you are going to call you must call. Don't think that the donor will be flattered that you thought of calling. Don't offer to call unless you are prepared to do so.

Upgrading the Gift

There are several methods to upgrade gifts; some are easy to implement, others take more time. The minimal effort that a group should undertake is to include the phrase "or more" in every suggestion of the amount to give. For example, in your letter asking for a renewal of a $50 gift, say, "I hope you will renew with a gift of $50 or more this year." The phrase "or more" can be tacked on to any suggested amount of gift.

The next level of upgrading involves doing more research on your current donors to determine which of them should be asked to raise the amount of their gift. From the records of your current donors, identify those in the following categories:

1. Donors who have given the same amount for three years or more, no matter what the size of the gift;
2. Donors who give several times a year in response to your extra appeals;
3. Donors whom you know are not giving at their level of ability.

The first step is to eliminate from the list those donors who are not candidates for an upgraded gift. For example, a person who has given the same amount for three years or more may not be able to afford more or may not have enough interest to upgrade. People giving frequently may not be able to give a larger gift at any one time.

You can narrow the list down to prospects who might be able to give more by using the principles of prospect identification outlined earlier in this chapter.

Once you have established how much a donor can give, based on his or her commitment, ability, and whom he or she knows in your organization who can ask for this higher gift, you must develop a strategy for approaching the person. You cannot simply say to the donor, "Our research has shown that you are only giving $250, and you could be giving $1,000 so please pay up." (Donors will rarely give more than twice the amount of their last gift, unless they are presented with a compelling reason.)

The reasons that you present to the donor for increasing the gift will vary greatly. Sometimes donors can be asked to set an example of giving more, which can be announced to other major donors. If the donor is respected and well known, his or her increased commitment will draw out a similar commitment in others. Sometimes a donor can be approached to support a special project or to give to a capital campaign. Sometimes it is enough to present them with the fact that your budget has increased by a certain percentage and you are hoping the donor's gift can also increase by that percentage.

Approaching donors for a larger gift is generally done the same way as approaching a first-time prospect. Send a letter outlining your need and why you think the donor would be interested. Then follow the letter with a phone call and a visit. This process should be much more informal than with a first-time prospect because you have established a relationship with the donor by being in touch with him or her frequently.

Sometimes board and staff feel shy about approaching a donor for a higher gift. They are afraid that the donor will feel taken advantage of and stop giving altogether. Of course this can happen but usually only when the approach is too aggressive or proper research on the donor's giving ability has not been done. When research is thorough and the approach is appropriate, the worst that can happen is that the donor will continue to give at his or her present level.

REMEMBER: Donors gravitate to organizations that help them feel noticed, sought out, and appreciated. While an organization may perceive that it is leaving the donor alone to make up his or her own mind about a gift, the donor may be likely to feel ignored. While an organization may fear that writing and calling donors frequently will make them feel "hounded," the donors will perceive that they are being noticed and appreciated.

We cannot overstate the importance of letting the donor make his or her own decision and not making assumptions on the donor's behalf about what the gift should be. You simply make your needs and your request plain to the donors, in a dignified and professional manner. If you respect the donors as people important to the organization and let them decide what to do, they will be likely both to repeat and to upgrade their gifts when asked.

Chapter 8

Capital Campaigns for Low-Budget Organizations

A "capital campaign" is a technique for raising money for a specific project that constitutes a one-time need over and above the annual budget of the organization. Usually the project involves buying, refurbishing, or constructing a building. Capital campaigns can also be used for money to buy equipment or to establish endowments. (An endowment is a large amount of money that is held as principle, with the interest used to finance the organization.)

Capital campaigns have usually seemed out of the range of low-budget organizations, which are often hard-pressed simply to meet their ongoing annual budget. Capital campaigns are normally associated with universities and hospitals, and the amount of money needed (almost always more than $1 million) seems beyond the scope of possibility for a low-budget organization.

However, there is no reason a capital campaign can't have a goal of $10,000, $5,000, or any other smaller amount. For low-budget organizations, a large part of the capital campaign's goal can be met with government or foundation grants.

Building Your Case

To begin a capital campaign an organization must have a one-time need. The board of directors must fully concur that this is a need and support the mechanism of a capital campaign to meet it. The first element of the campaign, then, is a strong case.

The case for the campaign is separate from the overall case statement for the organization. It focuses on the project alone, not on any other work of the organization. The case statement for the capital campaign discusses why the project is needed, how the building or equipment reflects the organization's goals and overall mission, and how the expenditure of money and time is absolutely critical to the best interests of the group. The case implies (or may state overtly) that the work of the group would be significantly slowed down or impaired by the lack of this facility or equipment.

A capital campaign puts a great strain on an organization's annual fundraising. Some of the people most loyal to the organization will be asked to contribute, often substantially, to the capital campaign. This means that they may not make their regular annual contribution or they may cut the amount of their annual gift. At the very least, they will not be increasing the amount of their gift during the time they are fulfilling their pledge to the capital campaign. All board members will need to make a financial contribution to the campaign in addition to their annual gift. The amount of the contribution will vary from member to member but must be significant for each. Board members will be doing face-to-face soliciting and other fundraising for the capital campaign, in addition to the fundraising they do for the annual budget.

Planning the Campaign

Budget and time line

Once the case is accepted and supported by staff and board, and the risks involved in such a campaign are understood, the planning for the campaign can begin. The first step is to prepare a budget for the campaign. A staff person or a small committee from the board can draw up this budget. Whoever undertakes it should be very aware of hidden costs: Building permits, fire insurance, earthquake-proofing, fire extinguishers, landscaping, etc. The budget should include a fair amount of money for the inevitable cost overruns. As anyone who has ever built or added onto a house knows, estimating cost overruns is not a simple proposition.

One cost that is difficult to calculate is the amount of staff and board time involved in the negotiation (and implementation) of the plans with the architect or contractor. If you are buying equipment, time must be spent thoroughly understanding the organization's needs, researching the best buys, discussing options, making the purchase, and learning how to use the equipment.

The final aspect of the budget is the fundraising costs for the campaign, which will include staff time, cost of the materials to promote the campaign, and establishment and maintenance of recordkeeping systems to keep the campaign's income and expenses separate from the annual budget.

You must also decide on the timing of the campaign. Your organization must have a solid annual fundraising program, in which you do not anticipate any serious cash flow problems or funding cutbacks. You will also need to discover what other capital campaigns are going on at the same time. While your campaign will not interfere with the capital campaign of a hospital or university, you would not want to launch it during a capital campaign for a related organization.

After the budget and time line for the campaign are worked out, bring the whole package back to the board for reapproval. While board members may have approved the concept of the campaign, when faced with the realities of the money and time involved, they may wish to change their minds. Without full board and staff ownership the campaign will fail. Taking the time to make sure that everyone understands the implications of the campaign is imperative, because once the campaign is launched it must be seen through to the end. It is extremely detrimental to the reputation of an organization to start a campaign and then abort it.

The fundraising plan

A gift range chart. With full board and staff enthusiasm, you are now ready to make the fundraising plan for the campaign. The first element of the program is the preparation of a gift range chart, similar in theory and purpose to the gift range chart for an annual campaign described in Chapter 7. However, a gift range chart for a capital campaign differs in two respects from that of an annual campaign: The lead gift is usually larger, and the top gifts must always be sought and received first. In fact, the lead gifts are sought even before the campaign is publicly announced. The lead or "pacesetting" gifts must be found first because the success of the campaign will depend mostly on the public's perception that the goal is achievable. The one element that makes the goal seem realizable is already having a good percentage of the total needed when the campaign is announced.

The following gift range chart for a capital campaign is based on studies of successful capital campaigns. Like all charts, it is not to be taken literally. If your chart is different it does not mean that your campaign will fail. The principles involved in putting together a gift range chart are: One gift should equal 10 percent of the goal and the next two gifts should each equal 5 percent each of the goal; 35-40 percent of the required goal is raised from 10-15 top gifts; the next 35 percent is raised from the next 100 gifts; and the rest of the money (25-30 percent) is raised from the rest of the donors. The lowest gift to a capital campaign is almost always greater than the lowest gifts to an annual campaign.

Low-budget organizations running small capital campaigns often use foundation or corporate grants as their lead gifts. Sometimes these grants are given as challenges. Whatever source you use, and however you decide how many gifts will make up the top 20-30 percent of gifts, you must have in hand or pledged 20-30 percent of the campaign goal before the campaign is announced far and wide—to members, in the newspapers, etc.

Here's an example of a gift range chart for a $100,000 capital campaign.

If you can find the lead gifts you can usually find the rest of the gifts. Finding prospects for the large lead gifts is the next step.

Prospects for lead gifts. Prospect research for a capital campaign is done the same way as for an annual campaign. Because the gifts are larger than in an annual campaign, however, many organizations use foundations and corporations for the top gifts. Look for foundations and corporations that have funded "bricks and mortar" campaigns in the past. Many foundations only give to building and equipment projects.

Gift Range Chart

	Gift Range	No. of Gifts	No. of Prospects	TOTAL
Pacesetting gifts:	$10,000	1	4	$10,000
	5,000	2	8	10,000
	TOTAL	20% of goal	12	$20,000
Major gifts:	$2,500-4,900	4-6	16	
	1,000-2,499	10-15	25	
	500-999	15-30	25-50	
	TOTAL	40-50% of goal		$40,000-$50,000
Other gifts:	$250-499	many		
	100-249	many		
	Under $100	many		
	TOTAL	40-50% of goal		$40,000-$50,000

In looking for individual prospects broaden your search to include research on individuals who have given to other capital campaigns in your community. Some of these individuals will be well known because their names appear on rooms in museums, stairways at the symphony, or in wings of the hospital. Do not discount these people as prospects, but be sure you have a link to them before you ask them to contribute to your campaign. From your own donor list identify those people who have ever supported other projects that required buying something specific. If you use a gift catalogue, research the donors who gave to that mail appeal. If you had a special appeal to buy equipment or supplies, research the people who gave to that. Some people prefer to give their charitable dollars to specific things; they will be your best prospects for a capital campaign.

The prospectus. While you are doing your prospect research you must prepare materials to be used in the fundraising solicitation. The most important of these is the "prospectus," which is taken from the case statement. The prospectus is a pamphlet, booklet, or folder that describes the project and includes an artist's rendering of the finished project, a statement of the need for the project, and a gift range chart showing the number of gifts needed to complete the project. Many organizations design their prospectus so that they can add updated pages as gifts are received, revising the remaining amount needed. The prospectus does not have to be an expensive, multicolored job, but it must be professionally designed, typeset, and printed on good quality stock. The board members and volunteers who are doing the soliciting must feel proud of the document, and it must be good enough to be taken anywhere and shown to anyone.

Securing the lead gift. With your prospectus and your lead prospects in place, you begin the campaign by soliciting the top gifts. People like to give the lead gifts because they like to be leaders, pacesetters whose example will inspire others to give. Foundations and corporations like this image too, especially when the group conducting the campaign is well respected by the community.

It may take some time to secure the lead gifts. Be patient, continue prospect research, and be sure you are doing enough other research before soliciting the gift. Pay close attention to the reasons for being turned down because they will help you to strengthen your case.

Full-scale solicitation
Once you have the lead gifts, announce the campaign to the press, in your newsletter, and to your donors. At this point full-scale solicitation of the smaller gifts begins. A time line should be set for completing this phase of solicitation. When you have 75 percent of your goal pledged or in hand, you can begin to build or do whatever you are going to do with the money raised. The final 25 percent will be raised easily once the project is under way. It can be raised through mail appeals, phone-a-thons, or from foundations and corporations that would like to put your organization over the top of its goal.

A small capital campaign is run with the same attention to detail required by a major gifts campaign. An organization should undertake such a campaign only when it has a loyal and repeating donor base, a firm ongoing major gifts program, and a working board of directors.

Chapter 9

Special Events

Correct Use of Special Events

Special events are social gatherings of many sorts that expand the reputation of the organization, giving those attending an amusing, interesting, or moving time, and that may make money for the organization sponsoring the event. The variety of special events is practically limitless, as are the possibilities for money earned or lost, amount of work put in, number of people participating, and so on. Special events are at one and the same time the most common fundraising device used by small organizations and the most misunderstood. They can do things for an organization that no other fundraising strategy can do as well, yet what they can best do is often the last thing that is expected or wanted.

Goals of a Special Event

Special events should have three goals:

◆ To generate publicity for the organization;
◆ To raise the visibility of the organization;
◆ To bring in (new) money.

Generating publicity means advertising the event for the purpose of calling the attention of a particular audience to the group for a limited time.

Enhancing visibility raises the profile of the organization in the community. Visibility is the cumulative effect of publicity. With each successive event, and in combination with other fundraising and organizing efforts, the organization will become known to more and more people. Eventually the organization becomes a household word, known just as well as the Red Cross, the American Cancer Society, or the March of Dimes.

Raising money is the last goal for a special event because there are many more effective ways simply to raise money than this one. In many cases special events can lose money or barely break even and still be successful because of the publicity and visibility they produced.

Who Attends Special Events?

Raising money from people who haven't given to your organization is the ideal fundraising goal for most special events. These people either come for the event or come to support your group. In the first category are people who would come to a particular event no matter who sponsored it. This audience is usually found at flea markets, dances, movie benefits, decorator showcases, auctions, and the like. Many times these people will not even know the name of the group sponsoring the event.

The second group of people are both interested in the event and believe in your group's work. They may not have heard of your organization before learning of this event or they may already know of your organization and want to support it while getting something important to them. For example, women wanting to take a self-defense class may choose one sponsored by the local rape relief program rather than a commercial gym in order to support the program. After the classes some of the participants may want to join the program as volunteers and paying members. Corporations, owners of small businesses, or politicians may only show their support of an organization by buying tables at a luncheon or ads in a program book. In addition to supporting the work of the organization, they want the advertising and the resulting good will. They cannot get that kind of publicity through any other fundraising strategy as easily or inexpensively.

Many of these new donors are people who appreciate your organization but can't afford or don't want to give more than a small amount. For them, buying a $1 raffle ticket or attending a $4 movie is a perfect way to show their support.

Choosing a Fundraising Event

Several criteria should be considered in choosing a fundraising event: The appropriateness of the event, the image of the organization the event promotes, the amount of volunteer energy required, the amount of front money needed, the repeatability of the event, and how the event fits into the overall fundraising plan.

Appropriateness of the event

Appropriateness is a major factor that, if overlooked, can result in a lot of trouble. To decide if an event is appropriate, ask yourself, "If people knew nothing about our organization except that it had sponsored this event, what would their opinion be?" If the answer is "neutral or good," then the event is appropriate. If you think that you would want them to know more about the group than just that event you should think again about the event. Examples of inappropriate events abound. In the extreme, if you are the symphony you don't sponsor a gong show; if you run an alcohol recovery program you don't have a beer bash. Often, however, the question of appropriateness is subtler than in those examples. The following are two case studies.

A question of timing. A community center in a factory town of 25,000 people held a yearly luncheon attended by about 500 people at $40-$75 a plate. The luncheon had been a successful fundraiser for three years. In 1980 the town's industry laid off half of its work force. Unemployment in the town rose from 4 percent to 25 percent. That year the community center still held its luncheon, and still 500 people came. By the end of 1982 the industry had shut down altogether. Unemployment was now up to 90 percent, with many people losing their homes and running out of unemployment benefits. The town was gloomy; businesses were also closing. The community center needed the money from the luncheon more than ever. Since there were still at least 200 people who could afford the price, they held the event. As a result they were sharply criticized for their ostentation in light of the severe economic austerity that most of the townspeople were facing. The yearly luncheon was an event that became inappropriate due to circumstances outside the control of the community center.

A question of judgment. A women's health organization in a large West Coast city offered as a top raffle prize a case of fine wine. During their promotion a number of studies were released showing the high rate of alcoholism among women. An internal debate ensued over whether it was appropriate for a group working to prevent dangerous drugs and devices from being given to women to offer alcohol—a potentially dangerous drug—as a raffle prize. Proponents argued that only 10 percent of the population is alcoholic and that alcohol, unlike the drugs that directly concerned the group, does not harm most people who use it. The chance of an alcoholic winning that prize was slim compared to how many people would be attracted to the raffle because of this prize. However, opponents swayed the group by reasoning that they would not approve of a contraceptive that hurt 10 percent of its users. The group withdrew the prize, not wanting to promote a drug with any potential for harm.

Image of the organization
Insofar as possible the special event should be in keeping with the image of the organization or should promote the image the organization wishes to have. Although considerations of appropriateness sometimes include those of image, this is a distinct issue. Many events that are appropriate for a group do not promote a positive image of it. For example, a library would choose a book sale over a garage sale, even though both are equally appropriate. An environmental organization would raffle a white-water rafting trip over a weekend at Disneyland. An organization promoting awareness of the problem of high blood pressure might choose a health fair over a dance.

Energy of volunteers
Looking at the volunteer energy required involves several considerations. How many people are required to put on this event? What would these volunteers be doing if they were not working on this event? Do you have enough volunteers who have the time required to produce this event—not

only to manage the event on the day of its occurrence but for all the details that must be carried out beforehand?

Volunteer time is a resource to be cultivated, guided, and used appropriately. For example, don't use someone with connections to possible large donors to sell raffle tickets at a shopping mall on Saturday afternoon. Similarly, a friendly, outgoing person who loves to talk on the phone should be the phone-a-thon coordinator or the solicitor of auction items and not be asked to bake brownies for the food booth at the county fair. Obviously, what the volunteer wants to do should be of primary concern. People generally like to do what they are good at and be involved where they can be most useful. (In the case study at the end of this section, we will show how an organization learned to use its volunteers effectively.)

Front money
Most special events require that some money be spent before there is assurance that any money will be raised. The front money needed for an event should be an amount your organization could afford to lose if the event had to be cancelled. This money should already be available—you should not, for example, use funds from advance ticket sales to rent the hall. If the event is cancelled most people will want their money back. Events that require a lot of front money can create a cash flow problem in the organization if the need for this money is not taken into account.

Repeatability of the event
You need to consider whether the event can be repeated annually. The best event is one that becomes a tradition in your community, so that every year people look forward to the event that your group sponsors. Using this criterion can save you from discarding an event simply because the turnout was small the first time you did it. Perhaps you got too little publicity and only a handful of people came: If each of those people had a great time, and you heard them saying, "I wish I had brought . . . ," or "I wish Alice had known about this," then it may be worth having next year. To decide if an event is repeatable, evaluate whether the same number of people working the same number of hours would produce a bigger event.

The big picture
The final consideration is the place of the event in the overall fundraising picture. An illustrative case study of a children's museum can be found at the end of this chapter. We will look at the museum's fundraising plan and its results before it knew how to plan special events, and then consider the plan and its successes after learning what has been presented here.

How to Plan a Special Event

Special events require more planning time than one would imagine. Nowhere is Murphy's Law more apparent; thus, "whatever can go wrong, will" events must be planned with more attention to minute detail than almost any other fundraising strategy.

The Committee for Special Events

First let's discuss the role of the committee in charge of the special event. There must be a committee of volunteers doing the bulk of the work for the event. Using paid staff time to organize a special event is expensive and does not help to train or involve volunteers in substantive fundraising tasks.

The job of the committee is to plan and coordinate the event, not to handle the entire process. It should delegate to others as many tasks as possible. With a larger committee planning the event, it is likely that some important element will be left out, that the planning process itself will take longer, and that the committee members will find themselves putting more time into the event than if just a few people had planned it and delegated the implementation to others.

Each special event should have its own committee, although there can be overlap from another. Special events are labor intensive, however, and people need to have a rest period between events and a chance *not* to participate in an event. The committee must have staff and board support, and everyone must agree that the chosen event is a good idea.

Tasks of the committee
There are three simple steps a special events committee should take to insure the success of the event or allow the organization to decide to cancel: detail a master-task list, prepare a budget, and develop a time line.

Detail a master-task list. First, list all the tasks that must be accomplished. Include everything—even those things you are sure no one would ever forget. Detail is all in this list. Take the list and put it into chronological order under the label "What." Then add three more columns to your list: "When," "Who," and "Done." Under "When," put the date by which the task must be completed. Under "Who," write to whom the task is assigned. When the task is completed check it off under "Done."

Second, to plan when things should be done, think backwards from the target date for your event. If you want to have a dance on August 10, what would have to be done on August 9? To do those things, what would have to have happened in early August? What would have to be in place by July 15? By this "backward planning," the committee may find out that it is impossible to put on the event in the time allowed. In that case they must either modify the event or change the date.

Before doing any other planning make sure the audience for this event will have no conflicts on the date selected. Check the calendar to make sure it is not Mother's Day or President's Day or Easter, unless you are deliberately choosing a holiday. Check a school calendar to make sure it is not the first or last day of school, or spring vacation, or commencement. Check as much as you can into other community events and see if anyone knows of an event that is traditionally held on that date. In some areas having an event during Lent would not be successful; in others you would have no participants during the World Series. Finally, you must think through whether you are going to be able to get the number of volunteers you need to accomplish those tasks that must be done just before the event. For example, few organizations can have a New Year's party as a fundraiser simply because they cannot get anyone to work during the two weeks preceding New Year's Day.

Prepare a budget. The budget should be simple but thorough, so that all costs are accounted for and planned on. The special events budget looks like the illustration below.

The items that go on the expense side of the budget are easily pulled from the tasks list. An estimate is not a guess: It is based on research and quotes of prices from vendors. As costs are incurred they can be noted under the column "actual." As much as possible, put off paying for anything until after the event and work in cancellation clauses for rentals or other contracts. For example, if a hall rents for $600 with $300 required as a deposit, try to reserve the right to get all or part of that $300 back, if necessary, as close to the date of the event as possible.

Ideally, of course, you will aim to get as many things as possible free, but don't plan on this.

The Special Events Budget

	Expenses	
Item	Estimated	Actual

	Income	
Item	Estimated (with justification)*	Actual

* Why do you think you will earn that much? Show how you arrive at this figure.

— 151 —

Develop a time line. Using your task list, make a timeline for the event and mark off task clusters—those groups of tasks that must be accomplished in order to evaluate your progress. (These might include all printing tasks or all mailing tasks or all tasks related to the place of the event, or determining how many tickets you would need to have sold to know that the event will be successful.) Note dates by which clusters of tasks must be accomplished:

* (today's date) . . . .   * (task cluster one) . . . .
* (task cluster 2) . . . .   * (task cluster 3) . . . .   * the event

These are your bailout dates. If everything that needs to happen by that date has not yet happened, reconsider the event altogether. Can you modify it? Move the date forward? Speed up the task process? Or should you bail out: Cancel, cut your losses now?

Once these three steps have been taken, you are ready to proceed. You can now assign tasks to other volunteers. When you do so, give the volunteer a date that is sooner than that in the "When" column of your task list. That way, in the best case you will always be ahead of your schedule; in the worst case—if the volunteer is unable to complete the task—you will have some time to get it done.

What Not to Forget

Here is a checklist of commonly forgotten items in planning an event:

◆ Liquor license.
◆ Insurance (on the hall, for the speaker, for participants). Contracts vary on this, but check it out. It often happens that a hall or auditorium is inexpensive because insurance is not included but is required of the renting organization. A one-night insurance policy or a rider on an existing policy can cost at least $600.
◆ Transportation (of food, drink, speakers, performers, from where to where).
◆ Lodging for performers or speaker.
◆ Parking.
◆ If there is food, plates, utensils, and napkins.

Here are some questions you may forget to ask before the event:

◆ Does the reply card fit into the return envelope?
◆ Has everything been read for typographical errors at least five times?
◆ Is the organization's address on the reply card, flier, poster, invitation, everything else?
◆ Are the price, date, time, place, and directions to the event on all advertising?

- Have you considered the necessity of child care, sign language translation, wheelchair accessibility, including in the bathrooms?
- How safe is the neighborhood? Will women feel safe coming alone?
- Can everyone see and hear from every seat? (Sit in a number of seats to make sure.)
- Who will open the room for you? Do you need a key?
- Where are the fire exits?

The Evaluation

The final step in planning a special event is evaluation. Within a few days after the event the planning committee should fill out an evaluation form, as illustrated below. Save this evaluation along with copies of the advertising, the invitations, and any other information that would be useful for next year's planning committee.

Special Event Report (evaluation form)

Approximately how much time did the committee spend on this event? (In evaluating this, try to subtract time spent fooling around and be sure to count time members spent driving around on errands and on the phone) _____

Did this event bring in any new members? _____ How many? _____

Can people be invited to be members who came to this event? _____

Did this event bring in new money? _____

Does this event have the capacity to grow every year? _____

What would you do exactly the same next time? _____

_____

What would you do differently? _____

_____

List sources of free or low cost items and who got them and indicate whether they will be available next year, in your opinion: _____

_____

What kind of follow-up needs to be done? _____

_____

Which committee members did what work? _____

Other comments: _____

_____

Which committee members would be willing to work on this event next year? _____

_____

Case Study: The Children's Museum

The Children's Museum is located in a small city of 250,000 people. Started two years ago, the museum is similar to those springing up all over the country in which children are encouraged to touch and interact with the exhibits. The museum has a board of 40 committed people from all walks of life. Most are married and have children. About half are involved as volunteers with other arts organizations in the community. All agree that board members should both give and help raise money.

Before learning the types of fundraising techniques discussed here, the fundraising committee (five board members and a staff person) presented monthly fundraising plans at board meetings. They never planned more than two or three months in advance. In one year they had the following activities:

January-February: A Japanese restaurant did a sushi benefit for the museum. Tickets were $10 each. Board members were expected to sell five tickets each, which they did. Net: $1,950.

March: An expert schooner donated his time and yacht for a day of sailing on a nearby lake. The museum provided food and drink. Board members were expected to sell two tickets each at $25. Most board members bought one ticket and sold the other to their spouses. Net: $1,800.

April: A pancake breakfast was held in cooperation with five other arts organizations. The breakfast was widely advertised, but each organization had to guarantee to bring in 100 participants. No requirements were set, but most of the board members came with their families and a few friends. Cost: $4 for adults, $2 for children. Overall net: $2,000; Children's Museum: $400.

April-June: Membership campaign: Board members came to one extra meeting that month in order to help send out 4,000 invitations to join the museum. In addition each board member was expected to enroll 15 new members at $15 each. All board members enrolled at least 3 new members and some got their full complement of 15. Total new members from all efforts: 410. Net: $400.

July: The museum contracted with a circus company to set up their tents with ferris wheels and other rides for the weekend of the Fourth of July. Admission was $1, with an additional charge for each ride. Booths for drinks, hot dogs, cotton candy and so on were staffed by museum board members and volunteers, with those proceeds going to the museum. Ten percent of the proceeds from the rest of the circus went to the museum. Anyone who worked at a booth could bring his or her family free, plus each child of a volunteer worker got three free rides. Fifty volunteers were needed during the weekend; board members and spouses worked. Net: $7,500.

August: A well-deserved breather, except for the fundraising committee that planned the September event. No board meeting.

September: An art auction was held with paintings and sculpture by local artists. The museum paid for the rental of the auction gallery and for the publicity. The artists paid for the auctioneer and split the price of each item sold with the museum. Board members were each given 50 posters announcing the auction to display around town. For this task the fundraising committee assigned each person several square blocks near their home or work. Further, board members were to help stuff invitations. These had to be mailed first class because, as the committee explained, "This all came together very fast." Front costs were high. Because the museum did not have the money to front, each board member was asked for an interest-free, one-month loan of $100. Net: $4,000.

October: Two wonderful opportunities arose, which the fundraising committee did not want to pass up. First, a fancy restaurant donated its opening to benefit the museum. Everything would be donated, that is, if the museum could keep the restaurant full all night. Capacity of the restaurant was 200. The event was free for board members, $20 for others. No children were allowed. Each board member was encouraged to bring at least five friends. The museum succeeded in its bargain. Net: $3,500. The other opportunity was selling bouquets of flowers at a shopping mall on three consecutive Saturdays. (The night of one of which was the event above). The museum would buy bunches of flowers at $1 and sell them for $2.50-$5.00. Two volunteers for two-hour shifts were needed for three shifts per Saturday, or six volunteers per Saturday. The board dutifully signed up. Net: $400.

December: The board evaluated their fundraising efforts. Every event had been successful. A total of $23,550 had been raised. Many events had brought in new people, some of whom had become members.

Not surprisingly, however, in spite of all their success, 36 Board members resigned at the end of the year, including 3 members of the fundraising committee. All cited overwork and too much fundraising as their primary reasons for leaving the board.

Almost miraculously, the museum recruited 36 more board members of the same high caliber. With the help of a consultant the museum board evaluated and changed its fundraising plans considerably. In the evaluation they decided that while all the events were appropriate, not all enhanced the image of the Museum. Therefore, the new fundraising committee scrapped those events that did not include children, except the art auction, which promoted the museum in other ways. They scrapped the sushi benefit, the sailing adventure, and the restaurant opening (an unrepeatable event in any case). The pancake breakfast, which had raised the least amount of money, was repeated with two changes: 1) as far as possible, the advertising was designed to attract new people, and 2) every family or adult attending would later be sent a fundraising appeal offering membership in all five arts organizations at a cost slightly higher than that of joining any two of them. Although this event would still not be a giant moneymaker, it would bring in many new members and increase visibility for all five organizations. Further, it promoted the sense that all the arts organizations were working in harmony. The flower selling was also repeated. Although labor intensive, the chance for volunteers to discuss the museum with so many people brought a notable rise in museum attendance in the weeks during and after the sale. Each bouquet was accompanied by a 3" by 5" card that briefly described the Museum and listed its hours.

Board members divided themselves into committees, each of which helped the fundraising committee in different ways. The membership committee worked all year to increase membership through mail and phone solicitation. The major gifts committee solicited major gifts. The rest of the board worked on the special events, with no board member working on more than three events. An auxiliary of volunteers is now being formed to help with the planning and work of these events.

The fundraising calendar is now prepared a year in advance and looks like this:

January-December: Ongoing membership recruitment. New members: 1,000. Net income: $12,000.

April: Pancake breakfast, with mail appeal follow-up. Net income: $1,000.

July: Circus with food booths. Net income: $9,500.

September: Art auction. Net income: $6,000.

September-November: Major gifts campaign. Net income: $8,000.

October-November: Three weekends of flower sales. Net income: $600.

Total expected income: $37,100

At the end of the first year of the new fundraising plan only five board members resigned, all citing personal reasons.

Special events are an important part of a diverse fundraising plan, if used properly. They have the greatest potential to be misused, causing frustration and burn-out in volunteers, and so must be carefully planned and evaluated. Because they also are the most enjoyable of all fundraising vehicles and one of the best ways for bringing in new donors, special events are worth holding, and worth doing properly.

FUNDRAISING MANAGEMENT SYSTEMS AND STRATEGIES

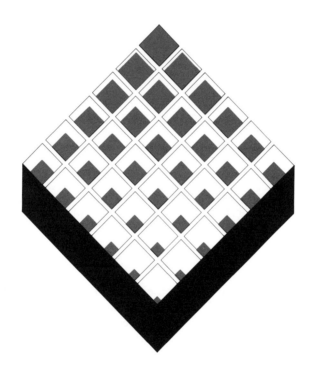

Chapter 10

The Fundraising Office

Basic Requirements for Fundraising Activities

Few offices of low-budget organizations are adequate in size, equipment, or support staff; none approaches the ideal. Short of buying expensive computer equipment or hiring more secretaries—probably neither is an option for your group—there are basic requirements for fundraising staff to carry out an effective fundraising program. The same requirements hold true whether your fundraising program is run by volunteers or by paid staff. All of these requirements cost money but will quickly pay for themselves. These costs should be seen as front money. You may not need these things all at once, but each item should be acquired as quickly as possible.

Space and Materials

Fundraising staff must have adequate space and materials. Most important, there must be a separate space in the office for fundraising staff, files, and materials. This would preferably be a room or at least a partitioned area. The space must be quiet, include a desk of adequate size (with drawers), a chair, a three-drawer (at least) filing cabinet, and a telephone. A bookshelf and other storage space, such as part of a closet, is also important. This space should not be used by people other than fundraising staff and volunteers. Too much of the information here is confidential; further, donor cards, mailing lists, reports, letters, etc., need to be kept in order and should not be touched by anyone who is not dealing with them. Fundraising staff should have access to a good typewriter, preferably a self-correcting one. All organizations should include obtaining a word processor in their long-range equipment acquisition plan.

The organization must take the fundraising process seriously. Both paid and volunteer fundraising staff should be seen as professionals, needing certain tools to carry out their job. A typewriter, desk, filing cabinet, phone, and separate space are the tools of a fundraiser in the same way, and with the same importance, that hammers, saws, levels, and the like are the tools of a carpenter. Just as you can't build a building without construction equipment, you can't build a donor base without fundraising equipment.

In addition to an adequate office setup, a fundraiser should have a basic library of fundraising books, as well as a dictionary, thesaurus and style manual to aid in writing and planning. (See the Bibliography for a recommended basic library.)

Managing Your Time

Every fundraiser should be skilled in time management. No absolute ways to manage time work for everyone, but there are certainly some guidelines that will help you keep abreast of your tasks. The most important thing to remember is that the fundraising job is never done, and you are never caught up. Another of Murphy's laws, "Expenses rise to meet income," is just as true for nonprofit organizations as it is for individuals and businesses. Consequently, many fundraisers feel that no amount of effort and no amount of money raised is ever quite enough. Time management, then, is in the context of always feeling behind. You must set your own limits, because no matter how supportive the organization may be of the fundraising staff's work, it is still relentless in its need for more money.

Guidelines for time management
Here are some guidelines for using your time to best advantage:

Every day:

◆ Reserve one to three hours during which you cannot be interrupted by phone calls. Either get someone else to answer the phone or use an answering machine.
◆ Spend fifteen to thirty minutes at the end of the day writing up a to-do list for the next day. At the beginning of the day review your to-do list. Unless something that can't wait comes up, do only those tasks already on your to-do list. Put new things on tomorrow's list.
◆ Write, or have a volunteer write, thank-you notes. Don't get behind on these.

Every week:

◆ Update your donor records.
◆ Go over your fundraising plan for the month and make sure you are on target. Don't put off tasks such as getting a letter to the printer, calling a foundation, setting up meetings of the major gifts committee or special events committee, etc. Do these tasks on time.

Every month:

◆ Call all board members, even if just to say hello. Make sure they feel needed and wanted by the organization. Those board members working on particular fundraising tasks need encouragement, gratitude, and sometimes help. (Sometimes you will need to call these people more frequently.)

◆ Look at your fundraising plan for the year and plan the details to be accomplished this month. Many people find it helpful to have a blank calendar for the month, with large boxes for each day. They then write in the tasks as they are due day by day. This helps in making weekly plans also.

◆ Get an income and expense report from the bookkeeper. The income should be broken down by category, i.e., major gifts—how many and what size; new members, old members—how many and what size; special events; sales; etc.

◆ Spend half a day just reading about fundraising strategies. If you have a foundation library in your community, go to it and browse through the materials available.

Many other time management tips can be learned from various courses, books, and other people. Develop a system that works well for you.

Working Conditions

Obviously, fundraising staff should not have nicer office space or fancier equipment than everyone else in the office, simply for the sake of being more comfortable. The whole organization should examine its working conditions from time to time, and make it a priority to improve them if needed. It is ironic that many social change or social service groups will work in conditions that include too much noise, dim light, inadequate equipment, and so on, when they would be outraged to read about such conditions for other workers. Good working conditions cost money, but poor working conditions cost money, too—in lower productivity, stress, loss of creativity, misfiling or loss of information, and the like.

Record Keeping

Donor Records

A complete list of donors, regularly updated and accurately kept, makes it possible to solicit repeat and upgraded gifts, to send multiple appeals to current donors, and to provide the membership benefits you have promised.

Categories of Records

Your records should include all donors, with a subcategory of records for major donors. You must be able to retrieve lists in several categories, including:

◆ a complete list of all donors in zip code order for mailings (also smaller lists of specific zip codes for mailing to specific towns or communities);

◆ a list of those donors needing renewal notices according to your renewal schedule;

◆ a list of donors who have not given for one year or more (called "lapsed" donors);

◆ a list of people who pledge, with their pledge amounts and when reminders should be sent to them; and

◆ a list of major donors with their gift amounts and renewal dates.

Recordkeeping by Computer

If you have access to a computer with software enabling it to hold donor records, or if you hire a mailing house or computer firm to handle your mailing list, the specific pieces of information are designated by a series of codes entered with each record.

If your donor list contains fewer than 500 names and you do not presently have or use a computer, there are other systems that will work well for you, discussed below. But once your list has more than 500 donors, any noncomputer method becomes extremely cumbersome. At that point it is usually cost effective either to hire a firm to keep your list on their computer or to acquire a computer for your organization. Cost effectiveness of computer systems varies substantially from area to area and organization to organization. (See Appendix 3 for a fuller discussion of the use of computers for fundraising.)

Recordkeeping by Hand

The by-hand methods for donor list maintenance fall into two categories. For very small lists (fewer than 250 names), most groups record the donors by zip code on master sheets for Avery labels. (One sheet for each 3- or 5-digit zip code, so that new names in the same zip code area can be added.) The master sheets are photocopied onto labels for materials to be mailed. A separate list with donor information is kept in alphabetical order on 3″ by 5″ cards.

Using sheets of labels quickly becomes unmanageable, and most groups move on to use either an addressograph or "730" cards, which print onto labels or directly onto the materials to be mailed. An addressograph holds the name and address on a metal plate, which is inked, and prints like a printing press. The metal address plates are typed with a special machine.

Whatever label or addressing system you have should contain only the donor's name and address. Information about their giving needs to be kept separately in the alphabetical list. The simplest noncomputer method is to record all the necessary information on 3″ by 5″ or 5″ by 7″ cards, which are kept in a card file. The card is set up as follows:

```
Name _____

Address _____ Zip _____

Phone Number (___)_____

Gift Record
Date of Gift              Amount
Given in response to


Other Information
```

These cards can be handwritten but must be readable. Use the category "other information" to record anything you know about the donor that might be useful in getting him or her to upgrade the gift, to introduce you to another prospect, to approach his or her business or corporation for gifts, etc. An example of other information would be: "Wife an attorney, active in civil rights; donor has been in plumbing business for 25 years."

Checks as Information Sources

Because many people have illegible handwriting, and because most donors are offended if you misspell their name, it is best to get the name, address, and phone number from the check that the donor sends, rather than relying solely on the return form. The phone number of the donor, which is rarely noted on the return form, is important for phone-a-thons. The other advantage of seeing the check is that other information printed on the check may be useful. For example, a check might be a joint account, with the profession of one or both account holders identified, such as Joe Cumberland, CPA; Janice Ruark, MD. If Joe is the donor, he may not have noted that he is a CPA on his donor form and certainly would not have mentioned anything about Janice. The fact that they seem to be in well-paid professions will be the first clue that they may be major gift prospects.

You may sometimes receive a membership check from a family foundation. While the return form might simply say, "Kate Wilkins," the check might say "Wilkins Family Foundation." Again, this is something to explore for bigger gifts.

Keeping Your List in Shape

Whether you use a computer or by-hand method, you should update your mailing list on a regular basis. Don't let more than 25 names go unrecorded or you will get careless with numbers and spelling. Many small, understaffed groups put off updating their mailing list until a few days before a mailing is to go out. When a staff person or volunteer then frantically tries to get it in order the list is inevitably full of errors.

As you do mailings watch for duplicate labels. Donors are annoyed when they receive duplicate mailings, which they see as a colossal waste of money. Duplicates usually come from misfiling an address and then making another card, or from not deleting an old address when a change of address is sent.

By-hand systems can be coded for more specific references. Some organizations use different color cards to identify major donors or donors who need to renew. Tabs can be added to individual donor cards or to signal a group of cards (i.e., an orange tab for all donors who need to renew in March, a green tab for all major donors, etc.)

Safety First

Whatever system you use, be sure to have a duplicate copy of your mailing list in a safe place, away from your office. Many groups rent a safe deposit box for this. They place an updated copy of the list in the safe place every six months. If your donor system is stored on a computer, you will want to protect your organization with two systems: First, always be sure that all information on a computer disk is also stored on a back-up disk. Second, print out a master list about every three months or so. Keep this list away from the office and the computer. Computers can malfunction, and human error can cause all or part of your mailing list to be erased.

Though it may seem pessimistic, you must consider what would happen to your donor information if your office was flooded, burned, or vandalized, and plan accordingly.

Major Donor Records

Even though records of all donors are kept on cards or within the memory of a computer, a fundraising staff person must also keep separate records on each major donor.

These records can be kept in notebooks or in individual file folders for each donor. A master list of major donors should be printed out from the computer or checked off the zip code list from time to time to insure that these people are "on the list" and that their names and addresses are correct.

Some fundraisers keep major gift information in two categories—a notebook for donors of $50-$250, and file folders for donors giving more than $250. In some cases information about the major donor is taken right from the prospect form, as many of your prospects will become donors. In many other cases, however, people will send major gifts through a mail appeal. Sometimes people give you large gifts that no one (to your knowledge) has solicited. Some of these gifts may come in from mail appeals, some from radio and TV shows, and some from referrals by other donors or foundations.

The cover sheet for each donor contains information in certain categories. Additional information, records of correspondence, items about the donor in the newspaper, etc., are then included with this sheet in the notebook, or kept in a file folder. The categories of information are: Name, Business address, Home address, Business and home phone, Gift record, and what you know about the donor. A complete form might look like this:

Hilary Morgan
1218 Nice Condominium
Suburb, State, ZIP

Business Address:
Morgan, Freedman and Holz, Stockbrokers
Downtown, State, ZIP

Home Phone _____ Business Phone _____

Occupation: Stockbroker. Has been a partner in her own firm for ten years. This firm handles the biggest clients in the county. She became a major donor at the request of Sally Parkinson, who used to be on the board (1979). Sally has been a major donor for years.

Other comments: Hilary would be a good person to talk to about investments and starting a capital campaign. She could probably introduce us to a lot of other well-to-do people and she might encourage some of her clients to give us gifts of stock. She is really friendly and easygoing, but overextended. Quite involved in child abuse programs.

Gift	Date
$500	12/18/84

REMEMBER: All donor records are confidential, but major donor records should be kept in a locked filing cabinet, and only be accessible to people who need to see them. Much information about major donors is given in confidence; it should be treated as privileged.

Chapter 11

Analyzing Your Constituency

To build an effective donor base an organization should periodically analyze the makeup of its current donor population. Try to assess what attracted these people to your organization and how you can attract more of them. Conversely, see what kinds of people you have not attracted but would expect to be represented.

The Demographic Survey

The first step in this analysis is a demographic survey. This involves compiling specific statistics, which can be anything from birth records to number of marriages. For fundraising purposes a demographic survey has these categories:

Number of donors who are:

◆ Men
◆ Women
◆ Couples

Gift ranges:

◆ Mode gift: (the gift you get most often)
◆ Highest gift from an individual
◆ Number of major donors
◆ Number of donors who pledge
◆ Number of donors who have not repeated their gift in the last year (lapsed donors)
◆ Number of donors who have given for more than two years, three years,
◆ five years

Strategies used for attracting donors:

◆ Number of donors recruited by mail
◆ Number of donors recruited by face-to-face solicitation
◆ Number of donors recruited by special events

◆ Number of donors recruited by other strategies
◆ Number of donors recruited by unknown solicitation method

Geographic Distribution:

Divide the area you serve in some way—neighborhoods, zip codes, regions—and count the number of donors in each division. From this count figure out the following percentages, which will give you your demographic report.

Our donor base is:

◆ Percent women, percent men, percent couples;
◆ Percent pledging, representing percent of total donor income;
◆ Percent major donors, representing percent of total donor income;
◆ Percent small donors, representing percent of total donor income;
◆ Percent lapses each year;
◆ Percent renews: percent renewed for two years, percent renewed for three years, percent renewed for five years;
◆ Percent recruited through mail; percent recruited through special events, percent recruited through face-to-face solicitation, etc.;
◆ Percent live in _____, percent live in _____, etc.

Uses of the Demographic Survey

This information should help assess which strategies are working well and which need strengthening. For example, if more than 33 percent of your donor list does not renew on a yearly basis, you should figure out what is keeping them from renewing. If 50 percent of your donor income is from mail but 80 percent of your fundraising efforts are in special events, you may want to put more effort into mail appeals or figure out better ways to attract donations from people who come to your special events.

If your mode gift is higher than your membership rate you can consider raising the basic membership fee. If yours is a regional or national organization, with chapters in various places, see if some chapters have a disproportionate number of donors compared to others. Use this information to analyze what each chapter is doing, and what some could do better. Size of population in each chapter's region will, of course, be a strong factor, but it may also be that some chapters have discovered some excellent fundraising strategies that other chapters should try.

Organizations sometimes make assumptions about who their donors will be and solicit only people in those categories. These assumptions can be incorrect, however. For example, a health clinic serving a small town assumed that all its donors would live in the neighborhoods surrounding the clinic and that few, if any, would live outside the town. Their demographic survey showed, however, that 13 percent of their donors lived 60 miles or more from the town and 8 percent even lived outside the state. Some of these donors were former patients, but many of them enjoyed the health clinic's informative newsletter. Based on the results of their survey, the clinic now seeks newsletter subscriptions from former clients and others who live outside the state.

The Donor Survey

More detailed demographic data can be compiled by surveying your donors. Information on average income, occupation, age, race, number of children, etc., will be important in drawing a profile of current donors and determining if you are reaching the people you want to reach. With this information you can plan for reaching more people of the kind you now attract as well as focus on other target populations. Many organizations send out such surveys every two years. The survey results are slightly skewed because usually only the most interested members respond, but a random telephoning of members can add to your data base. One needn't worry about insuring scientific validity, however; the survey is merely a way for you to know more about your donors.

A sample survey to be sent to members, which can also be used in a random telephone survey, would include these questions:

◆ Age
◆ Race
◆ Income level per year: $0-$5,000 $21,000-$35,000
                         $5,000-$12,000   over $35,000
                         $13,000-$20,000
◆ Marital status
◆ Number of children
◆ How many organizations do you belong to?
◆ Please name some of them
◆ How did you become a member (i.e., through the mail, a friend asked,
◆ don't remember)?
◆ Have you ever been to our office?
◆ Do you know other members of this organization?

You can also ask whether people like your newsletter, what issues they would like your group to work on, or for any other opinions of your organization you would like to know. Don't make the survey too long, or it will discourage response. As much as possible make the answer multiple choice so that people only have to mark a box rather than writing something out. Include a return envelope with the survey; do not send it with any other mailing. (In other words, don't include a survey and a fundraising appeal in one mailing—you will have fewer responses to both.)

Uses of the Donor Survey

Information of this sort is useful in determining what parts of your fundraising strategy are working best, what further mailing lists you should acquire, what special events should be repeated, etc. It is also useful to have this information when approaching foundations, corporations, or the United Way. Knowing the number and type of donors you represent can also be helpful in advocating legislation or testifying for or against regulations.

Student interns are often interested in conducting these surveys. If you have a college or university in your community, contact it to see if student interns (free) or work-study students (you pay only 40 percent or less of their salary) are available for this short-term project.

> The basic premise of building a donor base is that you cannot know too much about your donors and your prospects. If you want more donors, build into your fundraising plan every conceivable method to find out more about who is interested in your organization, and why.

Chapter 12

Looking to the Future

Keeping Track of New Ideas and Strategies

In addition to all the work required to analyze current strategies and keep up with current donors, fundraising staff must keep abreast of new ideas and develop ways to keep track of possible new prospects. Fortunately, there are fairly simple ways to gather and file this information.

Fundraising Strategies

File folders
Make all file folders for each strategy you use now, i.e., mail appeals, special events, sales, etc. These folders are different from the folders you should already be keeping for evaluations of your current uses of these strategies. The purpose of these folders is to gather new ideas, new ways of doing things, and examples set by other groups.

In some cases, such as special events, you may wish to have three file folders, labeled "Small Events—Under $2,000 Net Income;" "Medium Events—$2,000-$5,000 Net Income;" and "Large Events—At Least $5,100 Net Income." Into these folders put invitations from other groups, results of brainstorming sessions, and articles about special events.

Your folder on mail appeals might be similarly divided into "Letters," "Return Forms," "Enclosures," and "Outside Envelopes," or "Mail appeals from groups similar to ours," "Mail appeals from groups completely unlike ours," etc.

Having file folders divided into discrete topics and placed in order will aid in locating information. Alphabetical order is the most obvious way to arrange the information, but ordering files by subject, with alphabetical subcategories, works better. Noting on the outside of the folder what its contents are will save you from leafing through it.

In addition to folders on every fundraising strategy that you are interested in exploring, you need folders with the following information:

◆ Copies of your IRS letter designating your nonprofit status. This folder should be easily accessible to everyone in the office, as it is frequently needed.

- Copies of grant proposals, usually subdivided into program areas or by the name of the foundation being approached.
- Copies of lists of the board of directors and advisory board members.
- Copies of current budget and annual reports.
- Resumes of current staff.
- Support letters.
- Press clippings about your organization.

What to throw away

An important aspect of recordkeeping and research is throwing away things you no longer need. Once every six months spend a day cleaning out your files. You will be surprised at how unimportant formerly critical documents have become. Also, items that you may be reluctant to throw away or can see a need for at some point (such as receipts from your previous fiscal years, monthly fundraising reports from previous fiscal years, old grant proposals for projects that have been temporarily shelved, but may be revived, etc.) can be "retired" to a cardboard file box and put into storage. They do not need to take up room in your active files.

The following is a list of items you almost definitely do not need to keep:

- Mailing lists that are more than six months old. They will have too many addresses that are no longer correct.
- Resumes of staff who no longer work for your group.
- Foundation and corporation annual reports more than two years old.
- To-do lists more than a week old. (Make new ones.)
- More than two copies of any flier, mail appeal, or other dated materials.
- Lists of former board members. (The fact that someone used to be a board member should be noted on their donor card. If this person is not a donor you should prepare a prospect form on him or her.)
- Information on fundraising that is more than three years old. This information will either be out of date or something better will have since been written.

Sources of Possible Prospects

There are many ways to get names of new prospects for small and large donations. These are discussed below.

Small Donor Research

Make several files labeled "Mailing Lists," "Sources of Mailing Lists"— which might include catalogues and correspondence with groups who would trade mailing lists—and "Ideas for Recruiting Small Donors," which includes notes to yourself on the topic, ways that other groups get small donor prospects, and articles on the subject.

The file that contains mailing lists should be reviewed at least monthly, and the mailing lists should be used quickly, as they are soon out of date. American society is very mobile, and up to 15 percent of the addresses on a list can be incorrect after three or four months.

Sources of Major Donor Prospects

In conjunction with your prospect identification program, you will need to have other files that contain names or sources of names of people who are really "suspects"—that is, you suspect they may be prospects but you don't have enough information to justify lengthy prospect research.

Suspects are people about whom you have only hearsay information and no evidence that he or she knows anyone in your organization. Keeping track of names, however, is a valuable habit, because when a name is mentioned you can check your suspect file to see if you already have any information on the person. Many of your suspects will remain just that, but enough names will move onto prospect forms to make this a worthwhile endeavor.

These names can be kept on 5″ by 7″ cards, recording the following information:

Name _____

Address (business and home) _____

Source of name _____

Evidence that this person is a suspect: (newspaper articles, who mentioned him/her, well-known in community for philanthropy but has never heard of or shown any interest in your group) _____
_____
_____
_____

A second file should be kept for ideas of ways to recruit prospects, such as housemeetings, parties, and educational events. Looking at how other organizations recruit prospects will give you some good ideas.

Future Ideas

Your final file category is one loosely labeled "Future Ideas." This file is for those terrific ideas whose time has not yet come. Many times board members, volunteers, or staff will say, "Why don't we . . . " and the sentiment is, "What a great idea. In two years, we'll be ready to do that." This idea should not be lost. Write it up briefly and put it in this folder. If you go through your files frequently you will see the idea again and again, and it will develop. When it is time to implement that idea, a good deal of the conceptualizing will have already been done.

Each group will develop other files appropriate to its fundraising plans. What is most important about recordkeeping and research is that the information stored be used frequently and that time be built into a fundraiser's month to review new ideas. There is no point in creating such a wonderful system only to be intimidated because it is too vast to be practical.

Glossary of Fundraising Terms

The following words or phrases are the most common fundraising terms used both in this book and in the practice of fundraising. Many of these words are shortened versions of a whole phrase, such as "bulk," which might be used in this way: "Send it bulk," meaning, "Send the mailing using bulkmail rules," or "net," as in "What was the net?" which means, "What did you make after expenses are subtracted?"

This glossary is neither a dictionary nor a comprehensive list of all fundraising terms. Terms that do not appear here are either not commonly used or require a longer explanation than this format allows.

ACKNOWLEDGEMENT An expression of thanks for a contribution, usually a written note for a financial donation.

ANNUAL GIVING Setting up a system to seek donations on a yearly basis, bringing in new donors, and encouraging current donors to renew their gifts and to increase the amount of their gifts if possible. The planning and implementation of annual giving is often called the *annual campaign.*

APPEAL Short for "appeal letter," a written request for donations.

BENEFITS The tangible items that were sent to donors because of their donation. Common benefits include a newsletter, a membership card, a book, or a calendar.

BOARD OF DIRECTORS The people who are legally, morally, and fiscally responsible for insuring that the organization is able to carry out its mission, that the programs and services offered are appropriate to the statement of mission, and that

the statement of mission continues to reflect a true need.

BUDGET Statement of itemized expenses and income projected usually a year in advance.

BULKMAIL A Postal Service program for sending 200 or more pieces of mail for a much reduced rate of postage. Strict rules apply to the sorting and labeling of bulk mail; these may be obtained from the Post Office. Bulk mail is used to send appeal letters, invitations, newsletters, and the like.

CAMPAIGN Any intensive fundraising effort, with a specified goal and timeline, such as annual campaign, membership campaign, or CAPITAL CAMPAIGN.

CAPITAL CAMPAIGN An additional fundraising drive for special, often large expenses, usually for things such as a building, remodelling, equipment, and the like. Organizations also use a capital campaign to build endowments.

CASE The justification for the existence of the nonprofit organization, usually put together in a package called the CASE STATEMENT.

CASE STATEMENT A document containing the mission statement of the organization and documenting evidence for the mission. Often contains goals and objectives, brief history of the group, and accomplishments so far. The case statement is used in preparing brochures, mail appeals, and the like, and in educating new board members and volunteers.

CASH FLOW The amount of income and

expenses flowing through your organization on a monthly basis, and the planning for this flow. Cash flow problems occur when expenses exceed income for more than a month, even if the organization is not operating at a deficit but is waiting on a large grant, reimbursement, or donation.

CONSTITUENCY Those people who are or have been involved in your organization as donors, volunteers, clients, staff, etc., and anyone who is potentially involved in your organization.

CULTIVATION The process of encouraging and promoting a person's interest in an organization, usually with the goal of asking for a large gift.

DEFERRED GIVING Also called "planned giving." A legal mechanism to give money, stocks, property, and the like to an organization that will not be able to use the assets until the death of the donor and his or her beneficiaries.

DEFICIT Projecting that at the end of the fiscal year the organization will have spent more money than it raised.

DESIGNATED GIFT A contribution made for a specific purpose, which must be used for that purpose.

DEVELOPMENT Encompasses all aspects of fundraising, including planning, evaluation, long-term goals, etc., as in "director of development," "development plan," "development committee."

DIRECT MAIL Requesting financial contributions through appeal letters sent by bulk mail to a large audience. Used to solicit small donations and to acquire donors.

ENDOWMENT An amount of money set aside to provide income for an organization or one of its programs. The principle amount of the endowment is untouched, and the interest from it is used as income.

FISCAL YEAR The 12-month period for which budgets are made. This can coincide with the calendar year or begin with any month.

GIFT Contribution or donation, usually of money. Gifts are described as small, major, membership, lead, and so forth to differentiate them. The difference is usually one of size and sometimes of timing.

GROSS The amount of money brought in by a fundraising strategy before expenses are subtracted.

LAPSED DONOR A contributor who has not given for two or more years. The assumption is that the donor is no longer interested in giving.

LIST Refers to the collection of names of current donors or prospective donors. Often used as shorthand for acquiring a mailing list of interested prospects.

MAJOR DONOR The person who gives a gift larger than the average. Usually used to describe people giving $100 or more.

MAJOR GIFT A gift of $50, $100, and up. Low-budget organizations generally have major gifts of $100-$5,000 for an annual campaign.

MEMBERSHIP The group of people giving a yearly donation (sometimes called "dues"). Membership is also used as shorthand, such as "renew your membership," or "membership is down," or "a broad-based membership." All of these uses refer to the membership set-up and to the people who are members.

MEMORIAL Gift made to remember a person who is deceased, as distinguished from other tribute gifts.

NET The amount of money earned from a particular fundraising strategy after expenses have been subtracted—the profit.

PERCENT RESPONSE The number of people who gave money divided by the number of requests that were made gives the percent response and allows for evaluation of the relative success of the appeal.

PLEDGE A promise to give a certain amount of money in monthly or quarterly installments over a specific period of time, or a promise to give a lump sum of money by a certain date.

PREMIUMS Tangible items used to encourage a prospect to give a contribution by a certain date. Differ from benefits, which the donor will get any time he or she gives. For example, "Send your donation by Dec. 1, and we will send you a magnificent calendar for next year."

PROSPECT A person, corporation, foundation, business, service club, etc. that would seem to be interested in donating time or money to an organization but has not yet been approached.

PROSPECT IDENTIFICATION The process of researching which of the many possible funding sources (including people and agencies) will be interested in giving and what their giving ability is.

SPECIAL EVENT A fundraising benefit such as a party, dinner, dance, raffle, whose purpose is to draw attention to the organization and often to raise money.

SOLICITATION Asking for the gift.

STRATEGY The fundraising method to be used or the plan for cultivating a prospect.

TAX-EXEMPT STATUS The legal Internal Revenue Service designation for nonprofit organizations allowing them to solicit money without paying taxes on their income. The most common tax-exempt status is 501(c) (3), which also allows the donor to that organization to use his or her gift as a tax deduction.

VEHICLE The fundraising strategy or the form of the fundraising method, such as a mail appeal, special event, annual campaign, etc.

YTD Year-to-date, a shorthand phrase that is usually followed by an amount of money indicating how much has been raised or spent in the current fiscal year.

The following list of materials is divided into two categories: those that everyone engaged in fundraising, whether part-time or full-time, paid or volunteer, must read and preferably own or have access to, and those that supplement knowledge or are written on specific topics or would be more useful to some audiences than others.

This list is not exhaustive. It contains the books, magazines, and other materials that I have found helpful or important for effective fundraising. For a complete bibliography, I recommend **The Grass Roots Fundraising Book**, by Joan Flanagan (listed below).

One of the most valuable ways to read more about fundraising is to visit the Foundation Center collection nearest you. **The Foundation Center** (main office in New York) is a nonprofit library service supported by foundations, fees for service, products for sale, and other fundraising strategies, that collects and disseminates information about foundations, corporations, government, and all other types of fundraising and grant-writing. A list of Foundation Centers, and their cooperating collections (that is, public libraries or other locations that have materials from the Foundation Center) can be found at the end of this bibliography.

MUST READ

America's Wealthy and the Future of Foundations, Teresa Odendahl, ed., 1986. 325 pgs. $24.95. The Foundation Center, 79 Fifth Avenue, New York, NY 10003.

Designs for Fund-Raising: Principles, Patterns, Techniques, Harold J. Seymour, 1966. 210 pgs. $41.50. McGraw-Hill, 1221 Avenue of the Americas, New York, NY 10020.

Giving USA Annual Report, American Association of Fund Raising Counsel, Inc., published yearly. $30.00. AAFRC, 25 West 43rd St., New York, NY 10036.

Grassroots Fundraising Journal, a bi-monthly periodical, Lisa Honig and Kim Klein, publishers and editors. 16 pgs. $20 annual subscription. Grassroots Fundraising Journal, 517 Union Ave., Suite 206, Knoxville, TN 37902. (See below for reprint series and back issues.)

How to Get Control of Your Time and Life, Alan Lakein, 1974. 160 pgs. $2.95. Signet Paperbacks, available in most bookstores.

How to Make Meetings Work, Michael Doyle and David Straus, 1986. $3.95. Jove Publications, available in most bookstores.

How to Sell Anything to Anybody, Joe Girard and Stanley Brown, 1977. 240 pgs. $3.95. Warner Books, available in most bookstores.

On Being Board, or How Not to Be Dead Wood, 16 pgs. RAJ Publications, P.O. Box 150720, Lakewood, CO 80215. $1.50 for one copy, discounts for multiple orders.

Speaking Up, Janet Stone and Jane Bachner, 1977. $6.95. McGraw-Hill, available in bookstores and from People Speaking, 237 Crescent Road, San Anselmo, CA 94960.

The Grass Roots Fundraising Book: How to Raise Money in Your Community, Joan Flanagan, 1982. 320 pgs. $11.95. Contemporary Books, 180 N. Michigan Ave., Chicago, IL 60601.

ALSO RECOMMENDED

Activists Guide to Church Fundraising, Karen Livacoli, ed., 1987. 50 pgs. $5.95. Center for Third World Organizing, 3861 Martin Luther King Jr. Way, Oakland, CA 94609.

CBBB Standards for Charitable Solicitations. Free with SASE. Council of Better Business Bureaus, Inc., 1515 Wilson Blvd., Arlington, VA 22209.

Business Ventures of Citizen Groups, Charles Cagnon, 1982. $7.50. Northern Rockies Action Group, 9 Placer St., Helena, MT 59601.

Direct Mail on a Shoestring, Bruce P. Ballenger, 1984. $7.50. Northern Rockies Action Group, 9 Placer St., Helena, MT 59601.

Financial and Accounting Guide for Nonprofit Organizations, Malvern J. Gross, Jr., and William Warshauer, Jr. 1983. 568 pgs. $55. Wiley, 605 3rd Avenue, New York, NY 10158.

Gaining Momentum for Board Action, Judy Rauner and Arty Trost, 1983. $10.50. Marlborough Publications, PO. Box 16406, San Diego, CA 92116.

Insight and **Give But Give Wisely**, two newsletters available for one $20 annual subscription, from Council of Better Business Bureaus, Inc., 1515 Wilson Blvd., Arlington, VA 22209.

Looking at Income Generating Businesses for Small Non-Profit Organizations. 25 pgs. $3. Center for Community Change, 1000 Wisconsin Ave., NW, Washington, DC 20007.

The Membership Recruiting Manual, Bruce Ballenger, 1981. 52 pgs. $10. Northern Rockies Action Group, 9 Placer St., Helena, MT 59601.

Nonprofit Piggy Goes to Market, Robin Simons, Lisa Farber Miller and Peter Lengsselder, 1984. 32 pgs. $9.95. Denver Children's Museum, 2121 Crescent Drive, Denver, CO 80211.

Philanthropy and Cultural Imperialism: The Foundations at Home and Abroad, Robert F. Arnove, ed., 1982. 488 pgs. $10.95. Midland Books, available in bookstores.

Philanthropy and Voluntarism: An Annotated Bibliography, Daphne Niobe Layton, 1987. 308 pgs. The Foundation Center, 79 Fifth Avenue, New York, NY 10003.

Responsibilities of a Charity's Volunteer Board, (booklet). $1 from Council of Better Business Bureaus, Inc., 1515 Wilson Blvd., Arlington, VA 22209.

Robin Hood Was Right: A Guide to Giving Your Money for Social Change, 1977. 148 pgs. $5. Vanguard Public Foundation, 14 Precita Ave., San Francisco, CA 94110.

Securing Your Organization's Future, Michael Seltzer, 1987. 514 pgs. $19.95 plus $2 postage. The Foundation Center, 79 Fifth Avenue, New York, NY 10003.

Starting and Running a Nonprofit Organization, Joan Hummel, 1980. 147 pgs. $11.95. University of Minnesota Press, Minneapolis, MN.

The Successful Volunteer Organization, Joan Flanagan, 1981. 376 pgs. $13.95. Contemporary Books, 180 N. Michigan Ave., Chicago, IL 60601.

Workplace Solicitation. For books and other information on this topic, write to National Committee for Responsive Philanthropy, 2001 S Street, #620, Washington DC 20009.

Available from the **Grassroots Fundraising Journal**:

Reprint series:

> **Annotated Index**, 1982-86 ($2.50)
> **The Board of Directors** ($6)
> **Major Gifts Campaigns** ($7)
> **Planning for Fundraising** ($6)

Back Issues. Write for listing and order form. Grassroots Fundraising Journal, 517 Union Ave., Suite 206, Knoxville, TN 37902.

The Foundation Center is an independent national service organization established by foundations to provide an authoritative source of information on private philanthropic giving. In fulfilling its mission, The Center disseminates information on private giving through public service programs, publications and through a national network of library reference collections for free public use. The New York, Washington, DC, Cleveland and San Francisco reference collections operated by The Foundation Center offer a wide variety of services and comprehensive collections of information on foundations and grants. The Cooperating Collections are libraries, community foundations and other nonprofit agencies that provide a core collection of Foundation Center publications and a variety of supplementary materials and services in subject areas useful to grantseekers.

Over 100 of the network members have sets of private foundation information returns (IRS Form 990-PF) for their states or regions which are available for public use. A complete set of U.S. foundation returns can be found at the New York and Washington, DC offices of The Foundation Center. The Cleveland and San Francisco offices contain IRS returns for those foundations in the midwestern and western states, respectively.

Because the collections vary in their hours, materials and services, IT IS RECOMMENDED THAT YOU CALL EACH COLLECTION IN ADVANCE. To check on new locations or current information, call toll-free 1-800-424-9836.

Those collections marked with a bullet (●) have sets of private foundation information returns (IRS Form 990-PF) for their states or regions, available for public reference.

Reference collections operated by The Foundation Center are in **boldface.**

ALABAMA

● Birmingham Public Library
2100 Park Place
Birmingham 35203
205-226-3600

Huntsville-Madison County
Public Library
108 Fountain Circle
P.O. Box 443
Huntsville 35804
205-536-0021

University of South Alabama
Library Building
Reference Department
Mobile 36688
205-460-7025

● Auburn University at
Montgomery Library
Montgomery 36193-0401
205-271-9649

ALASKA

● University of Alaska,
Anchorage Library
3211 Providence Drive
Anchorage 99508
907-786-1848

ARIZONA

● Phoenix Public Library Business
and Sciences Department
12 East McDowell Road
Phoenix 85004
602-262-4636

● Tucson Public Library
Main Library
200 South Sixth Avenue
Tucson 85701
602-791-4393

ARKANSAS

● Westark Community College
Library
Grand Avenue at Waldron Road
Fort Smith 72913
501-785-7000

● Little Rock Public Library
Reference Department
700 Louisiana Street
Little Rock 72201
501-370-5950

CALIFORNIA

● California Community
Foundation Funding Information
Center
3580 Wilshire Blvd., Suite 1660
Los Angeles 90010
213-413-4042

● Community Foundation for
Monterey County
420 Pacific Street
Monterey 93940
408-375-9712

California Community
Foundation
4050 Metropolitan Drive #300
Orange 92668
714-937-9077

Riverside Public Library
3581 7th Street
Riverside 92501
714-787-7201

California State Library
Reference Services, Rm. 309
914 Capital Mall
Sacramento 95814
916-322-4570

● San Diego Community
Foundation
525 "B" Street, Suite 410
San Diego 92101
619-239-8815

● **The Foundation Center**
312 Sutter Street, Room 312
San Francisco 94108
415-397-0902

● Grantsmanship Resource Center
Junior League of San Jose, Inc.
Community Foundation of Santa
Clara County
960 West Hedding, Suite 220
San Jose 95126
408-244-5280

● Orange County Community
Developmental Council
1440 East First Street, 4th Floor
Santa Ana 92701
714-547-6801

● Peninsula Community
Foundation
1204 Burlingame Avenue
Burlingame 94011-0627
415-342-2505

● Santa Barbara Public Library
Reference Section
40 East Anapamu
P.O. Box 1019
Santa Barbara 93102
805-962-7653

Santa Monica Public Library
1343 Sixth Street
Santa Monica 90401-1603
213-458-8603

Tuolomne County Library
465 S. Washington Street
Sonora 95370
209-533-5707

COLORADO

Pikes Peak Library District
20 North Cascade Avenue
Colorado Springs 80901
303-473-2780

● Denver Public Library
Sociology Division
1357 Broadway
Denver 80203
303-571-2190

CONNECTICUT

Danbury Public Library
170 Main Street
Danbury 06810
203-797-4527

● Hartford Public Library
Reference Department
500 Main Street
Hartford 06103
203-525-9121

D.A.T.A.
30 Arbor Street
Hartford 06106
203-232-6619

D.A.T.A.
25 Science Park
Suite 502
New Haven 06513
203-786-5225

DELAWARE

● Hugh Morris Library
University of Delaware
Newark 19717-5267
302-451-2965

● Santa Barbara Public Library

DISTRICT OF COLUMBIA

● **The Foundation Center**
1001 Connecticut Avenue, NW
Washington 20036
202-331-1400

FLORIDA

Volusia County Public Library
City Island
Daytona Beach 32014
904-252-8374

● Jacksonville Public Library
Business, Science, and Industry
Department
122 North Ocean Street
Jacksonville 32202
904-633-3926

● Miami–Dade Public Library
Humanities Department
101 W. Flagler St.
Miami 33132
305-375-2665

● Orlando Public Library
101 E. Central Blvd.
Orlando 32801
305-425-4694

Selby Public Library
1001 Boulevard of the Arts
Sarasota 33577
813-366-7303

● Leon County Public Library
Community Funding Resources
Center
1940 North Monroe Street
Tallahassee 32303
904-478-2665

Palm Beach County Community
Foundation
324 Datura Street, Suite 340
West Palm Beach 33401
305-659-6800

GEORGIA

● Atlanta–Fulton Public Library
Ivan Allen Department
1 Margaret Mitchell Square
Atlanta 30303
404-688-4636

HAWAII

- Thomas Hale Hamilton Library
General Reference
University of Hawaii
2550 The Mall
Honolulu 96822
808-948-7214

The Hawaiian Foundation
Resource Room
130 Merchant Street
Bancorp Tower, Suite 901
Honolulu 96813
808-538-4540

IDAHO

- Caldwell Public Library
1010 Dearborn Street
Caldwell 83605
208-459-3242

ILLINOIS

Belleville Public Library
121 East Washington Street
Belleville 62220
618-234-0441

DuPage Township
300 Briarcliff Road
Bolingbrook 60439
312-759-1317

- Donor's Forum of Chicago
53 W. Jackson Blvd., Rm. 430
Chicago 60604
312-431-0265

- Evanston Public Library
1703 Orrington Avenue
Evanston 60201
312-866-0305

- Sangamon State University
Library
Shepherd Road
Springfield 62708
217-786-6633

INDIANA

Allen County Public Library
900 Webster Street
Fort Wayne 46802
219-424-7241

Indiana University Northwest
Library
3400 Broadway
Gary 46408
219-980-6580

- Indianapolis-Marion County
Public Library
40 East St. Clair Street
Indianapolis 46204
317-269-1733

IOWA

- Public Library of Des Moines
100 Locust Street
Des Moines 50308
515-283-4259

KANSAS

- Topeka Public Library
Adult Services Department
1515 West Tenth Street
Topeka 66604
913-233-2040

- Wichita Public Library
223 South Main
Wichita 67202
316-262-0611

KENTUCKY

Western Kentucky University
Division of Library Services
Helm-Cravens Library
Bowling Green 42101
502-745-3951

- Louisville Free Public Library
Fourth and York Streets
Louisville 40203
502-561-8600

LOUISIANA

- East Baton Rouge Parish Library
Centroplex Library
120 St. Louis Street
Baton Rouge 70821
504-389-4960

- New Orleans Public Library
Business and Science Division
219 Loyola Avenue
New Orleans 70140
504-596-2583

- Shreve Memorial Library
424 Texas Street
Shreveport 71101
318-226-5894

MAINE

- University of Southern Maine
Center for Research and
Advanced Study
246 Deering Avenue
Portland 04102
207-780-4411

MARYLAND

- Enoch Pratt Free Library
Social Science and History
Department
400 Cathedral Street
Baltimore 21201
301-396-5320

MASSACHUSETTS

- Associated Grantmakers of
Massachusetts
294 Washington Street
Suite 501
Boston 02108
617-426-2608

- Boston Public Library
Copley Square
Boston 02117
617-536-5400

Walpole Public Library
Common Street
Walpole 02081
617-668-5497 ext. 340

- Western Massachusetts Funding
Resource Center
Campaign for Human
Development
Chancery Annex
73 Chestnut Street
Springfield 01103
413-732-3175 ext. 67

- Grants Resource Center
Worcester Public Library
Salem Square
Worcester 01608
617-799-1655

MICHIGAN

- Alpena County Library
211 North First Avenue
Alpena 49707
517-356-6188

University of Michigan-Ann
Arbor
Reference Department
209 Hatcher Graduate Library
Ann Arbor 48109-1205
313-764-1149

- Henry Ford Centennial Library
16301 Michigan Avenue
Dearborn 48126
313-943-2337

- Purdy Library
Wayne State University
Detroit 48202
313-577-4040

- Michigan State University
Libraries
Reference Library
East Lansing 48824
517-353-9184

- Farmington Community Library
32737 West 12 Mile Road
Farmington Hills 48018
313-553-0300

- University of Michigan-Flint
Library
Reference Department
Flint 48503
313-762-3408

- Grand Rapids Public Library
Sociology and Education Dept.
Library Plaza
Grand Rapids 49502
616-456-4411

- Michigan Technological
University Library
Highway U.S. 41
Houghton 49931
906-487-2507

MINNESOTA

- Duluth Public Library
520 Superior Street
Duluth 55802
218-723-3802

- Southwest State University
Library
Marshall 56258
507-537-7278

- Minneapolis Public Library
Sociology Department
300 Nicollet Mall
Minneapolis 55401
612-372-6555

Rochester Public Library
Broadway at First Street, SE
Rochester 55901
507-285-8002

Saint Paul Public Library
90 West Fourth Street
Saint Paul 55102
612-292-6311

MISSISSIPPI

Jackson Metropolitan Library
301 North State Street
Jackson 39201
601-944-1120

MISSOURI

- Clearinghouse for Midcontinent
Foundations
P.O. Box 22680
Univ. of Missouri, Kansas City
Law School, Suite 1-300
52nd Street and Oak
Kansas City 64113
816-276-1176

- Kansas City Public Library
311 East 12th Street
Kansas City 64106
816-221-2685

- Metropolitan Association for
Philanthropy, Inc.
5585 Pershing Avenue
Suite 150
St. Louis 63112
314-361-3900

- Springfield-Greene County
Library
397 East Central Street
Springfield 65801
417-866-4636

MONTANA

- Eastern Montana College Library
Reference Department
1500 N. 30th Street
Billings 59101-0298
406-657-2262

- Montana State Library
Reference Department
1515 E. 6th Avenue
Helena 59620
406-444-3004

NEBRASKA

University of Nebraska, Lincoln
106 Love Library
Lincoln 68588-0410
402-472-2526

- W. Dale Clark Library
Social Sciences Department
215 South 15th Street
Omaha 68102
402-444-4826

NEVADA

- Las Vegas-Clark County Library
District
1401 East Flamingo Road
Las Vegas 89119
702-733-7810

- Washoe County Library
301 South Center Street
Reno 89505
702-785-4190

NEW HAMPSHIRE

- The New Hampshire Charitable
Fund
One South Street
Concord 03301
603-225-6641

Littleton Public Library
109 Main Street
Littleton 03561
603-444-5741

Cumberland County Library
800 E. Commerce Street
Bridgeton 08302
609-455-0080

The Support Center
17 Academy Street, Suite 1101
Newark 07102
201-643-5774

County College of Morris
Masten Learning Resource
 Center
Route 10 and Center Grove Rd.
Randolph 07869
201-361-5000 ext. 470

• New Jersey State Library
Governmental Reference
185 West State Street
Trenton 08625
609-292-6220

Albuquerque Community
 Foundation
6400 Uptown Boulevard N.E.
Suite 500-W
Albuquerque 87110
505-883-6240

• New Mexico State Library
325 Don Gaspar Street
Santa Fe 87503
505-827-3824

• New York State Library
Cultural Education Center
Humanities Section
Empire State Plaza
Albany 12230
518-474-7645

Bronx Reference Center
New York Public Library
2556 Bainbridge Avenue
Bronx 10458
212-220-6575

Brooklyn in Touch
101 Willoughby Street
Room 1508
Brooklyn 11201
718-237-9300

• Buffalo and Erie County Public
 Library
Lafayette Square
Buffalo 14203
716-856-7525

Huntington Public Library
338 Main Street
Huntington 11743
516-427-5165

• Levittown Public Library
Reference Department
One Bluegrass Lane
Levittown 11756
516-731-5728

• **The Foundation Center**
79 Fifth Avenue
New York 10003
212-620-4230

SUNY/College at Old Westbury
 Library
223 Store Hill Road
Old Westbury 11568
516-876-3156

• Plattsburgh Public Library
Reference Department
15 Oak Street
Plattsburgh 12901
518-563-0921

Adriance Memorial Library
93 Market Street
Poughkeepsie 12601
914-485-4790

Queens Borough Public Library
89-11 Merrick Boulevard
Jamaica 11432
718-990-0700

• Rochester Public Library
Business and Social Sciences
 Division
115 South Avenue
Rochester 14604
716-428-7328

Staten Island Council on the Arts
One Edgewater Plaza Rm. 311
Staten Island 10305
718-447-4485

• Onondaga County Public Library
335 Montgomery Street
Syracuse 13202
315-473-4493

• White Plains Public Library
100 Martine Avenue
White Plains 10601
914-682-4488

• Suffolk Cooperative Library
 System
627 North Sunrise Service Road
Bellport 11713
516-286-1600

• The Duke Endowment
200 S. Tryon Street, Ste. 1100
Charlotte 28202
704-376-0291

Durham County Library
300 N. Roxboro Street
Durham 27701
919-683-2626

• North Carolina State Library
109 East Jones Street
Raleigh 27611
919-733-3270

• The Winston-Salem Foundation
229 First Union National Bank
 Building
Winston-Salem 27101
919-725-2382

Western Dakota Grants Resource
 Center
Bismarck Junior College Library
Bismarck 58501
701-224-5450

• The Library
North Dakota State University
Fargo 58105
701-237-8876

• Public Library of Cincinnati and
 Hamilton County
Education Department
800 Vine Street
Cincinnati 45202
513-369-6940

• **The Foundation Center**
Kent H. Smith Library
1442 Hanna Building
1422 Euclid Avenue
Cleveland 44115
216-861-1933

The Public Library of Columbus
and Franklin County
Main Library
96 S. Grant Avenue
Columbus 43215
614-227-9500

• Dayton and Montgomery County
 Public Library
Grants Information Center
215 E. Third Street
Dayton 45402-2103
513-227-9500 ext. 211

• Toledo–Lucas County Public
 Library
Social Science Department
325 Michigan Street
Toledo 43624
419-255-7055 ext. 221

Ohio University–Zanesville
Community Education and
 Development
1425 Newark Road
Zanesville 43701
614-453-0762

Stark County District Library
715 Market Avenue North
Canton 44702-1080
216-452-0665

• Oklahoma City University Library
NW 23rd at North Blackwelder
Oklahoma City 73106
405-521-5072

• Tulsa City–County Library System
400 Civic Center
Tulsa 74103
918-592-7944

• Library Association of Portland
Government Documents Room
801 S.W. Tenth Avenue
Portland 97205
503-223-7201

Oregon State Library
State Library Building
Salem 97310
503-378-4274

Northampton County Area
Community College
Learning Resources Center
3835 Green Pond Road
Bethlehem 18017
215-865-5358

• Erie County Public Library
3 South Perry Square
Erie 16501
814-452-2333 ext. 54

• Dauphin County Library System
Central Library
101 Walnut Street
Harrisburg 17101
717-234-4961

Lancaster County Public Library
125 North Duke Street
Lancaster 17602
717-394-2651

• The Free Library of Philadelphia
Logan Square
Philadelphia 19103
215-686-5423

• Hillman Library
University of Pittsburgh
Pittsburgh 15260
412-624-4423

Economic Development Council
of Northeastern Pennsylvania
1151 Oak Street
Pittston 18640
717-655-5581

James V. Brown Library
12 E. 4th Street
Williamsport 17701
717-326-0536

• Providence Public Library
Reference Department
150 Empire Street
Providence 02903
401-521-7722

• Charleston County Public Library
404 King Street
Charleston 29403
803-723-1645

• South Carolina State Library
Reader Services Department
1500 Senate Street
Columbia 29201
803-734-8666

• South Dakota State Library
State Library Building
800 North Illinois Street
Pierre 57501
605-773-3131

Sioux Falls Area Foundation
404 Boyce Greeley Building
321 South Phillips Avenue
Sioux Falls 57102-0781
605-336-7055

• Knoxville-Knox County Public
 Library
500 West Church Avenue
Knoxville 37902
615-523-0781

• Memphis Shelby County Public
 Library
1850 Peabody Avenue
Memphis 38104
901-725-8876

- Public Library of Nashville and
  Davidson County
  8th Avenue, North and Union
  Street
  Nashville 37203
  615-244-4700

TEXAS

Amarillo Area Foundation
1000 Polk
P.O. Box 25569
Amarillo 79105-269
806-376-4521

- The Hogg Foundation for Mental
  Health
  The University of Texas
  Austin 78712
  512-471-5041

- Corpus Christi State University
  Library
  6300 Ocean Drive
  Corpus Christi 78412
  512-991-6810

- El Paso Community Foundation
  El Paso National Bank Building
  Suite 1616
  El Paso 79901
  915-533-4020

- Funding Information Center
  Texas Christian University Library
  Ft. Worth 76129
  817-921-7664

- Houston Public Library
  Bibliographic & Information
  Center
  500 McKinney Avenue
  Houston 77002
  713-224-5441 ext. 265

- Lubbock Area Foundation
  502 Commerce Bank Building
  Lubbock 79401
  806-762-8061

- Funding Information Library
  507 Brooklyn
  San Antonio 78215
  512-227-4333

- Dallas Public Library
  Grants Information Service
  1515 Young Street
  Dallas 75201
  214-670-1487

- Pan American University
  Learning Resource Center
  1201 W. University Drive
  Edinburg 78539
  512-381-3304

UTAH

- Salt Lake City Public Library
  Business and Science
  Department
  209 East Fifth South
  Salt Lake City 84111
  801-363-5733

VERMONT

- State of Vermont Department of
  Libraries
  Reference Services Unit
  111 State Street
  Montpelier 05602
  802-828-3261

VIRGINIA

- Grants Resources Collection
  Hampton Public Library
  4207 Victoria Blvd.
  Hampton 23669
  804-727-6234

- Richmond Public Library
  Business, Science, & Technology
  Department
  101 East Franklin Street
  Richmond 23219
  804-780-8223

WASHINGTON

- Seattle Public Library
  1000 Fourth Avenue
  Seattle 98104
  206-625-4881

- Spokane Public Library
  Funding Information Center
  West 906 Main Avenue
  Spokane 99201
  509-838-3364

WEST VIRGINIA

- Kanawha County Public Library
  123 Capital Street
  Charleston 25301
  304-343-4646

WISCONSIN

- Marquette University Memorial
  Library
  1415 West Wisconsin Avenue
  Milwaukee 53233
  414-224-1515

- University of Wisconsin-Madison
  Memorial Library
  728 State Street
  Madison 53706
  608-262-3647

WYOMING

- Laramie County Community
  College Library
  1400 East College Drive
  Cheyenne 82007
  509-838-3364

AUSTRALIA

Victorian Community Foundation
94 Queen Street
Melbourne Vic 3000
607-5922

CANADA

Canadian Center for Philanthropy
3080 Yonge Street
Suite 4080
Toronto, Ontario M4N3N1
416-484-4118

ENGLAND

Charities Aid Foundation
14 Bloomsbury Square
London WC1A 2LP
01-430-1798

MEXICO

Biblioteca Benjamin Franklin
Londres 16
Mexico City 6, D.F.
525-591-0244

PUERTO RICO

Universidad Del Sagrado
Corazon
M.M.T. Guevarra Library
Correo Calle Loiza
Santurce 00914
809-728-1515 ext. 357

VIRGIN ISLANDS

College of the Virgin Islands
Library
Saint Thomas
U.S. Virgin Islands 00801
809-774-9200 ext. 487

THE FOUNDATION CENTER AFFILIATES PROGRAM

As participants in the cooperating collection network, affiliates are libraries or nonprofit agencies that provide fundraising information or other funding-related technical assistance in their communities. Affiliates agree to provide free public access to a basic collection of Foundation Center publications during a regular schedule of hours, offering free funding research guidance to all visitors. Many also provide a variety of special services for local nonprofit organizations using staff or volunteers to prepare special materials, organize workshops, or conduct library orientations.

The affiliates program began in 1981 to continue the expansion of The Foundation Center's funding information network of 90 funding information collections. Since its inception, over 80 organizations have been designated Foundation Center affiliates. Affiliate collections have been established in a wide variety of host organizations, including public and university libraries, technical assistance agencies, and community foundations. The Center maintains strong ties with its affiliates through regular news bulletins, the provision of supporting materials, the sponsorship of regional meetings, and by referring the many nonprofits that call or write to The Foundation Center to the affiliate nearest them.

The Foundation Center welcomes inquiries from agencies interested in providing this type of public information service. If you are interested in establishing a funding information library for the use of nonprofit agencies in your area or in learning more about the program, we would like to hear from you.

The first step is for the director of your organization to write to Zeke Kilbride, Network Coordinator, explaining why the collection is needed and how the responsibilities of network participation would be met. The Center will contact you to review the details of the relationship. If your agency is designated an affiliate, you will then be entitled to purchase a core collection of Foundation Center materials at a 20% discount rate (annual cost of approx. $410). Center staff will be happy to assist in identifying supplementary titles for funding information libraries. A core collection, which must be maintained from year to year, consists of current editions to the following publications:

The Foundation Directory	Source Book Profiles
The Foundation Directory Supplement	The National Data Book
The Foundation Grants Index	Foundation Fundamentals
The Foundation Grants Index Bimonthly	

For more information, please write to: Zeke Kilbride, The Foundation Center, 79 Fifth Avenue, New York, NY 10003.

12/87

Appendix 1

Raising Money in Rural Areas

Just as cities and towns vary greatly from one to another, so do rural areas, but there are some things many of them have in common. In this appendix, I discuss those commonalities, and suggest some fundraising strategies that are effective in rural communities.

Five factors must be taken into account in doing any kind of work in a rural community.

1. **Everything takes longer.** This applies not only to the obvious time involved in getting from one place to another when vast distances separate homes or towns, but also to rural hospitality, which is much more deliberate than that of citydwellers. For example, suppose you decide to visit a major donor on his/her ranch. You make an appointment, then drive three or more hours to the ranch. Once there, you do not chat briefly, ask for the gift and leave in 30 minutes, as you would in a city. The graciousness often customary in rural areas may lead your host or hostess to give you a tour of the ranch, invite you to stay for lunch or dinner, and perhaps encourage you to spend the night. This graciousness is wonderful but time-consuming.

   The necessities of ranch life can also be obstacles. Depending on the main economy of the area, there may be times—such as planting, harvesting, lambing or calving—where contact must be limited because people are working almost around the clock. Then, when none of those things are going on, the weather may make driving conditions so hazardous that volunteers cannot get to meetings, people cannot attend special events, and prospects cannot be visited.

2. **Fundraising costs may be higher in rural communities.** The cityperson's idyllic notion that everything is inexpensive or free in a rural area is false. Almost all supplies have to be shipped in, adding freight to their cost. Lack of competition among businesses can also cause high prices. While office space may be less expensive, there may not be any available. The distances between people and places make driving costs high, and the price of gasoline is higher per gallon.

3. **Logistics are complicated.** If you wish to print a newsletter, mail appeal, or flier, you may have to send it to the nearest city. If you need something sent or received quickly, there may be no overnight Express Mail from or to your community. If your rural community or your constituency is made up of low-income families or individuals, details can take on nightmarish proportions. For example, a small organization covering 20 counties in a southern state held an annual meeting. The meeting was timed perfectly between planting season and the onset of unbearably hot weather, and the organization offered to pay transportation costs for their low-income members. Five members decided to drive to the meeting together; none of them, however, had a car that could

be trusted for the eight-hour trip. After the organization encouraged them to rent a car, they drove two hours to the nearest rental-car facility, only to be told that they must present a credit card, which none of them had. Finally, the organization called a credit card number to the rental car agency and the group made it to the meeting.

4. **The culture plays an important role.** In organizing and fundraising in a rural community, one must keep in mind that people often have known each other for many years; sometimes families have known each other for generations. People depend on each other for help in hard times or for assistance in emergencies. Thus, rural people are cautious about doing anything that might cause offense. If you live down the road from someone who is dumping effluent into your water source, you will think twice about publicly confronting this person when you know that if you have a medical emergency in the middle of winter and can't get your car started you may need to call on him or her.

This reluctance to challenge other people's actions often includes a hesitation to fundraise assertively or ask people for money directly. Fundraisers and organizers mistakenly interpret this reluctance on the part of volunteers as a sign that they are either conservative (wishing to maintain the status quo) or passive (willing to sit by while land is destroyed or people's rights are violated). In fact. this reluctance is a survival mechanism, and must be respected and taken into account. Because of this and other factors, change comes more slowly in rural communities.

5. **Not everyone has equal loyalty to the area.** Some rural areas, such as those around Asheville, North Carolina or many parts of Florida, are retirement communities. Many of the people living in these communities are not from the region, and have little loyalty to it. Many of them do have money, and, being retired, also have time to volunteer. Other rural communities, such as those within a few hours of major cities such as San Francisco, Washington, D.C., or Boston are bedroom communities for commuters who work in those cities. The increasingly common use of the personal computer and modem for business means that people can live in rural communities two or three hours' drive from their workplace and still carry on their business, commuting to the city one or two days each week. Their loyalty to their local community may depend on whether they are raising families there and how strongly they wish to be accepted and involved. While their time may be limited, they may have significant disposable income. The back-to-the-land "hippies" or small farmers are another population type in rural communities. Finances and values of these people are extremely varied.

One often thinks of residents of rural communities as people who have lived in the same place all their lives and make their living from farming or ranching. This, of course, is common. But there are also many rural communities where people make their living from mining (many of these people are now unemployed) or as workers on other people's farms or ranches, in some instances as sharecroppers. Increasingly, there are rural communities where the majority of the population are non-English-speaking immigrants or refugees from Mexico, Latin America, Cambodia and other countries.

It is important to analyze your rural community in terms of all these considerations. People raising money in rural Mississippi have little in common with those raising money in rural Mendocino, California, where the primary crop is the extremely lucrative but illegal marijuana.

Strategies for Raising Money

For groups in communities located near cities with populations of 100,000 or more, focus attention on raising money in those towns and cities where the financial base is strongest. Form support groups with people living in the town or city. Hold special events there, and use direct mail to locate donors there.

In addition to raising money in the nearest population center, try to discover ways to raise money from people who pass through the community, particularly tourists and visitors. Some communities mount events just to attract tourists. For example, many communities have county fairs or various kinds of festivals, such as the Garlic Festival in California, the Ramp Festival in Georgia, the Storytellers' Convention in North Carolina. These attract tourists.

If you live in a place where tourists come to see the natural beauty or to vacation (such as the coasts, or near national parks or monuments), consider developing products that tourists will buy. Local crafts and homemade jellies and jams are always appealing.

If you live near a freeway or a frequently travelled road, set up a rest stop where truckers and tired drivers can buy coffee and doughnuts. This can be very lucrative in the cold, winter months, particularly at night. It is also a community service which helps keep people from falling asleep at the wheel.

You can raise money from your local community as well. It is important to note that even in the poorest and most rural areas churches, volunteer fire departments, rescue squads, service clubs and the like are supported by local residents. Even the smallest, poorest towns in Appalachia, for example, support at least two churches. Certainly, they may not have full-time paid clergy, but the people manage to support a building.

Money can be raised locally through special events. This helps counter the reluctance rural people have for asking for money directly by providing a way to give something in return. Raffles, car washes, bake sales and the like can be good money-makers. Many times people from rural community groups simply stand with buckets at busy crossroads and ask drivers to drop in spare change. Three hours at a crossroads on a shopping day can bring in $200-300.

Flea markets are also very popular. It is often easier for rural people to donate items rather than cash, and people always seem willing to buy each other's castoffs.

All of these are labor-intensive activities, and make fundraising in rural communities even harder than it is elsewhere. We must face the fact that an organization located in a low-income, rural area doing work related to social justice issues (tax or land reform, appropriate economic development, peace and disarmament work, or opposing such things as hazardous waste dumping, clearcutting, or wildcat strip-mining) will need to seek funding from foundations and from outside their immediate region. Unless the organization has a very low budget and no paid staff, it is unlikely that it will be able to become entirely self-sufficient. However, your community will support you, and your work will be more successful, if community members have bought into it with a donation.

Appendix 2

Dealing with Anxiety

During the thirteen years I have been in fundraising, I have observed that the greatest factor causing people to leave fundraising, or to "burn out," is not the work itself, or even the challenge of having to ask for money. It is the constant, gnawing anxiety that the money won't come in, and the knowledge that once you have raised money for one month or one quarter you must simply turn around and begin raising it for the next period of time. There is never a rest, and lack of success shows up immediately.

Many paid fundraising staff have told me that they wake up in the middle of the night worrying, that they never feel really free to take a weekend off, let alone a vacation. Fundraising staff often watch their self-esteem eaten away by the constant pressure of a job that by its nature can never be finished.

There are four ways to deal with this anxiety short of psychotherapy or quitting one's job.

First, remember that if you do your job, the money will come in. Of course some mail appeals will fail, some donors won't give, and some grant proposals will be turned down. But your job is to generate enough requests for money that even when only a small portion are successful you will have the money you need. Fundraising is basically a numbers game—get the word out in as many ways and to as many people as you can, and you will get money back.

Second, if your primary responsibility is to raise money, then every day that you come to work you need to set your priorities around that goal. Ask yourself, "Of all the tasks that I have to do today, which one will raise the most money?" Do that task first, then do the task that will raise the next most money, and so on. No one ever gets their whole job done. Make sure that the things you don't get done are things not related to fundraising. In one organization, the director was the only staffperson. Feeling responsible for everything, she did those things she knew how to do, and which she could finish. She kept accurate and excellent books, paid bills on time, got out minutes and agendas for meetings, and wrote, edited and produced the newsletter. The Board did a lot of program work under her direction. Soon, the group had little money and was in danger of going out of business. This director quickly learned to change her priorities; now she works on fundraising at least five hours every day. If she has time, she does the books. Board meeting minutes and agendas are handled by the Board secretary. At each Board meeting, the director brings a fundraising to-do list for the Board. While some Board members object that they want to work on program, not fundraising, the Director is teaching them that without money there is no program and no group. The first and primary responsibility of the Board and staff of any organization is to keep the group going, and this usually means active ongoing participation in fundraising.

Third, try to detach from the results of your work. An unsuccessful proposal or mailing does not mean that you are a failure as a person or as a fundraiser. Not being able to do everything is not a condemnation of your worth as a person Ask yourself whether it will be important in ten years that you got the thank you notes out today or next week. One person can only do so much. Do what you can do in the time allotted, and let the rest go. Too often, groups have fundraising goals that no one could reach. Re-evaluate your goal setting, instead of trying to live up to impossible expectations.

Some people have found it helpful to form support groups: either informal gatherings over happy hour, or more formal, structured meetings at a specific time and place. If you do use a support group, make sure it supports your work and helps with strategies. Do not use it as a gripe session to compare notes on how awful everyone's job is. That will only make you more depressed.

Finally, take care of yourself. Don't always work overtime. Take vacations. Ask for help. Delegate tasks. The overall work of social justice is the empowerment of people as they move to a humane and just society. If your work is none of those things for you, it is unlikely that your organization will effect long-lasting social change.

Appendix 3

Using Computers in Fundraising

Not long ago I drove into rural West Virginia, down and up windy roads with no towns for 40 and 50 miles at a stretch, into a valley between two mountains (called a "holler"). The group I was visiting has their office in a converted barn, with newspaper providing much of the insulation. The desks were planks of plywood on sawhorses, the filing cabinets were wooden boxes. Part of the floor was dirt. On top of one long plank of plywood sat an IBM-compatible, hard disk drive computer, and nearby the letter-quality printer that went with it. A sign-up sheet over the computer was full, with each person allowed up to two hours before having to surrender to the next person.

Computers are a fact of life. Today in the United States, it is difficult not to know how to use one. However, they have not and will not revolutionize fundraising. Quality fundraising will always depend for success on people asking people for money. Nevertheless, computers can make the back-up work required for fundraising faster and easier.

This appendix comments on what computers can do for fundraising and what you should look for in getting a computer and buying software for it. No brand names will be recommended; the field is changing too fast for any recommendations to be current. Groups buying a computer and software will need to do further research in order to feel ready to go exploring for what they need.

For small non-profit organizations, there are four important factors in getting a computer and software. (Large non-profits such as hospitals and universities, as well as small for-profit businesses and corporations have entirely different computer needs.)

1. **The computer and its basic programs need to be user-friendly.** This means your computer should be fairly simple to learn to use, and it should be easy for

someone to teach its methods to others. Certain programs ought to be simple enough that volunteers can be taught to use them for data entry, thank you notes, printing mailing labels and the like. As you explore what computer to buy or to seek as a donation, remember the high turnover small groups generally have in their clerical staff (if they have clerical staff), the limited time each volunteer puts in, and the fact that paid staff will need to take the time to learn how to use the computer—time they don't have and will feel pressed to find.

Often groups are given a computer as a donation. Most of the time this is a wonderful gift, but occasionally it is a way for a manufacturer or business to get rid of a computer that is old or difficult to use, or that has no compatible software. Through careful reading of the manual, a group may figure out a little about how to use their donated computer, but mostly it sits enshrined as the group's effort to modernize, while all records are still kept by hand and letters and proposals are written on the typewriter.

2. **The computer needs to have enough memory to hold all the information your group would wish to store.** For many groups, this means going to a hard disk drive because of its much greater storage space. The size of your computer's memory is also a factor in selecting software, as you don't want programs that are so complex they take all the available space just to run.

3. **The printer the computer uses needs to be able to do letter-quality printing in addition to the much faster dot-matrix printing.**

4. **The organization needs to have someone who will understand all the ways the computer can be used.** When someone in the organization understands how to use the computer, modify software for it, set up the menu, create back-up systems, and so forth, and can show everyone else how to use it, as well as be available when the screen won't erase or the printer won't print, then the computer is much more likely to be used.

Using the Computer in Fundraising

With regard to fundraising, small non-profits will use a computer basically to help with two fundraising tasks: word processing and keeping donor records, which includes the mailing list.

I recently visited a group that had just spent a good deal of money on a word-processing program that was in large part a "desktop-publishing" program. They were very excited that they would now be able to do their newsletter and some of their brochures on the computer, saving them "bundles" of typesetting and layout costs. As they described the wonders of this program, I noticed that a secretary was laboriously typing the same letter to more than 50 different prospects. When I asked why they didn't use their computer for that function they confessed, "The program can't do mail merge."

For fundraising purposes, the word-processing program you buy must be able to do mail merge: that is, to type the same letter to a number of different people, with each letter individualized to the recipient. The program also must have the capacity to move paragraphs around inside a document, to change margins and page length easily, and to have easy-to-understand print commands.

If word processing were the only need, a much less expensive memory typewriter would probably suffice, or renting time on a computer in any number of copy shops that now make that service available. But most groups switch their systems to a computer in order to organize their mailing list. If your mailing list is over 500 names, a computer will be useful and will be easier than a paper system.

There are dozens, perhaps even hundreds of mailing-list programs. It is important to get one that will serve you well for fundraising. You want a program that can do all of the following:

- Hold up to 10,000 names and addresses.
- Sort those names and addresses by alphabet, zip code, and donor status (new, renewing, lapsed; major donor, pledge, direct-mail donor, or prospect).
- In addition, it is very helpful if the program can keep track of pledge payments, interest areas of the donor, source of the name, who the contact person is for the donor, and the like.

Sometimes groups get a program that can hold an enormous number of names and addresses—30,000 or more—but accommodates little information on each donor. For most small groups, there is little likelihood of having a mailing list of 30,000 or more names. Therefore, you need a program that holds lots of information on fewer donors. Most small nonprofits are working with lists of 5,000 names at the most, including not more than 500 major donors, 100 or so pledge donors, 2,000 direct-mail donors, and so forth.

The sheet on the following page shows what one program can do. When a donation comes in, a fundraising staff person or volunteer fills out this sheet of paper on the donor. A clerical person then enters this data into the computer. The paper is saved as a back up, and is put into a file or notebook about donors. The program has an almost unlimited capacity to sort data; the organization simply creates the categories that would be useful for it to have.

Reasonably sophisticated data bases should be able to sort all this information. Using this system, you can invite all the people who came to your auction every year to attend again, send out special emphasis mailings to those people most concerned about a particular issue, and send special mailings only, for example, to major donors or to volunteers. Also, the system can sort by several categories. Suppose a leading union organizer is in town—you can invite all the people who come to special events, or who are interested in labor, or who live nearby (zip code), or who are volunteers or Board members to come to a special meeting with this person.

By thinking the way the computer thinks, you can be selective in putting together a list. For example, suppose a famous author of a book related to the work of your group agrees to meet some members of your organization in a small gathering. You can ask the computer to give you the names of those people who are Board members or volunteers, interested in the topic of the book, living nearby, and who also have given $50 or more. You can also ask the computer to give you the same information on prospects. This gives you a nice, small group of perhaps 25 people, sorted for you in 30 seconds or less. You can then add others who should be invited.

The effective use of the computer depends not only on the computer selected and the software to be used, but also on the willingness of the staff (paid or unpaid) to learn how the computer works and to use it properly. Even so, paper records will still be necessary, and someone must type in all the data on any particular donor—the computer knows nothing it is not told. Thus, while computers don't really save time, they allow you to use your time in a wider variety of ways.

For fundraising purposes, the main advantages of a computer are: to expand the number of ways you can be in contact with your donors, to personalize donor contact with more specialized mailings or invitations, and to expand the contacts with prospects by using the information stored in the data base more effectively than you could if you had to sort through it by hand.

DATA SHEET ON DONOR

NAME AND ADDRESS:

PHONE:

AMOUNT GIVEN:

METHOD OF PAYMENT:
(*cash, credit card, pledge, stock, property, etc.*)

WORKER:
(*the person who solicited the gift*)

SOURCE:
(*what mailing list, contact person, special event, did this donor come from?*)

FORM OF ADDRESS:
(DEAR Ms., Mr., Mrs., First Name, Mr. and Mrs., Friend)

RENEWAL DATE:

CATEGORIES: (*People can be coded for more than one category*)

M   Major Donor

P   Prospect (*contact has been made but no solicitation has occurred*)

U   Uncontacted prospect (*research complete, no contact yet*)

FD Foundation

C   Pledge (*gift promised but not received, or payment plan set up*)

S   Special event donor

D   Direct mail donor (*gift was received as a result of direct mail, and future gifts should be sought this way for now*)

F   Friends (*non-donors*)

I   Inactive

G   General donor (*doesn't fit other categories*)

B   Board member

V   Volunteer

FO Former Board member or founder

X   Do not trade this name

LISTS:
(*indicates interest areas; people can be coded for any number*)

H   Health

R   Civil Rights

W   Women's Rights

P   Peace

E   Environment

L   Labor

D   Economic Development

Q   Endowment

COMMENTS:
(*Narrative comments that don't fit above categories.*)

Appendix 4

Annotated Glossary of Special Events

Introduction

The following 28 events are divided into three categories: those that can be done in one month, those that can be done in three months, and those that require five or more months of preparation. Needless to say, some of the events that can be done in one month by several people would take much longer if only one or two people were working on them, or could be much bigger if more time were taken. Conversely, some of the events requiring more preparation could be considerably shortened with the help of paid staff or more volunteers. Although, as has been repeatedly emphasized, special events should not be held primarily to raise funds, they do play an important part in the plans of low-budget, grass roots organizations as a fundraising strategy. Therefore, knowing a few general points about a number of special events will aid in choosing appropriate activities for your organization.

Each event listed is followed by a brief description of the event, the number of planners and other volunteers needed, and the principal costs of the event. All of these descriptions assume little or no paid staff involvement. "Planners" are the volunteers in charge of the special event who then delegate as many tasks as possible to other volunteers. Clearly, these are only a small sampling of all possible special events. However, they represent the major types of special events held by small nonprofit organizations; most other special events are variations on these.

Events That Can Be Done in One Month

SUMMERTIME BARBECUE. Choose any weekend or holiday, find a park or beach, and invite as many people as you want to an "all-you-can-eat" barbecue. Volleyball, softball, and games for children round out this afternoon event.

Planners: 2 or 3—to reserve a space for the barbecue, and to prepare and distribute advertising fliers or invitations. (City parks generally need to be reserved through City Hall or the park commissioner.)

Other Volunteers: 2 or 3—to help with publicity and to cook and clean up on the day of the barbecue.

Main Costs: Permits for the barbecue, paper plates and utensils, and advertising fliers. Food can be an expense, but often a store or several stores will donate some or all of it if you will hang a large sign at the picnic noting their donation.

Charge: $10 per adult, $5 for children under 12, free under 5.

DINNER IN A PRIVATE HOME. Have someone among your board, staff, or volunteers who lives in a nice or unusual home or setting and/or is a gourmet cook invite 10-25 people (depending on what the house will hold) to a sit-down dinner.

Planners: 1 or 2—The person doing the event may be the only planner. His or her job is to write the invitations and the guest list and to cook the food for the event.

Volunteers: 2 or 3—to address invitations, tabulate RSVPs, and help serve and clean up the night of the event.

Main Costs: Invitations, which need to be fancy or elegant.

Generally, the person putting on the event donates some or all of the food and drink; if not, food and drink will be the only other large cost.

Charge: $25 per person/$40 per couple. Children are not generally included in such an event.

GARAGE SALE. On a small scale, garage sales are easy to organize and reasonably lucrative. Simply ask 5-10 people to clear out their closets and bookshelves and bring their donations to one garage or yard located on a highly trafficked street.

Planners: 1—who calls the donors, who are usually board or staff members, and determines the location of the sale.

Volunteers: 4—who prepare signs noting the place and time of the sale, help to price the items for sale, staff the sale, collect money, refold clothes, answer questions of prospective buyers, and clean up, taking leftover items to Goodwill or the like.

Main Costs: None. Everything is free.

Charge: Price items well below their actual worth and attempt to sell everything that has been donated. Be prepared to bargain with buyers. In the last two hours of the sale, mark everything down 50 percent.

HOUSE MEETING. This device can be used in any number of ways. As a quick fundraiser, it simply means that one individual who is already a donor to the organization invites 5 to 10 friends over for an evening or afternoon. A staff member describes the organization and its needs, and asks everyone there to make a donation. A basket is passed or left by the door. Coffee and dessert are served. The event takes about 2 hours.

Planners: 2—the person in whose house the event will take place, and the speaker to arrange the agenda.

Volunteers: Often none; sometimes one person helps make coffee and dessert and helps clean up.

Main Costs: Usually there are no costs. Should the host/hostess wish reimbursement for refreshments, food is the only cost.

Charge: Nothing. The pitch for money should include some specific financial suggestions, but the people invited can come and go without giving anything.

PANCAKE BREAKFAST. Serve from 7:30-11 at a public location, such as a church or service club. Usually pancake breakfasts are all you can eat.

Planners: 2 or 3—in charge of finding a place, setting a date, and preparing advertising.

Volunteers: 6—to distribute fliers and help with any other invitations; cook and clean up.

Main Costs: The food, eating utensils, and advertising. The volunteers should seek to get the food donated or sold at cost, which will keep the costs down.

Charge: $5 for adults, $2.50 for children. Try for volume of people, and make it cheap enough for a family to afford to go out for breakfast.

PROGRESSIVE DINNER. This event starts at one person's house for drinks and hors d'oeuvres, moves to a second house for dinner, and a third house for dessert. Sometimes, two more stops are added, for appetizers or soup, and a final stop for coffee and liqueur after dessert. The houses need to be near each other, and the guests are transported from house to house, and then returned to the house they started in.

Planners: 3—to line up the homes and help plan the menus. Generally, the three planners are also the people in whose homes the various parts of the dinner will take place.

Volunteers: 3—one or two people need to call all the people who are invited (keep costs down by preparing a guest list of friends and by phoning rather than mailing invitations) and then help to set up each house. One or two people will be in charge of driving the guests from house to house.

Main Costs: Again, the only cost is food if the hosts do not wish to donate it.

Charge: $20 per person; more if the food is very fancy or the homes very elegant or unusual.

PHONE-A-THON. See Chapter 5 for full description.

RAFFLE.

Planners: 1 or 2—to find prizes and have the tickets printed.

Volunteers: As many as possible; at least 12 to sell the tickets.

Main Costs: The cost of the tickets, and, if cash is a prize, the cost of the cash. Do not buy raffle prizes.

Charge: $1 per ticket, or 6 for $5. Again, attempt volume sales. A raffle can be run for up to 6 months from the date of making the tickets available to the final drawing. Money is coming in the whole time, so the organization does not have to wait for the funds.

Events That Can be Done in Three Months

BOOK SALE. The same idea as a garage

sale, but having only books for sale.

Planners: 3 or 4—to get the books. Usually a mailing to all local donors asking for books will bring in a large number. Ask people to bring them to a central location, or offer to pick them up if you have people to do that. The planners must also get a place for the sale and arrange for publicity.

Volunteers: 6 to 12, depending on the number of books. They must be sorted into hard- and soft-cover and usually into broad categories such as fiction, travel, self-help, cookbooks, children's books, religion, philosophy, history, etc. It is a good idea to have someone familiar with books to pull out rare ones such as first editions, old books, and out-of-print books, and put higher prices on these, as well as keeping them on a separate table. Usually, a set price for paper and hardback books makes accounting easier and encourages sales. Set the price of nonrare books low so that you sell as many as possible. Volunteers also staff the booksale and clean up.

Main Costs: Advertising.

Charge: No admission charge, various prices for the books.

COCKTAIL PARTY. Held at a large and elegant house, or a banquet room of a hotel, or a small restaurant. The "draw" (that is, why people come) is the setting or a person or persons who will be there. Generally, someone of note should ostensibly be the guest of honor.

Planners: 3 or 4—to secure a place, find the person to honor, and design the invitation.

Volunteers: 3 or 4—to send the invitations, welcome people as they arrive, and, unless you have hired bartenders, to serve the drinks.

Main Costs: Renting the place, if it is not someone's house, and the invitations and liquor.

Charge: $15-$25 per person.

CRAFTS FAIR. Give local artists a chance to display their wares while promoting yourselves to the public.

Planners: 3—to identify a place to hold the fair, set the date, and design the publicity. The place should be big enough for the number of crafts booths needed, and in a highly trafficked area, preferably with its own parking lot. A church or community center is an excellent site.

Volunteers: 5—to send out invitations to artists to display at the fair, and then advertise the fair to the general public. The day of the fair they will need to help set up the showroom.

Main Costs: The place for the fair, the invitations, and publicity.

Charge: Varies, depending on how you decide to do it. Generally artists are charged a booth fee, and there is a small admission charge for the general public. Sometimes artists give a percentage of their sales for that day to the organization.

HAUNTED HOUSE. A great Halloween event. Convert an old house or church into a haunted house by filling it with cardboard or plastic skeletons, spiders, vampires, and the like, and setting up lighting and sound systems for appropriate scary ambience. Some volunteers should dress up as mad scientists, vampires, witches, and so forth, and make occasional unannounced appearances to groups touring the house. Two or more volunteers must lead groups tours of the house, telling a story, which they must make up, about the various parts of the house.

Planners: 3 or 4—to find a site, secure permission to use it, and plan the publicity and the house setup.

Volunteers: 6 to 10—to be in charge of various parts of the operation. Publicity beforehand is extremely important. One or two volunteers to set up the house; a lighting and sound expert, volunteers to dress up and to lead groups through the house. One or two volunteers need to collect the entrance fees, and then everyone must participate in getting the house back to normal at the end of the day.

Main Costs: Publicity and sound and light systems, unless they can be hooked up with simple stereos and light fixtures already installed.

Charge: $.50-$1.00 per person, less for children under 7. The ideal is for the children and their parents to want to take several tours through the house during the day.

MOVIE BENEFIT. A theater donates an evening to your group.

Planners: 2 or 3—to find the theater and then work with its staff to select a movie. Also, to design publicity in cooperation with the theater.

Volunteers: 2 to 3—to help get publicity out, and depending on your arrangement with the theater, to collect tickets or work the concession stand.

Main Costs: Publicity.

Charge: The same price as the movie theater normally charges, or more. Bill it as a donation.

OPEN HOUSE. An opportunity to invite donors and prospects to your office to meet the staff and board. An open house is not technically a fundraiser, but you can prominently display donation cans and sell your organization's products. You can also add a no-host wet bar.

Planners: 2—to set the date and prepare the invitations.

Volunteers: 2 to 4—to send the invitations, bring in the refreshments (usually finger foods, soft drinks, and wine), set up, welcome guests, and clean up the day of the open house.

Main Costs: Food and publicity.

Charge: No charge at the door. Have things for sale (T-Shirts, bumper stickers, etc.) and encourage people who are not already donors to join. (Have a lot of membership information available.)

SIDEWALK SALE. A much larger version of the previously described garage sale.

Planners: 2 or 3—to coordinate announcements to people to donate items to the sale, to find a busy sidewalk or parking lot for the sale and secure permission to use it, and to design the advertising for the day of the sale.

Volunteers: 6 to 10—to sort and price the items for sale, transport them to the sale, set everything up, and staff the sale. After the sale is over, volunteers will be needed to clean up and take unsold items to Goodwill or the like.

Main Costs: Advertising.

Charge: No admission charge. Again, underprice items so that you sell as many as possible.

TASTING. Any exotic, sophisticated or popular food or drink can be brought in many varieties for tasting. Wine, chocolate, liqueurs and cordials, fancy candy, and ethnic foods all lend themselves to this format.

Planners: 2 or 3—to find a place, decide on a theme, and prepare advertising.

Volunteers: 4—to distribute advertising and mail invitations; set up a place where tasting is to occur, collect money at the door, and make sure everyone has a chance to taste.

Main Costs: Advertising. The food or drink is donated by the manufacturers, who gain a great deal of publicity through this event. You may have to provide snacks at the wine tasting, or coffee and tea for a chocolate or candy tasting.

Charge: Varies depending on what you are serving, but usually you do not charge less than $8 per person. Children are generally not encouraged to come to such an event.

TOUR. A guided tour of a historic part of town or architecturally interesting houses, churches, or other places, or a nature walk.

Planners: 1 or 2—to find someone to lead an appropriate tour and to design the advertising.

Volunteers: To greet people as they arrive and provide refreshments at the end of the tour.

Main Costs: Advertising. Possibly an honorarium for the tour guide.

Charge: $5-$15 a person, depending on how exotic the tour is or how knowledgeable the tour guide.

WORKSHOP OR CLASS. On almost any topic that people want to know about and that you have a qualified teacher to teach. Topics might include organic gardening, sewing, knitting, fundraising, tennis, judo, auto mechanics, aerobics, etc.

Planners: 1 or 2—to find the teacher, get a place, and design publicity.

Volunteers: 1 or 2—to help with publicity and registration, to introduce the teacher, and to clean up after the class.

Main Costs: The place and the publicity. Try to get the teacher to donate his or her time and try to get a free place.

Charge: The going rate for similar classes; usually at least $10/person, going as high as $75-$100.

Events Requiring Five or More Months of Planning

AUCTION.

Planners: 3 to 5—to find a place and secure an auctioneer, design publicity, and help get prizes to auction.

Volunteers: 10 or more—The main task is getting good items to be auctioned and getting adequate publicity. A list of items for each participant, with their value, and their minimum bid must be prepared. The day of the auction there should be food and drink available, chairs must be set up, and a two or more volunteers must be available to collect money and arrange for delivery of auction items.

Main Costs: The place and the publicity. You may also have to pay a professional auctioneer, although usually a volunteer can be found.

Charge: Charge an admission price and charge for food and drink. The bulk of the money is made from the auctioned items.

BINGO. Many groups now run bingo games 1 or 2 nights a week. Check with your community's laws to insure compliance.

Planners: 1 to 4—to set up the bingo game, which generally means renting out an evening of an ongoing bingo game, advertising, and recruiting volunteers to manage the game. Some organizations prefer to pay the person running the game.

Volunteers: To run the bingo game, collect money, set up, and clean up.

Main Costs and Charge: Varies from community to community. Check with other groups doing bingo as a fundraising device.

CONCERT. One of the most common fantasies of a low-budget group is the idea of having a concert with a famous performer. This is one of the most difficult fundraising events to carry out successfully.

Planners: 5—to find the performer (which can take months of research and cultivation) and to set a time and place.

Volunteers: Unlimited number to do publicity, sell tickets, set up food and drink at the performance hall (if allowed), etc. Many organizations choose to pay someone to handle the details of planning and implementing.

Main Costs: Rental of the performance space, publicity, and the performer's expenses (assuming that his/her/their fees are waived, you will still be charged for plane fare, hotel, food, etc.).

Charge: Whatever is the going rate for similar performances, or more.

CONFERENCE. An expanded version of the workshop or class discussed earlier. A conference is held on a particular topic, usually for one or more days, and can include a series of speakers and workshops. Ideally, some continuing education credits should be offered.

Planners: 4 or 5—to decide on the theme, arrange for a conference space, contact speakers and workshop leaders, and plan publicity.

Volunteers: 12—to advertise the conference, mail packets to conference participants, set up and clean up, pick up speakers at airport, bus station, etc., register attendees, and to answer questions, solve problems, and act as runners for any items needed at the last minute.

Main Costs: Advertising and conference materials, honoraria for speakers, rental of conference space.

Charge: Depends on the number of days and the type of conference. Charge the going rate for similar conferences. Do not undercharge.

DANCE.

Planners: 3 or 4—to find a space, hire performers, and plan advertising.

Volunteers: 8-10—to promote the dance, arrange for food and drink the night of the dance, get liquor licenses, take money at the door, staff the food and drink booths, and set up and clean up.

Main Costs: The performers (unless donated), rental of dance hall, security guard(s), publicity.

Charge: Depending on how popular the dance band is, charge at least $5 per person. Some groups charge $8-$10 and include free munchies and one free drink. (This encourages people to buy more drinks, and is a lucrative strategy.)

DECORATOR SHOWCASE. Have each room of a house decorated by a different interior designer, then charge people to come through the house. Ideally, the house should be large, architecturally elegant or unusual, and belong to a famous person.

Planners: 5 or 6—Details seem almost infinite for this event. The main ones are to line up the house, the decorators, and plan publicity. There is a tremendous amount of work involved in coordinating the schedules and permission of the homeowners and the decorators and giving the decorators time to do their work with minimum inconvenience to the homeowners (who must have another home to use).

Volunteers: Unlimited numbers can be used. They must promote the showcase, collect money, conduct the tours, arrange for parking for people coming to the showcase, and assist the planners in coordinating the whole thing.

Main Costs: Publicity.

Charge: $10-$20 per person, depending on how fancy the house and the decorations are.

DINNER DANCE. An elegant affair usually held at a hotel, with a fancy dinner and excellent dance band.

Planners: 4-5. As with the decorator showcase, details are everything here, and a comprehensive task list is imperative. Aside from the obvious details of renting the hotel, the band, etc., having sponsors listed on the invitation is important. The invitation is thus a list of 25-100 socially prominent people who join in inviting the rest of the community to a dinner dance in honor of your organization.

Volunteers: Again, as many as possible to send out the invitations, collate the RSVPs, make a seating chart for the dinner, coordinate with the hotel's catering service, and oversee the setup of the dinner and dance.

Main Costs: The hotel, food, invitations, and performers' fees. This is a costly event.

Charge: $50-$250 per couple.

FASHION SHOW. Can be done in the traditional sense of having models wear the latest fashions, but is more fun if it is a take-off on that idea, such as a "working woman's fashion show," which would show professional-looking but comfortable fashions for upwardly mobile working women, or ethnic fashion shows that feature clothes

from other countries, or as a spoof on a fashion show, which might be things that are out of fashion, what to never wear in public, etc. The models can be professionals, or, for fun, board and volunteers, or politicians and well-known people in the community.

Planners: 2 or 3—to plan theme of fashion show, find appropriate models, find a place, and plan publicity.

Volunteers: (not including models) 4 or 5—to help with publicity, coordinate the show itself, write up descriptions of the fashions, describe the models and what they are wearing, set up and clean up. If food and drink are sold volunteers need to staff those booths.

Main Costs: Rental of hall and publicity. If the models are paid that will be a main cost.

Charge: Depends on the theme of the fashion show and the intended audience. Charge at least $5.

TRIBUTE LUNCHEON. A fancy luncheon usually held at a hotel, which honors one or more people and features a speaker.

Planners: 4 to 5—to decide whom to honor and why, find an appropriate speaker, and design the invitation. Also, planners must get a "committee" of 50-100 people who will let their names be used on the invitation as joining in inviting the community to the luncheon.

Volunteers: As many as needed to reserve the hotel, arrange the food, send out invitations, collate responses, solicit corporations and businesses to reserve tables at the luncheon, arrange the seating, and see that things go smoothly the day of the luncheon.

Main Costs: The hotel, food, and invitations, all of which are very expensive. Like others in this section, this event is heavy on front money, and must be planned with great care.

Charge: $35-$500 per person, depending on how fancy it is, and who the audience is. Charge separately for full tables, and allow people to give more in order to be "sponsors" or "benefactors." The main money is made from "selling" tables at $1,000 and getting donations above the individual price.

WALK; JOG; BIKE; ROCK; ETC-A-THON. Participants collect pledges for every mile they walk, jog, or bike, or every hour they rock in a rocking chair, or for some other measurement of endurance.

Planners: 2 or 3—to plot the course of the marathon, get any needed permission from the police department or City Hall for using the streets, and design publicity.

Volunteers: 12 or more—to help with publicity, to monitor and mark the pledge sheets of participants as they go by their checkpoints, to collect money from partici-pants, (who must collect it from their pledges). Also, volunteers skilled in first aid must be on hand in case of injuries.

Main Costs: Publicity, permits, and prizes for those who participate. (Prizes are usually a T-shirt or certificate of participa-tion.)

Charge: There is usually no charge to en-ter, unless the 'thon is done as a race be-tween participants, in which case an entry fee is charged. Participants get whatever they can for each mile; usually a minimum pledge of 10 cents is suggested.

Appendix 5

What To Do In Case of Financial Trouble

First, don't panic. Every organization gets into financial straits from time to time. Cash-flow problems are common among small nonprofit groups.

Next, carefully analyze the nature of the financial problem and how you got into it.

There are several kinds of financial troubles, ranging from simple cash-flow problems to serious mismanagement or even embezzlement of funds. We will discuss each of these major types of financial problems below. First, however, it is important to recognize that financial problems are usually symptomatic of deeper management difficulties. These difficulties usually show up first, and often most seriously, in the areas of fundraising and spending. The root cause may be the failure of the board of directors to plan the year thoroughly and thus anticipate the financial crisis; or it could be the reluctance of a staff person to discuss the finances of the organization honestly and fully with the board, leading them to approve an unrealistic budget. Sometimes the deeper problem is that fundraising projections are inaccurate, because there was not enough research to make reasonable estimates of income. Whatever the problem turns out to be, it must be addressed and solved. If only the financial problem is solved and the underlying organizational issues remain unaddressed the financial problems will recur, each time with increasing severity.

There are three main types of financial problems:

Cash-flow problems: Anticipated income is not coming in fast enough, creating a temporary lag in income in relation to spending. A cash-flow problem has an end in sight. You know that when a certain major donation or grant comes in, or reimbursement from the city, county, or state is received, you will be able to pay your bills, and say goodbye to your problem. Until that time, however, the organization has to draw on its reserves; once the organization exhausts any savings it might have, then it is in a bind.

You have several choices at that point. You can put a freeze on spending and even up your income and expenses by ceasing to incur expenses. You can attempt to stall your creditors by paying bills in installments and by postponing as many bills as possible. (Call creditors and explain your situation, giving them a date by which you will pay the bill. Many times creditors will allow you to postpone payment if they believe you will have the money soon.)

A third choice is to borrow money to cover your expenses and repay the loan when your cash flow improves. Depending on the size of the loan, you may be able to borrow the money from a loyal board member or major donor with little or no interest and no publicity. Foundations and corporations in some communities have "emergency loan funds" to help groups through cash-flow difficulties when those problems are not the organization's fault.

Deficit spending: A deficit is a chronic cash-flow problem or a cash-flow problem with no end in sight. Every month your organization spends more than it brings in. Some organizations finance their deficit with money from their savings or money earmarked for special programs. At some point, however, you will run out of money and no longer be able to finance the deficit. There is only one solution to deficit spending: spend only as much money as you raise. Permanently cutting down on spending may require radical alteration of the organization's spending habits. Examine where you are overspending and put a freeze on those areas. Designate one or two staff people to authorize all expenditures over $5. In a low-budget organization, careful attention to costs of photocopying, postage, and office supplies can make a big difference.

Obviously, the fundraising plan and the income reports will have to be carefully examined and strengthened. Raising more money, however, is a long-term solution;

deficits require immediate attention because the longer they continue the worse they get.

Serious accounting errors or embezzlement of funds. In these cases, the entire board must be notified immediately, and the people responsible for the error or crime must be fired. In the case of fraud or theft, the board will have to decide whether to take legal action against the person responsible.

Board members should prepare a brief statement on what happened and what the organization is doing about it. This statement can be sent to funding sources and used should the story get into the newspapers or other media. Honesty and swift action are the best ways to insure the fewest repercussions.

The harder problem to solve is how to make up the loss of money that this error or crime has caused. Loans, spending freezes, vacation without pay, or pay defer-ments for staff (in the last resort, staff lay-off may be necessary) are some options.

If the financial situation cannot be improved by any of the above means, the organization should consider closing. An organizational development consultant or a facilitator will be helpful in leading the board to a proper decision.

The most serious problem in this third case is the morale of all the people involved. Very little work goes on when the entire organization is depressed and shocked. Morale will be boosted when the staff and board have decided on a course of action. If the organization is to stay alive, this must be decided quickly, and the plan implemented immediately. A crisis of this magnitude can pull people together and strengthen the organization, as long as those who stay with it agree that keeping the organization going is of the utmost importance.

Appendix 6

Hiring a Fundraising Consultant

There are times in the lives of all people and all organizations when they need help from someone not involved in their day-to-day life; help from someone who has no investment in the outcome of the situation beyond a general wish for it to be improved or resolved. Individual people generally go to friends, teachers, or therapists for this help. Organizations go to consultants.

An organization that has reached an impasse in its fundraising efforts or lacks the knowledge of how to proceed with a particular strategy is wise to hire a fundraising consultant. Sometimes organizations hire fundraising consultants simply to train their board to identify prospective major donors and ask for money, or to review their fundraising plan and suggest ways to make the plan more effective.

There are five steps to hiring a consultant that will insure that neither the consultant's nor the organization's time and money will be wasted.

Clarify your goals. Remember that consultants are not miracle-workers. They cannot guarantee results and they cannot control people's actions. All they can do is make recommendations, help clarify issues, and give people information. What anyone does with the consultant's information is beyond the control of the consultant.

Shop around. There are many fundraising consultants in the United States. Some are good, many are excellent, and a few are truly bad.

Some consultants are better for some organizations than others, and some are better for certain organizational and fundraising issues than others. A consultant who is superb in setting up a major gifts program and helping boards accept their role as fundraisers may be very poor at planning large special events. Call several consultants before making a decision. Be very straightforward about your situation and ask if the consultant believes he or she can help. Unless the consultant comes highly recommended, ask for the last three places he or she has worked, and call them for a reference.

Be realistic about cost. A consultant's daily or hourly rate is high compared to what you make for the same amount of time. The prices consultants charge are extremely varied. Just because someone is very expensive does not necessarily mean that he or she is better; on the other hand, people charging bargain-basement prices may be no better if they waste your time. Good consultants are generally booked for three or four months in advance, and this factor may be more of a clue to their relative excellence than their fee.

Sign a contract. Be sure either you or the consultant write down everything the consultant will do. If the written contract is not agreeable to you, modify it. In particular be sure that the consultant's fee and expenses are understood, as well as the length of time the contract covers.

Trust the consultant. Once you have gone through the process of deciding to hire someone, checking out references, and signing a contract, do not spend valuable time second-guessing the consultant, thinking up reasons why something he or she has recommended won't work or talking about how "we've tried that and it doesn't work."

Used appropriately, consultants can be invaluable in helping an organization expand its fundraising program.